DYNAMICS OF CHANGE IN EAST ASIA

Over the past forty years, East Asia has been radically transformed from a war-damaged sub-continent to a region of global pre-eminence. With new, highly developed scientific resources, great economic strengths, significant global trading links and equally powerful financial resources, East Asia is now one of the most dynamic regions in the global system.

This book illuminates the historical development trajectory and contemporary circumstances of the countries of the region. Embracing a cross-disciplinary perspective, it summarizes the history of the region and goes on to focus upon the rise of East Asia since the ruins of the Pacific War. Analysing the region's basic strengths and the distinctive elite development strategies across the various countries, it also examines areas of domestic, intra-regional and international conflict. It covers the basic ground of political economy, society, culture and politics, whilst also taking care to locate the contemporary region in its own history and asking, what further change can be expected in the future?

Providing an excellent introduction to the study of the region, this book is an important read for students and scholars of East Asian politics, history and development.

P.W. Preston is Emeritus Professor of Political Sociology at the University of Birmingham, UK. His recent publications include *Political-Cultural Developments in East Asia* (2017) and *The Logic of Chinese Politics* (2016).

DYNAMICS OF CHANGE IN EAST ASIA

Historical Trajectories and Contemporary Development

P.W. Preston

LONDON AND NEW YORK

First published 2018
by Routledge
2 Park Square, Milton Park, Abingdon, Oxon OX14 4RN

and by Routledge
711 Third Avenue, New York, NY 10017

Routledge is an imprint of the Taylor & Francis Group, an informa business

© 2018 P.W. Preston

The right of P.W. Preston to be identified as author of this work has been asserted by him in accordance with sections 77 and 78 of the Copyright, Designs and Patents Act 1988.

All rights reserved. No part of this book may be reprinted or reproduced or utilized in any form or by any electronic, mechanical, or other means, now known or hereafter invented, including photocopying and recording, or in any information storage or retrieval system, without permission in writing from the publishers.

Trademark notice: Product or corporate names may be trademarks or registered trademarks, and are used only for identification and explanation without intent to infringe.

British Library Cataloguing-in-Publication Data
A catalogue record for this book is available from the British Library

Library of Congress Cataloging-in-Publication Data
Names: Preston, P. W. (Peter Wallace), 1949– author.
Title: Dynamics of change in East Asia : historical trajectories and contemporary development / P.W. Preston.
Description: New York : Routledge, 2018. | Includes bibliographical references and index.
Identifiers: LCCN 2017052378| ISBN 9780415424370 (hardback) | ISBN 9780415424882 (pbk.) | ISBN 9781315227993 (ebook)
Subjects: LCSH: Economic development–East Asia. | East Asia–Strategic aspects. | Nationalism–East Asia. | East Asia–Commerce. | Information technology–Economic aspects. | East Asia–Economic conditions–21st century.
Classification: LCC HC460.5 .P74 2018 | DDC 338.95–dc23
LC record available at https://lccn.loc.gov/2017052378

ISBN: 978-0-415-42437-0 (hbk)
ISBN: 978-0-415-42488-2 (pbk)
ISBN: 978-1-315-22799-3 (ebk)

Typeset in Bembo
by Wearset Ltd, Boldon, Tyne and Wear

CONTENTS

List of figures and maps viii
List of tables x
Maps of East Asia xi
Preface xiv
Acknowledgements xv

PART I
Complex change and the logics of forms of life   1

  1 Argument making in social science   3

  2 Substantive approaches: the resources of current disciplines   20

  3 Grasping the core logics of forms of life   32

PART II
The shift to the modern world in East Asia   49

  4 Colonialism and modernity: the overall trajectory   51

  5 Colonialism and modernity: disentangling the issues   76

PART III
Successor elites and the pursuit of national development   93

  6 The dissolution of state-empires   95

  7 The formation of successor elites   114

  8 Elites and masses: domestic power, authority and dissent   130

  9 Development issues faced   144

PART IV
East Asia in the changing global system   171

10 Three spheres of concern: domestic, regional and international   173

11 Globalization, the end of history and the debate about regions   188

PART V
East Asia: success and its costs   203

12 Elite projects and post-colonial goals   205

13 Elites, masses and the ideal of democracy   217

14 Imagined communities, collective memory and the national past   235

15 Performance, problems and mooted reforms   253

     Afterword   278

     Annex 1: Population, GDP and Gini coefficient   280

     Annex 2: Health and education   281

     Annex 3: Rural and urban employment   282

     Annex 4: Military expenditures   283

Annex 5: China's twentieth century in twelve films	284
Annex 6: East Asia's twentieth century in twenty films	285
Bibliography and further reading	*286*
Index	*292*

FIGURES AND MAPS

Map 1	South Asia, Southeast Asia and East Asia	xi
Map 2	Southeast Asia and East Asia	xii
Map 3	China – provinces	xiii
P.1	Roadside flowers, author and friends, outside Zhenjiang	xvi
4.1	A tea warehouse in Canton, 1790	53
4.2	A view of Batavia (no date)	53
4.2(a)	Batavia Plan, 1897	54
4.3	Singapore: view from Government Hill, 1830	55
4.4	Rangoon: storming the principal stockades, 1824	59
4.5	Interior of the North Taku Fort during Second Opium War, 1860	59
4.6	Pu Yi	60
5.1	Chinese snipers, 1894	77
5.2	Japanese Navy, 1894	78
5.3	Combined Japanese and British attack on Ching Tao, 1914	88
5.3(a)	Ching Tao Plan, 1912	89
6.1	Battle of Shanghai, 1932	96
6.2	HMS Prince of Wales and HMS Repulse, 1941	97
6.3	Mountbatten, Chiang Kai Shek and T.V. Soong	99
6.4	Allied reoccupation of French Indo-China, 1945	107
9.1	Village field, Sichuan	151
9.2	Washing leeks, Sichuan	152
9.3	Farming, Zhenjiang	153
9.4	Village, Zhenjiang	155
9.5	Ramkhamhaeng Road, Bangkok	157
9.6	Café, Ramkhamhaeng Road	158
9.7	Public housing, Singapore	159

14.1	Lim Bo Seng Memorial, Singapore	249
14.2	Kranji, Singapore	250
14.3	School, Sichuan	251
15.1	Hong Kong Central	256
15.2	Changi Airport	259
15.3	Beijing Airport	260
15.4	Consumption, Singapore	266
15.5	Recycling, Zhenjiang	268
15.6	Beijing smog	269
A.1	Café, Bangkok	279

TABLES

4.1	Wars of colonial expansion	63
4.2	The career of Imperial Japan	63
4.3	Overlapping wars: multiple participants, experiences and memories	67
4.4	Wars of colonial withdrawal, 1945–75	73
6.1	China: the shift to the modern world, some costs	112
10.1	East Asia – states	175
10.2	ASEAN membership, 1967–99	176
14.1	East Asia: major conflicts, 1911–91	246
14.2	East Asia: casualties, 1911–91	247

MAPS OF EAST ASIA

MAP 1 South Asia, Southeast Asia and East Asia.

Source: d-maps.com/carte.php?num_car=66580&lang=en.

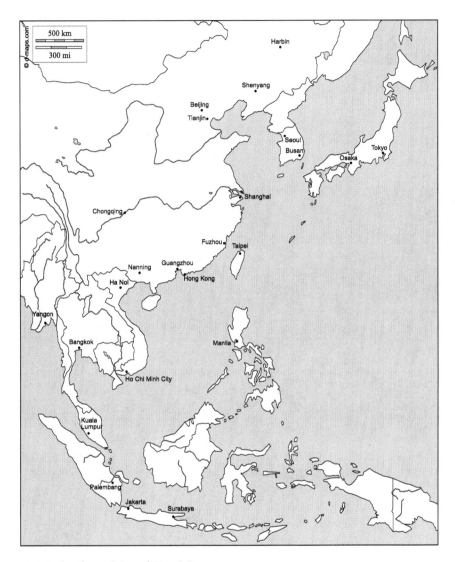

MAP 2 Southeast Asia and East Asia.

Source: d-maps.com/carte.php?num_car=28781&lang=en.

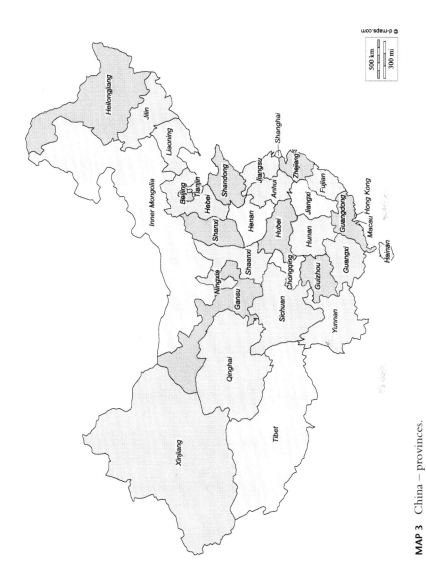

MAP 3 China – provinces.

Source: d-maps.com/carte.php?num_car=27748&lang=en.

PREFACE

East Asia is a key region in the contemporary global system. In the last forty or so years it has gone from war-damaged, conflict-riddled and poor to a position of global pre-eminence. It is a remarkable success story. At the present time, the early twenty-first century, the region has highly developed scientific resources, great economic strengths, global trading links and equally powerful financial resources. East Asia is now one of the most dynamic regions in the global system. This book is intended to serve as a first stop for scholars, students and others who are more or less new to the study of the region. It covers the basic ground of political economy, society, culture and politics. It also takes care to locate the contemporary region in its own history and that of the much wider global shift to the modern world.

The book includes written material (blocks of text), maps, lists, data tables and photographs, both historical and contemporary. The book can be read as a straightforward narrative; that is, it tells the tale of the unfolding shift to the modern world of the present countries of East Asia. It can also be used as a starting point for more specific enquiries, into development or democracy or historical memory and so on. The main text has been built on lecture courses, given in various universities. It is constructed without all the usual machinery of footnotes but all the names mentioned are fully referenced in the bibliography. The annexes to the book contain tables of basic data, taken from mainstream UN and similar bodies, along with lists of books and films that might profitably be consulted as readers plan the next steps of their enquiries in the unfolding development trajectories of the countries of East Asia.

ACKNOWLEDGEMENTS

Scholarship is always a collective endeavour and so my thanks go to friends, colleagues and students both in Europe and also in East Asia, and to the numerous creative figures whose monographs, academic papers, journalistic commentary, images, novels and films have helped me disentangle some of the issues relating to the historical development trajectory of the countries of the region. Much of the initial writing was done whilst sitting in various local coffee shops, an institution that is a boon to any scholar, but as might be expected the bulk of the research work was done in the context of local universities, in particular: the Chinese University of Hong Kong, Beijing Normal University, Ramkhamhaeng University in Bangkok and Jiangsu University in Zhenjiang; once again, my thanks to friends and colleagues.

I would like to acknowledge permission to reproduce the following images:

Figures 4.2(a) and 5.3(a) are reproduced courtesy of the Perry-Casteneda Library, University of Texas Libraries, The University of Texas at Austin (USA).

Figures 5.3, 6.1, 6.3 and 6.4 are Crown Copyright and reproduced by permission of the Imperial War Museum (UK).

Figures 4.1, 4.2, 4.3, 4.4, 4.5, 4.6, 5.1 and 5.2 are reproduced by permission of the British Library (UK).

Figure 6.2 (NH 60566) is reproduced courtesy of the Naval History and Heritage Command (USA).

All other images are by the author.

FIGURE P.1 Roadside flowers, author and friends, outside Zhenjiang, China, spring 2017.

PART I
Complex change and the logics of forms of life

The classical European tradition of social theory is concerned with the analysis of complex change in the unfolding shift to the modern world. This intellectual tradition, which has its roots in the period of the Enlightenment, offers political analysts, and members of wider European societies, an elaborate repertoire of concepts: science, progress, development, industry, democracy and so on. It is a long-established and very rich tradition. In Part I of this book the nature, status and utility of these materials will be considered; the manner in which they might be deployed in respect of other cultures will be noted; and, thereafter, these resources will be turned to the interpretive and critical analysis of the historical trajectories and contemporary logics of the many discrete forms of life that together constitute modern East Asia.[1]

Note
1 I have written about these issues elsewhere and references are given in the bibliography and further reading section.

1
ARGUMENT MAKING IN SOCIAL SCIENCE

As the world of religion-informed agrarian society gave way to natural science-based industrial society, a process dramatic in its practical and philosophical impacts, commentators dealing with the sphere of the social looked to the natural sciences for lessons. As natural science was so successful in respect of its claims to knowledge, it made sense to see if its assumptions and procedures could be shifted to the sphere of the social, a sphere, moreover, that was now in process of sweeping change. This argument by analogy, that is, borrowing the assumptions and procedures of the natural sciences and deploying them in the sphere of the social, has been pursued and debated for at least three centuries. In a recognizably modern form, it reaches back to Thomas Hobbes and his contemporaries writing in seventeenth-century England, and it has been presented in various combinations down all the subsequent years. It has been strongly criticized; some have looked to language-carried human understanding, whilst others have looked to the political nature of human social life. This chapter on argument making notes these debates and indicates that this particular text is constructed within and with reference to the classical European tradition of social theorizing, which in form is taken to be interpretive and critical and which can be deployed in a dialogic form when addressing other cultures.

The shift to the modern world

The shift to the modern world took its earliest form in Europe, from (roughly) the seventeenth through to the late nineteenth centuries, and it encompassed the shift from an agrarian feudalism informed by the rhythms of the natural world (seasons), and grasped in its totality by religious schemes that identified the pervasive presences of gods, through to an industrial capitalism that fused reason-centred natural science with a competitive, market-oriented approach to the provision of the means to human livelihood.

The shift to the modern world began in Europe but it was the product of a series of accidents, including the tentative rise of natural science, the emergence of trading cities, the creation of restrictions on the absolute power of monarchs, and agricultural improvements, which, along with imported food, raised the levels of living of whole populations (less subsistence, more production). As these changes ran through northwestern Europe, attended by multiple conflicts, domestic and international, they began to be exported, at first in the guise of what Europeans remember as voyages of discovery, then later as the trading voyages that created the long-distance links that served to facilitate later colonial expansion. In sum, the shift to the modern world involved great changes in culture (sets of ideas) and social practice (the ways in which people lived), and the modern world turned out to be very dynamic with intensification, as it increased its demands on its local population (ever greater 'efficiency'), and expansion, as it sought wider areas of activity, overseas trade, later colonies (and much later still, tales of globalization).

This complex process was not planned, rather it unfolded over several generations and it enfolded the social worlds that it successively remade. The patterns of life of the people within these territories were changed. The shift to the modern world was not something that happened off to one side of the social world. It remade existing social worlds. It made new social worlds. And the growth of the intellectual and practical power of natural science underscored the novelty of the unfolding changes. Unsurprisingly, making sense of these sweeping changes came to be a key concern for social commentary; in England this began with Thomas Hobbes and his contemporaries, and was picked up in the Scottish Enlightenment, and thereafter the French and German Enlightenments. Overall these changes amounted to a novel celebration of the power of human reason.

All this work is the root of contemporary European social science, and it inaugurated a rich tradition: the ideas presented by seventeenth-century English thinkers and by later French and German Enlightenment scholars have been picked up and advanced by later generations across Europe. These communities of scholars have often been bounded by nations and so national traditions emerged; matters shaped by accidents of intellectual inheritance, local social circumstances and the business of institutionalization. For Europeans these traditions have subsequently been overlain by external influences: during the Cold War, with the competing claims of the USA and USSR; and, more recently, with the development of the European Union. Here, this has involved, in particular, the high public politics of reaffirming Europe, the corporate world's contribution via trade and the cultural consequences of widespread popular movement for work, or pleasure or lifestyle, thus the creation of a somewhat scattered European reading public and thus a sense of collective belonging. All these shifting, overlapping processes feed into contemporary social science disciplines. And all this means that the substantive claims of the various social science disciplines are rooted in complex sets of assumptions about the nature and possibilities of knowledge of the social world.

In this chapter, with some simplifications (thus it offers a general overview, not a country by country or decade by decade survey, coupled to a notion of a 'classical European tradition of social theorizing'), these deep-seated assumptions are made clear. Thus there are three broad strategies of grasping the nature of the social sciences and each has been adopted at various times and in various ways:

- arguments from natural science – here the received model of the natural sciences is invoked in order to cast the social sciences in an analogous form, both procedures of enquiry and utility of knowledge outputs, hence the output of technical knowledge of the social system able to inform expert intervention and planning;
- arguments from human understanding – here the resources of the humanities are invoked in order to establish that human beings are inhabitants of structured webs of meaning, which might be unpacked using strategies of enquiry from history, language and ordinary social practice, hence enquiry serves greater self-understanding, individual and collective;
- arguments from human political organization – here the resources of humanities and social sciences are turned to issue of pursuit of self-understandings within structurally unequal social worlds and the strategy of critique addresses such inequalities – hence an orientation towards the pursuit of the active utopia of a social environment where all can flourish, that is, unpack and put to use both inherent and acquired skills.

Arguments from natural science

The social sciences lodged within the European tradition grew and took shape during the early phases of the shift to the modern world and during this early phase around the seventeenth century a number of key shifts in thinking took place. The old intellectual and practical world dominated by religious schemes gave way to a novel intellectual and practical world shaped by material forces.

One complex package of ideas and practice was replaced by another. The process was difficult, contested and slow. The shift in thinking can be summarized in this way:

- ontological – the nature of the world changes, from theism (gods/spirits) to materialism (matter/causes);
- epistemological – the nature of knowledge changes, from submissive reflection upon the word of god (medieval religious teaching) to the active use of human reason to understand the ordinary material world;
- methodological – the getting of knowledge changes, from systematic reflection on the timeless truths of sacred texts (theology) to the accumulation of the mundane details of the material world (empiricism);
- ethical – the ends of human life change, from the search for final perfection to the accumulation of piecemeal advance, progress;
- pragmatic – the nature of practical activity changes, from acquiescence in the given to a concern for what can be crafted as reason informs mundane practice and human progress.

The evident success of the natural sciences invited an obvious intellectual movement; if the intellectual strategies of the natural sciences can produce such dazzling results why should they not be transferred to the social sphere in the expectation of similarly outstanding results?

The idea has been pursued down the generations and a long list of great names could be assembled, starting with the theorists of the retrospectively identified British Enlightenment and moving on to the theorists of the Scottish and French Enlightenments before adding in figures from the later German Enlightenment. And thereafter, debate typically moves to the late nineteenth- and early twentieth-century theorists associated with the notion of positivism.

The equation of reliable knowledge with the products of the natural sciences reached its apogee in the work of the logical positivists of the early part of the twentieth century, the logical positivism of the Vienna Circle and Bertrand Russell's Cambridge. These essentially philosophical discussions have run on: into post-empiricism, into social constructivist models of the assumptions, work and claims of the community of natural scientists, and into pragmatist informed characterizations of natural science.

The notion of positivism embraces a spread of ideas and a clutch of theorists could be mentioned, and they have it in common that they look to the model of the natural sciences as exemplars of the getting of knowledge. The character of the debate changes over time. Early enthusiasts for natural science presented the activity as essentially context-free, natural science was a matter of turning human reason to the task of deciphering the processes of the natural world. Later theorists noted that the community of natural scientists was embedded within their own social communities, that is, the pursuit of natural science was not context-free, it was one more social activity (and thus shaped in part by the influence of funding agencies, institutional power structures and the vagaries of political or public attitudes).

A number of key figures could be mentioned, together covering the spread of debates:

- Vienna Circle's logical positivism;
- Karl Popper's critical rationalism;
- Thomas Kuhn's post-empiricist discussions of paradigms.

Vienna and the programme of logical positivism

Vienna at the turn of the twentieth century was home to a number of intellectuals and artists and they constituted a distinctive grouping, which turned its attention to life in the modern world, to questions of the nature of urban life, mass production and the longer-term implications of the rise of science. They were critical of the form of life of turn-of-the-century Austro-Hungarian Hapsburg Empire, which they viewed as decadent, a failing empire ruled by an intellectually and morally bankrupt elite. These critics sought an intellectual and moral clarity in their work. This was also a central theme in modernism, the art world's response to the rise of the modern world. This search for clarity was picked up by the philosophers of the Vienna Circle and they turned their attention to clarity in language itself, for this was understood to be the basis of all other social activities, including science.

The philosophical theorists of the Vienna Circle extended late nineteenth-century ideas about scientific enquiry: first, they picked up on the idea that the natural world was in principle available to unbiased enquiry using unclouded human senses, and that facts could be described, accumulated and made the basis for reliable generalizations or more reliably, universal laws, and endeavoured to make these claimed procedures clearer; second, they picked up late nineteenth-century ideas about formal logic, new ways of thinking about formal logic, and they endeavoured to make the logic of scientific argument clearer; finally, they also embraced a concern for the nature of language and sought to make the language of science clearer. The three themes ran together: thus the logical positivists sought to elucidate the language of natural science, the better to understand it and maybe to inform its work.

There were key differences between proponents of positivism and logical positivism: the former took the business of the description of facts to be essentially unproblematic – a matter of careful procedures of enquiry, whereas the latter granted that any and all claims about the natural world had to be made using language and that being so it was important to be clear just how language grasped the world, both in general, the matter of relationship of words and things, and also, more particularly, the relationship between the language of natural science and the natural world.

Detailed philosophical debates ensued about language, the nature of science and the status of the work of the logical positivists themselves. The logical positivists came up with a number of attempts to answer these questions. Centrally, they claimed that for a sentence to be meaningful it had to be analysable down to empirical claims, that is, words had sense because they were underpinned by reality. The principle of verification showed how scientific sentences could have meaning: any sentence could in principle be analysed down to claims about facts, the way it was verified. A number of other claims were made: thus a distinction between formal and substantive claims (as clearly mathematics and logic were not empirically verifiable, but were equally clearly crucial to science); and a distinction between claims that could be reduced to facts (meaningful) and claims that could not (meaningless). This last noted distinction had the effect of ruling out large areas of human reflection such as the humanities, ethics, politics and the like, where many sentences were found that did not state facts and so these sentences were strictly speaking meaningless; all they did was express simple subjective approval or disapproval.

The school comprised a number of members and they looked in particular to the work of a Viennese intellectual, Ludwig Wittgenstein. In an early published work he offered an elaborate theory of the relation of atomic facts to atomic propositions; language had meaning because it was underpinned by reality and so far as he was concerned he had demonstrated how language at base was simple, thus contributing to the modernist drive for simplicity and clarity.

Karl Popper's objections and counter proposal

The logical positivist approach to the analysis of the fundamental nature of natural science was criticized by another pre-war Viennese scholar, Karl Popper, who took the view that empirical reduction was impossible; it was not what natural scientists actually did and it also meant that the procedure of verification could not work either, so the core of the logical positivist programme failed. Popper, however, remained a great enthusiast for natural science, and with good reason, for in the early years of the twentieth century scientists made great strides in chemistry and physics. Popper was also a social reformer and worked for a while with the psychologist Alfred Adler, a student of Freud. Yet Popper became increasingly disenchanted with psychology and with then fashionable Marxism; he compared both unfavourably to the work of contemporary physicists.

In this way the distinction that the logical positivists had made between natural science and everything else was sustained. However, Popper offers an alternative view of the logic of natural scientific argument by first returning to an issue long debated by philosophers, the idea of inductive reasoning; the process whereby the accumulation of particular observations of facts will permit an intellectual act of generalization. Popper argues that this process – a shift from particulars to the general – does not work. This strategy of argument is not a matter of logic; it is only a psychological habit. Humans expect things to go on as they always have, so if they are used to seeing white swans they will argue (falsely) that all swans are white. Popper points to what he calls a logical asymmetry: it does not matter how many white swans you see because you cannot logically move to the general statement, however, if you begin with the statement all swans are white you only have to see one black swan in order to show your opening claim was false. Popper inverts induction; now natural science proceeds by making clever guesses, deriving ways of testing these guesses and if they survive the attempt to falsify them, then they survive, but only until the next test.

This gives us the notion of falsification: a statement is a scientific statement if it can in principle be falsified and, conversely, if there is no way for the statement to be falsified then it is not scientific. Popper's variant form of empiricism has proved very influential. It allows scholars to draw a distinction between scientific and non-scientific claims. It offers a model of what it is to be scientific (empirical hypotheses subject to empirical test – in the social sciences this points to a preference for quantification – qualitative work resists test/falsification). It downgrades the humanities and social sciences because however useful they may be, they do not have the clarity and surety of natural science. The distinction also has the subsidiary utility of ruling out Marxism as a strategy of securing social reform, and here Popper preferred to speak of piecemeal social engineering. Popper's work was tagged critical rationalism. It celebrated active reason, not passive fact gathering, and it made the natural scientist an active being, intellectually progressive, not conservative. It was, in sum, an optimistic view of the nature and utility of natural science. It was also, it might be noted, produced before the war. Later, Popper moved to London, where his work assumed something of a politically reactionary tone.

Finally, in similar sceptical vein, W.V.O Quine rejected positivism in favour of pragmatism. Quine argues that any substantive claim to facts rests on a whole web of prior commitments and any one of these can be abandoned, but at some likely cost. The body of work of natural sciences advances in an ad hoc fashion, reductive schemes don't help and the claims made within the realms of natural science exemplify what counts as knowledge.

It is this early twentieth-century celebration of natural science that has subsequently been modified, challenged and also rejected, so too, efforts to argue from the natural to the social sciences.

Thomas Kuhn and the idea of paradigms

Later scholars were somewhat more radical in their discussions of the nature of the sciences, moving away from reflections on abstract logic towards seeing natural science as a practical human pursuit. Theorists put natural scientific work back into its routine social context. All the pressures of institutional life impacted the research process: individual careers, office politics and the vagaries of outside demands (funding agency policies, institutional hierarchies and their priorities, links with the corporate world and more generally the attitudes of government agencies – for natural science is in the main very expensive).

So far as Kuhn was concerned natural scientists were not disembodied intellects and their professional interactions determined the pace and direction of natural science. Kuhn argued that natural scientists worked within socially created paradigms, sets of ideas built around a particularly interesting experimental procedure, which told scientists what there was to investigate and how to go about it (the paradigm established the parameters of the currently thinkable). The paradigm informed the practice of the discipline: the work of its practitioners, the training of its students, the contents of its papers and textbooks and so on. The community affirmed the dominant paradigm and ignored or explained away experimental results which did not fit within the paradigm framework; however, anomalous results could accumulate until eventually a younger generations of researchers would rebel, rejecting the old paradigm in favour of a new one. A period of revolutionary science would interrupt the flow of normal science. The implication of Kuhn's work was that natural science results were not simply established by getting the facts straight but also upon inter-subjective agreement; natural science was not a body of truths, rather it was a body of agreed truths.

There were two broad reactions to the work. First, proponents of positivism reacted negatively for they did not welcome the intrusion of social relations into the realm of scientific truths. Second, proponents of positivism within the social sciences welcomed the idea for if paradigms were so important then the failure of the social sciences to live up to the standards of the natural sciences could be explained. The social sciences were in a pre-paradigm state and all that needed to happen was agreement on a paradigm and then scientific output would begin.

The debates in respect of the social nature of the natural sciences and the implications of this evident situation for the research programmes, procedures and results of the sciences were all long debated. For the social sciences, it is with Kuhn's work that a slow movement away from arguments based on the received model began; social science, it was felt, could more readily accommodate the social aspect of their work – it marked a move towards historical and interpretive styles of work.

Some objections to invoking natural science

All these debates – and they are on-going – are aimed at elucidating the logic of natural science. As it is the brightest jewel in the cultural crown of modern civilization, such attention is not surprising, and that other disciplines should look to learn its lessons and apply them to their own concerns is to be expected. However, there have been objections to attempts to shift the assumptions and procedures of the natural sciences into the sphere of the social and such criticisms have been repeated down the years.

There have been two main lines of criticism (again, to anticipate later material):

- first, that even if social science could accumulate something that looked like facts, it would not add up to a natural science type activity because its core concern – humans – have the ability always and everywhere to refuse the proffered knowledge or evade the deployed expertise or over time, to simply change their minds and thus related social practices; in brief, as Alasdair MacIntyre has pointed out, human beings can judge the social world for themselves and answer back, and so human social life is not a material system;
- second, relatedly, where the natural scientists can operate with the notion of cause (natural systems can be characterized in terms of elaborate sets of causal relations built, finally, around the reductive core work of physics and chemistry with the resultant body of work expressed in the formal language of mathematics), social scientists cannot, for the human social world is shaped by the exchange of reasons in conversation – in brief, as Peter Winch has made clear, reasons not causes underpin human social action and interaction.

Alongside this high-level work there has been a less clearly articulated notion of the nature of the natural sciences and this it can be argued has fed most directly into the realms of the social sciences. It revolves around a double claim, or set of taken-for-granted ideas, first realism, that the world is disclosed directly to the senses (what you see is what there is), and second, induction (what you see are facts and these can be gathered up), pointing to a particular procedure of the accumulation of discrete descriptions of facts, the basis thereafter of generalizations and eventually the establishment of the fixed laws underpinning reality.

This received model offers a particular image of the practice of natural science (one that has been criticized, as noted above) as technical, accumulative and reliable. The practice discloses the facts of the world. It might also be said that the received model offers a curiously bloodless image of a breathtakingly ambitious and dazzlingly successful human cultural-intellectual endeavour. So when this narrow model is unpacked in the sphere of the social it produces a quite specific set of preferences for procedures (limited, restricted empirical studies) that in turn inform particular (often unspoken) forms of social practice (thus, policy science, arguments for figures of authority lodged within bureaucratic machines, state and corporate).

The positivistic style of social science has found expression in many areas of the social sciences (the institutional organization of the social sciences differs in various European countries – much influenced also by post-1945 American practices; here again, the tale is simplified):

- in economics – the practitioners of mainstream liberal market economics embrace a status akin to that of natural scientists (as they understand them) – thus, economic science studies the facts and processes of a self-subsisting, self-regulating system and its results are akin to those of the natural sciences (hence, the Nobel Prize for Economic Science – with most recipients American or based in US universities);
- in political science – with American scholars similarly influential – but with the claims to status weakened by equally influential traditions of political philosophy;
- in international relations work – again, commentators have noted a shift from European to US work – pre-war, with figures such as E.H. Carr, rooted in philosophy, sociology and history, and post-war, concerned with its intellectual status as it crossed the Atlantic;
- other disciplines have been more resistant – thus sociology or anthropology – their professional status suffers as a result – the arts and humanities have also resisted, their status is also (in the eyes of positivists) lower – some of these disciplines find that they are lodged outside the social sciences, thus, most obviously, history.

In sum, it is clear that arguments from the natural sciences to the social sciences have been influential and they continue to be influential and, given the dazzling success of the natural sciences and their central place in contemporary social world (a world unimaginable without the contribution of the natural sciences), it is entirely sensible to try to argue from the natural sciences to the social sciences. However, critics say quite clearly that these arguments do not work.

Arguments from human understanding

An alternative line of reflection on the nature, value and utility of social science is available from those philosophers and social theorists who have called attention to the centrality in human experience of language; in brief the claim made is that humankind inhabits language. These theorists argue that language is constitutive of our social world and that we move within the ambit of the conceptual repertoire of our ordinary language. This can change as new technologies and new forms of livelihood generate new ways of thinking and acting. And so new ideas suggest new ways of apprehending and acting in the world.

In sum, language is fundamentally social, it is carried in tradition, it shifts and changes down the generation, but is always central to human social life. A number of lines of reflection have been presented: first, hermeneutics; second, ordinary language philosophy; and third, cultural studies.

Hermeneutics: culture as text

The tradition of hermeneutics begins with nineteenth-century Christian biblical scholarship where a quite particular issue arose for some adherents to the religion. Protestantism had broken away from the Catholic Church for at the time of the split the former saw the latter as corrupt (institutionally and in terms of theology). Protestants had to accomplish two tasks (what we could tag as political): distancing themselves from the institutional machinery of the Catholic Church and at the same time finding a way to legitimize their version of the religion. The key was the sacred text. Adherents of the faith working within the Protestant tradition were committed to using the sacred text, the Bible, as direct personal access to their God. In this way believers could by-pass the church machinery that was crucial to Catholicism and access the revealed truths that legitimated their activities directly.

But this created a problem as the sacred text in question was some 2,000-years old and had been translated and retranslated and copied and recopied over this lengthy period. So, the question was, which text amongst the many versions available was the correct word of God. If the sacred text revealed the word of God, then it was no use reading a faulty translation or miscopied version. It had to be an accurate text. The question produced techniques of close textual analysis: language use, grammar, vocabularies and so on. It was a strategy of interpretation and it allowed scholars to determine which text was correct, which the less satisfactory version.

The scholar Wilhelm Dilthey took these ideas and shifted them into the territory of history, arguing that history was an interpretive science; the business of the historian was to sift through the available materials and produce the most reliable statement about the past. An early version of his approach stressed the task of the psychological grasp of historical actors' thought. Studying the available documents and artefacts was a route into the thoughts of the actors themselves; however Dilthey backed away from this appeal to psychology and in later work shifted away from human psychology to human language. Human social practices carried meaning and so they could be read and their meanings uncovered. Interpretation was a familiar skill. So for the social scientist, in this case, historian, human social practice could be analysed as a text-analogue.

Dilthey's work established a way of unpacking the nature of the social sciences, offered a coherent intellectual grounding and showed how they could be put to use – in brief, the basis for a non-natural science referring social science – an interpretive social science – one that was concerned to unpack the ways in which groups of people understood their worlds, worlds lodged in history.

A more recent figure offered stronger claims – presenting what has been called a philosophical hermeneutics. Where Dilthey offered hermeneutics as a strategy of interpretive research, unpacking patterns of meanings, Hans-Georg Gadamer goes one step further and argues that hermeneutics does not offer a new technique of interpretation; rather it offers an insight into the fundamental nature of human being.

Gadamer made human language central to the idea of what it is to be human. With Gadamer all experience is enfolded within the conceptual framework of received language. In brief, we inhabit language, and interpretation or understanding is not a technique to be learned, rather it is a fundamental characteristic of language-carried communication. No-one has to be taught how to interpret language, once the language is acquired (thus, mother-tongue acquired during infanthood), interpretation is automatic; cast in everyday terms, interpretation is an entirely taken-for-granted skill; humans have legs, they can walk, humans have language, they can talk/interpret.

The grounding for social science offered by the tradition of hermeneutics is thereby significantly reinforced; interpretation in conversation is central to human life and to human social practices, it is not a technique to be learned, rather it is central to human social practice, a routine social accomplishment. For the social sciences, human life becomes a complex conversation running down through time; ideas and social practice are embedded in language and history and the task of social science becomes interpretive commentary.

The philosophers of ordinary language

Similar work has been done by scholars of ordinary language and this line of work has its beginnings in the reflections on the nature of language pursued by Wittgenstein. As noted earlier in connection with logical positivism, working in early twentieth-century Vienna, Wittgenstein sought to contribute to then current intellectual concerns with intellectual and moral clarity in human reflection and he went to the heart of the issue and offered a model of language which, he claimed, revealed its elementary simplicity; language modelled the world, that was how it worked; at which point he retired from philosophy.

However, Wittgenstein came to realize that he had the story backwards and so he presented a second philosophy. Instead of language modelling the world (after the style of the natural sciences), it is taken to be thoroughly social in character. Language does not model the world, rather it is threaded through our ordinary social practice and it is the means whereby we constitute our social world and formulate our own myriad projects. It is a dramatic reversal and it put him in the same intellectual area as the hermeneutic theorists, for now language was key to human life. Wittgenstein argued that language games (patterns of language use) underpinned forms of life (patterns of social activity).

In the community of professional philosophers this was tagged ordinary language philosophy and they argued that familiar intractable philosophical problems could be dissolved away by attending very carefully to the way they were dealt with in ordinary language.

These ideas were moved into the territory of the social sciences by Peter Winch who looked at sociology (as a specimen social science) and argued that it had to be seen as an adjunct to philosophy – essentially interpretive – and not a second-class cousin of the natural sciences. Winch argued that both philosophy and sociology were doing essentially the same thing: the one elucidated the nature of rule following in general (after Wittgenstein, language as a socially embedded rule-governed system), the other elucidated examples of rule following in practice (the interpretive study of assorted language-carried social practices).

Winch made two central and overlapping arguments: first, to resist attempts to import the model of the natural sciences into the social sciences; and second, to establish the interpretive character of all social life and thus of a science of the social.

In regard to the first task, Winch made one central argument: that the notion of cause did not work within the social sciences; where relations between atoms and so on can be cast in terms of a notion of cause, relations between people cannot, for people act for reasons and these are always dependent upon social context. In brief, reasons are not causes, they are moves within a rational conversation. In regard to the second task, Winch looked at the nature of human interactions and notes that for most people most of the time the social world is perfectly intelligible, we know how to act and interact. Winch argues that social interaction is best thought of as moves in a conversation, not exchanges in a causal system.

In this work, once again, social science is given a grounding and role that does not refer to the natural sciences. Social science can elucidate the sets of ideas with which people make and remake their social worlds.

A further development of this line, influenced by the American tradition of pragmatism, was offered by Richard Rorty who followed up Wittgenstein's work by arguing that human language had no reductively identifiable base, it was social through and through, and so the fundamental contingency of human language had to be granted; thereafter human social life had no identifiable base for it too was social through and through, and so the fundamental contingency of human life had to be granted, and all this pointed towards an ironist's stance in regard to the forms of the social world, and in turn all this pointed to a distinctive way of dealing with the politics of the social world. Again, there were no guarantees and, that being so, sympathy for those less fortunate seemed like a good stance.

The work of cultural studies

A related line of reflection has been presented in the guise of cultural studies and here a number of strands of work can be identified. All are turned to the task of spelling out the patterns of understanding lodged in ordinary life: thus, the notions of subaltern cultures, popular cultures and media-carried commercial cultures; and in particular the idea of ordinary life, where such patterns of life and understanding were shaped by their system context, in particular, the demands of industrial capitalism.

Fred Inglis has identified three lines of work underpinning cultural studies: first, the critical English literature studies associated with F.R. Leavis (literature as a serious source of reflection upon human life); second, mainland European work influenced by humanist Marxism, thus, Antonio Gramsci and the Frankfurt School (plus, as an adjunct, work in hermeneutics); and third, work concerned with the nature of language, hence Ludwig Wittgenstein.

In its Birmingham School version cultural studies combined a language-informed sociology of subaltern classes with a strand of humanist Marxism, and the upshot was the detailed study of the cultural forms of ordinary life: in the first case, the work of Richard Hoggart, in the latter the work of Stuart Hall.

In sum, human social life is informed by language: it is the vehicle of human consciousness and self-consciousness; it offers the repertoire of concepts needed to inform ordinary social life; and it provides the start-point for the construction of the technical languages of particular disciplines. All of which may be true, but critics go on to say that attention should not be paid to language-in-general but to the actual circumstances of human argument, and here it is clear that there are systematic patterns within a language community – that is, issues of power and authority.

Arguments from human political organization

The work of scholars in hermeneutics attracted considerable attention: those disposed to copy across from the natural sciences dismissed the approach as subjective, unreliable and not amenable to clear empirical test or falsification – these criticisms are clear and have fuelled a long-running debate (positivism and anti-positivism) – those who were sympathetic saw a way of making social scientific enquiries that escaped the straightjacket of copied procedures and attended directly to the core of social life, that is, self-conscious, knowledgeable and routinely skilled interactions. All this has left the community of the social sciences somewhat split – broadly speaking, on the one hand, some scholars cling to the model of the natural sciences, thus mainstream liberal market economics, whilst others reject the model in favour of a variety of interpretive concerns, thus, sociology or history or cultural studies, and some seemingly dither, unable to decide one way or the other, thus, political science or international relations.

Stepping outside these debates, a further line of criticism of interpretive work has been made by scholars working with reference to the work of Karl Marx.

In brief, the line of criticism suggests that interpretive work is correct to seek to unpack the logics of forms of life (the ways in which people constitute their social environments), but it is wrong to treat such forms of life as simple givens, for they are not, rather they inherit earlier versions of the extant form of life (that is, they are lodged in history) and they are elaborately structured (they are ordered), and this opens up the question of the historical constitution and contemporary operation of forms of life, that is, their structures of power. These reflections inform the work of critical theory.

Marx is available in varieties – intellectual and official – and these variants can be noted: positivistic Marxism (the scientific analysis of the logic of capitalism), along with a closely related official Marxism (the official guiding theory adopted by the state, thus, the USSR (Soviet Union) or PRC (People's Republic of China)); plus a related line tagged humanist Marxism.

The tradition of scientific socialism

The former tradition has invoked a positivistic Marx usually associated with the work of his long-time collaborator Friedrich Engels; it reads Marx as an empirical social theorist and his work as a model of the unfolding logic of history so the past is described and the implications of the system's logic for the future is spelled out. Thereafter the tradition was embraced by the state machineries of the Soviet Union and later the PRC; positivistic Marxism is conjoined with official statements as to the nature and direction of the society (official ideologies, national pasts and the like) and these are taken to inform the policy stances of the state. Social theorists operating within these political systems therefore cast their work in appropriate terms, unpacking and elucidating the historical logic of the system and in the light of shifting circumstances determining appropriate pragmatic policy advice.

Proponents of this line of work understand their task in fundamentally technical terms; social scientific research work unpacks as policy advice, and such advice will be deployed (or not) by the denizens of the party-state system. There is no room in this scheme for a public sphere, for this idea belongs to the very different tradition of humanist or critical Marxism.

Humanist Marxism and critical theory

A reaction to this style of work, in its European guise, began in the early years of the twentieth century when the outbreak of the Great War saw a surge in popular nationalism and so Marxist hopes for an international solidarity of the working classes were dashed. Later, following the 1917 revolution in Russia, similar attempts, such as they were, in other European states failed as a result of lack of popular support plus effective elite repression. In the wake of these events scholars working within or with reference to the work of Marx and his successors turned to the issue of culture and they embraced the argument that individuals and groups acted in the light of their understanding of their circumstances; they were not the simple carriers of trans-individual system pressures.

Humanist Marxism is usually said to have its roots in the early work of Marx. This work was explicitly ethically engaged (notions of alienation); it was rooted in philosophy (the idea of dialectical analysis); and it was turned towards involvement with public arguments (critique of ideology). All this in contrast to later positivistic Marxism, which tried to model capitalism as a species of natural system, hence production relations and the dynamics of class conflict, together generating pressures for inevitable evolutionary, progressive change. Two comments are necessary, first, the positivistic line can be recycled in terms of ideas of structures (sets of circumstances confronting any one agent, hence pressures to act, but no mechanism); and second, the humanist strand of work was present in all the work created by Marx (thus, the *Grundrisse*).

The tradition was picked up by the members of the Frankfurt School: Max Horkheimer, Theodor Adorno, plus others such as Herbert Marcuse and Erich Fromm. They worked in the 1930s and constructed an approach to analysis characterized as critical; adopting a variant hermeneutic interpretive approach they added the socio-political context of any interpretive exchange, thus all conversations take place within given contexts and these are always suffused with power relations. So communication is distorted. Critical analysis can dissolve these distortions, showing how ruling elites shape popular thinking in order to buttress their privileged positions (ideologies) and in the context of the 1930s they offered criticisms of advanced capitalism endeavouring to show how its ideological and cultural superstructure served to sustain the system as a whole.

The members of the Frankfurt School were scattered by the episode of the rise of National Socialism and the subsequent warfare in Europe; after the Second World War the school was reconstituted in West Germany. A key figure over many years has been Jürgen Habermas who, in a series of intellectual exchanges with Marx, wider groups of European thinkers and the work of American scholars, constructed an influential novel restatement of the critical Marxist tradition, offering a diagnosis of the costs of the demands of the system of industrial capitalism upon the life-world of those working within the system. Habermas proposed a strategy of reform centred upon the notion of democracy, arguing that building up the strength of the public sphere (a realm of free debate amongst citizens) would enable the collective control of the system and its redirection in ways that better serve the majority of the population.

The substantive work has been influential but for present purposes it is enough to note that Critical Theory offers grounding for a social science that does not rely upon borrowing from the received model of the natural sciences.

The social sciences: talking amongst ourselves, talking with others

Stephen Gudeman, writing about the anthropological analysis of forms of human livelihood, offers a distinction between universal models and local models, where the former have often been embraced by First World theorists, before going on to make the point that purported universal models are really just one more type of local model. Or, put another way, it is not possible to step out of one's received culture because there is nowhere to step to – all social theorizing is informed by tradition and bound by context – that said, the aspiration of scholarship remains to 'get the story straight'.

The social sciences: nature, status and utility

Overall, reviewing discussions of the social sciences, three key issues can be addressed: the nature, status and utility of the social sciences.

It can be argued that the core of the European tradition of social theorizing is the interpretive-critical elucidation of the dynamics of complex change in the ongoing shift to the modern world. This world is read in philosophical materialist terms – the central business of human beings is with the social production of livelihood or forms of life and the materials of the social sciences are just one more attempt to make sense of the social world, here cast in terms of scholarship – the whole informing the public sphere.

The status of the social sciences is in principle clear. It is one more attempt to make sense of the social world alongside the efforts of witch doctors, shamans, policy analysts, politicians and every drunk in every bar in every country on earth. What distinguishes the social sciences is not any sort of borrowing from the natural sciences, rather it is the make-up and commitments of a discrete community. Within the community of social scientists there is a common commitment to the dispassionate display of the truth (getting the story straight) and to the environment of mutual public criticism, and its status within the wider realm of makers of sense derives from this tradition of disciplined enquiry.

The utility – getting the story straight – in European contexts feeds into the public sphere; optimistically, the self-understandings and social knowledge of elite and mass figures will be enhanced and thus the social world might be better ordered. Or, cast in substantive terms, social sciences is centrally concerned with elucidating the dynamics of complex change in the on-going shift to the modern world.

Other cultures: talking with other people

There are particular difficulties when dealing with other cultures. First, as there is no context-free point from which the social world may be viewed, enquiry into other cultures will be cast in terms of available domestic resources and these add up to a wealth of taken-for-granted assumptions. The core idea in the classical tradition is the notion of the shift to the modern world – moving from its European core in order to embrace other cultures, so that numerous local trajectories embodying their local models are drawn into the unfolding project of the shift to the modern world. It is one more local model and it orders enquiry.

The materials of the classical European tradition of social science are bound up with the unfolding shift to the modern world; they have their origins and subsequent development in the work of generations of scholars attempting with greater or lesser insight to decipher the logic of this unfolding process. The materials are shaped by and have shaped these processes. Consequently, they are not culturally neutral.

The materials of the classical European tradition of social science are rooted in long established traditions of reflection upon the nature and possibilities of human knowing and the territory of the social sciences are one part of this wider field. It means that the tradition – as described – is freighted with cultural assumptions. The discussion here has revolved around one set of assumptions, the nature of science; the other crucial idea embedded in these materials is the idea of progress.

It is possible to look for analogues in other cultures; thus, as all communities have to be ordered somehow it is not unreasonable to look for the logics of local politics. However, these logics are likely to be lodged deeply within forms of life. Two closely related strategies of enquiry can be deployed: ethnographic work, thick description of patterns of life, thereafter interrogated to pull out underlying logics; and dialogue with local agents where such dialogue requires a reflexive awareness of the assumptions brought to these exchanges. In this way (some) knowledge of the political logics and shifting historical trajectories of other communities can be uncovered.

It is clear that there are other cultures within the global system. It is also clear that the classical European work is interpretive. It cannot make a claim to culture-free technical expertise. It is not a natural science (setting aside debates about the way those endeavours are shaped by their circumstances) so the materials of the tradition cannot be applied to other cultures, they can only be the basis of interpretations proffered in the hope of conversation, that is, dialogue with others.

An orientation towards East Asia

The discussion of the historical development trajectories of the countries of the broad area of East Asia are made with these materials and presented with this orientation in mind. It is a view of East Asia made using the materials of the tradition, which this author inhabits. There is no culturally neutral point but dialogue is available; scholars in other places write and their work is available, other places may be visited and local life grasped directly, so much can be said. But the result – inevitably – will be shaped by the culture of the writer. What follows, therefore, is an inevitably partial view, but it is informed by the core ethic of European scholarship, trying to get the story straight, and it is offered as a contribution to dialogue with those inhabiting other traditions.

2

SUBSTANTIVE APPROACHES

The resources of current disciplines

The analysis of political life encompasses many discrete strategies. Particular issues can and are addressed using a variety of techniques. However, first, the broad spread of available approaches can be noted, where each sets up enquiry in a particular way, resting on domain assumptions, and these basic intellectual machineries establish what questions can and cannot be asked. A short survey is useful because, in brief, the history of the social sciences gives contemporary theorists both a tradition and a repertoire of concepts. And this text rests on a particular reading of the received classical European tradition of social theorizing – concerned, at heart, with the elucidation of complex change in the on-going shift to the modern world.

In this text, in regard to handling the detail of the records of the countries of East Asia, a particular approach is utilized that focuses on the dynamic interplay between structures and agents. The approach draws on available intellectual resources in regard to interpretation and critique, but, in brief, it is best thought of as a species of historical institutionalism coupled to culture-critical analysis. It allows an analyst to uncover structural patterns and the ways in which groups, including social scientists, have read and reacted to enfolding circumstances, arguments that can be presented dialogically in exchanges with other cultures.

Reading complex change: the materials of the classical European tradition

C. Wright Mills, in the appendix to his famous book *The Sociological Imagination*, remarks that the work of a scholar begins at the imaginative intersection of private concerns and public issues. It is here that a question or problem or issue is given preliminary shape, vague at the outset, becoming clearer during the process of research. The initial problem is addressed in terms of the available resources of the social sciences (the aspiration is to scholarship, not journalism, or diary-keeping or novel writing and so on) and these resources are found in the established set of disciplines, which have their own areas of concern and typically make claims for the status of the work they produce. The whole bundle of disciplinary enquiries can then be lodged in history and their provenance uncovered (that is, how and why they developed when and as they did); what then emerges in view is a tradition of enquiry. Any tradition (European, American, East Asian, Latin American or wherever) will have diverse elements (debates), will show phases of activity (particular concerns at various times) and have a discernible core concern and a spread of related concepts. These resources are the raw materials that any scholar, confronting current problems, must call on in order to advance enquiry. The process of enquiry deploys these materials and in doing so both reaffirms and advances the tradition of enquiry in which it is lodged: a reflexive and iterative process.

This text is lodged in the classical European tradition of social science.

The core concern of the tradition is with the analysis of complex change in the unfolding shift to the modern world.

The tradition takes shape in the early modern period, roughly, from the seventeenth century through to the nineteenth. In the nineteenth century it takes the particular form of political economy, that is, a holistic enquiry into the logic of the system and its dynamic interactions with the lives of ordinary people (lately cast as the dynamic of structure and agents). It takes its present form in the early twentieth century as political economy gave way to a spread of specialist disciplines. It is a live tradition and enquiry is on-going, so disciplinary work continues but areas of work are not fixed and nor are their results. Circumstances can embarrass or even overturn the claims of specialists: thus mainstream international relations in the 1980s when only marginal and disregarded figures thought the Soviet Union could reform, so that the events of 1989 were consequently wholly unexpected, and so too the 1991 collapse of the Soviet Union; more recently, mainstream neo-classical economics was unprepared for the 2008–10 financial crisis, regarding such events as a near impossibility. In regard to these matters the roots of contemporary disciplines can be sketched out; their construction, along with their particular sets of ideas and the institutional bases for their professional pursuit. The upshot of this review will be a reaffirmation of the core classical European tradition, a tradition rooted in political economy and available to be turned to the task of uncovering patterns of complex change in the on-going shift to the modern world.

Work in the early modern period

Any summary of the work of several centuries will offer a radically simplified story; the comments here are presented to recall that the European tradition is long established, rich and intellectually vigorous.

The eighteenth century

The earliest contributions to the European tradition of social sciences were made in the seventeenth and eighteenth centuries in the work of those tagged Enlightenment scholars. The earliest work was done in England. It was arguably pre-Enlightenment, but it was concerned both with the rise of natural science and the nature of ordered social life. It was characterized by the historian Roy Porter as a philosophy of expediency: Thomas Hobbes, John Locke and Isaac Newton.

Hobbes invoked the Newtonian scientific method of reductive analysis in order to deal with the political situation of England in the wake of civil warfare. Hobbes reduced society to individuals, social atoms, each pursuing their own desires, resulting in an inherent situation of conflict, such conflict needing the discipline of an overarching sovereign power. In a similar fashion, Locke, an English gentleman farmer, reduced the social world to families, thereafter reconstructing the social world in a more cooperative contractual fashion. These two theorists are regarded, today, as the founding fathers of the tradition of philosophical liberalism, a richly developed tradition that looks to the rich detail and difficulties of human life in terms that one way or another can be reduced to the lives of individuals.

During the eighteenth century the example of England was invoked by the French theorists of the Enlightenment as they looked to England and saw a prosperous orderly society, thus as an example. In respect of the French social world these social critics confronted the institutional and intellectual power of the Catholic Church and the Monarchy. The line of argument that they made celebrated human reason in place of received traditions and authorities (thus the religious claims of the church or the claims to the correctness of tradition in respect of royal authority). They sought to overturn traditional authority, not merely to make an abstract argument but to make a social revolution: reason could be deployed to analyse the social world – its history, institutions and, crucially, possibilities for the future. These theorists were tagged the *philosophes* and their work was turned to the ideas of republican democracy (no mere philosophy of expediency) and they can be taken to have been the theorists of the French Revolution.

The early nineteenth century saw the publication of materials that are now taken as founding texts in the contemporary social sciences. The process of the shift to the modern world had been established and natural science-based industrial society was taking shape, processes usually labelled the industrial revolution together with the democratic revolution. The movement away from intellectual received authority had been secured, the shift away from abstract philosophical reasoning had been made, and what now emerged was a theoretically informed analysis of the contemporary social world, the rapidly changing world that these theorists endeavoured to understand.

The first version of recognizably modern social science was cast in terms of political economy, which was a holistic analysis of the social production of human livelihood, concerned with both the logic of the system and its interchange with ordinary people, what much later came to be tagged the life-world.

The nineteenth century

The nineteenth century saw the rapid development of industry and later in the century the natural sciences advanced rapidly. In the early years of the century debates in Britain revolved around political economy, later Darwinism was influential and mainland scholars learned from these experiences whilst advancing their own lines of argument.

1 Debates in Britain: political economy: Smith, Ricardo and Marx

The nineteenth century saw the rise of industrial-capitalist society; the paradigm case was that of Britain and social scientific reflection upon this process was cast in terms of political economy. This was an enquiry into the social production of livelihood; that is, holistic analyses of system logics and the nature of the lives of people. The late eighteenth century pre-industrial work of Adam Smith was followed by David Ricardo, Thomas Malthus and later J.S. Mill; a locally based émigré critic, not much noted at the time, also contributed, Karl Marx.

Work in political economy was theoretically informed and basic arguments were made formally: thus, for example, the key contributors to the production of social wealth were identified as land, labour and capital. Each class made a distinctive contribution to the system as a whole (resources, labour power and finance), each class received rewards in a particular fashion (rent, wages and profits) and each had a particular interest in the political situation and future (the status quo, radical change and future advantage). The system worked overall. Thereafter, supplementing the analysis, many intellectual novelties were introduced; thus, again for example, Ricardo's iron law of wages (the labouring classes were destined not to rise) and the idea of comparative advantage (some places could do some jobs, best that they specialize and then exchange products with other places); similarly, Malthus's ideas about agricultural production (arithmetic growth) and human population (geometric growth) leading inevitably to population decline courtesy of disease, famine and war.

The work was formally structured and empirically rich, as data and examples were accumulated. The work was engaged and the distributive character of the contemporary form of economic life was discussed; that is, the political and ethical implications of the system logic were clarified. However, that said, it was in overall character, positivistic, thus it was supposed that reason could unpack the logic of the contemporary social world the better to control its direction. It was also in overall character, optimistic, expectations of the future shifted from received theological concerns with perfection, the ends of human life in heaven, to the mundane concerns of social analysts and reformers with accumulative advance, that is, with progress.

Adam Smith is usually taken to be the precursor of political economy. Writing in the late eighteenth century during the Scottish Enlightenment, essentially a pre-industrial period, Smith invokes both moral sentiment and material interests in people in order to discuss the social creation of wealth. He opposed mercantilism in favour of open commercial trade, thus the individual pursuit of material gain, disciplined by social rules, will produce the greatest benefit for all members of the community. Smith is writing for the new commercial bourgeoisie in Scotland and

England. Later, a fully developed political economy was offered by David Ricardo. Working in the early nineteenth century, Ricardo was a key figure in the creation of the tradition of English political economy. He analysed the social production of livelihood in terms of class groups, land, labour and capital, noted their contributions to the economy, noted their resultant income flows and, thereafter, economic interests. Ricardo presented the notions of labour theory of value (social creation of value), comparative advantage (such that trade benefits all) and the subsistence theory of wages (which suggested that those with only their labour to sell would not do very well, earning only enough for material survival and reproduction).

An influential figure, later in the nineteenth century, was Karl Marx. Writing in the middle of the nineteenth century, during a period of rapid social change as industrial capitalism flourished, his work was rooted in philosophy and the core of his approach was historical materialism. Marx offered a critique of existing political economy, which in his view underestimated the role of social class, and offered a discussion of class dynamics as the driving logic of the system. Karl Marx is writing for the newly created mass working classes of Europe.

2 Charles Darwin and Social Darwinism

These ideas were buttressed by the influential work of Charles Darwin. The cross-links between Darwin and the extant social sciences were many, intellectual influences flowed both ways; thus, the idea of competition. But Darwin was read as a theorist of the evolution in the natural world and in these terms his work was spectacularly original. It also cut directly against still influential religious doctrinal positions and thus caused considerable controversy. However, social theorists, following Darwin, looked in a similar fashion for competition and evolution in the social world. Here there were awkward debates. Darwin was read into the social sciences with mixtures of understanding, misunderstanding and extension – in particular, some theorists picked up the ideas of race, race competition, survival of the fittest and related ideas of eugenics. It was not only an ambiguous contribution to social scientific thinking but also an ambiguous contribution to social practice. And notwithstanding that Darwinian evolution is a mix of chance and necessity as the organism adapts to changing circumstances (thus 'survival of the fittest' is signalled only by the fact of survival), the idea that survival meant that the organism was somehow 'better' fed into a notion of evolution-as-progress – a social misreading stuck – it suited the English 'Whig' interpretation of history as a process of slow inevitable improvement. These ideas were codified, so to say, by Stanley Spencer with the idea of Social Darwinism; they were also picked up by the eugenics movement, with social reformers dedicated to welfare measures oriented towards improving the human stock. And some of these ideas fed into the thinking of scholars in Japan and other parts of East Asia around the turn of the twentieth century, although in Europe they ran into the sands after the cultural debacle of National Socialism.

3 Mainland scholars: Durkheim, List and Weber

All this work in building the European tradition of social theorizing was further buttressed by the work of mainland European scholars: for example, in France, the work of August Comte and Emile Durkheim, the former offering an ambitious scheme designed to order the new industrial world, with the latter arguing on behalf of the progressive bourgeois.

In France, Emile Durkheim, writing in the late nineteenth century during a period of rapid change with industrialization becoming important, deploys an organic metaphor to grasp the nature of the changing social world. Just as a living organism can be analysed in terms of the function of each part in sustaining the whole organism, so the social world can be analysed in terms of its functional components. Durkheim presented an analysis of the social world cast in terms of social causes: the logic of the social system could be grasped in terms of an organic metaphor where function was the key. Thus the social world of industrial life had produced an elaborate division of labour where each sector contributed to the whole, which was integrated by the new ethos of individualism. Durkheim identified a complex division of labour as the core of the industrial system and the refinement of the division of labour ensured evolutionary progress in the social world. Durkheim argued that social solidarity was not (as critics said) breaking down, rather the growth of individualism was a new source of social order, that is, it functioned to bind people together in a novel fashion. The social problems that could be seen were summed up as anomie; they flowed from failed or less than satisfactory integration into the social whole. Durkheim was writing for those who wished France to become a modern republic.

In Germany, further contributions to the tradition were made by Max Weber and Friedrich List. List was a key figure within the German Historical School. He argued that those countries that came to industrial capitalism late were confronted with a global system that was already controlled by those countries that had already developed, and from this he drew the conclusion that late development required protection such that local economic upgrading could be accomplished. Again, these ideas were influential in late nineteenth-century Japan. And, later, Max Weber, writing in the earliest years of the twentieth century, was a German nationalist who was both anxious about the behaviour of the German bourgeoisie (too complacent, leaving political space for traditional reactionaries) and concerned with the nature of industrial capitalist society (shaped by rigid bureaucratic rules). Weber rejected schemes that made human thought secondary to economic status and looked to the business of individuals thinking and acting. Weber is pessimistic about the future but thinks that the German bourgeoisie, his audience, have to take control of the direction of the country.

Late nineteenth- and early twentieth-century reaction

As the nineteenth century drew to a close, natural science-based industrial society moved ahead rapidly: new sciences were developed (chemistry, physics) and new industries emerged. There were significant flows of people: some moved from rural to urban areas, and rural society began a long slow decline, as did the status of the churches; there was heavy migration to North America. In time all this produced a reaction. First, substantive/practical: thus it was clear that there were problems in the social world; the practical downsides of rapid industrialization were flagged by a variety of both progressive social reformers and reactionary groups looking to a rapidly receding past. Second, intellectual/speculative: it was clear that new thinking was needed; an intellectual reply to changing circumstances was made in the social sciences, arts and humanities in the guise of a wide philosophical and moral reaction against positivism and the apparent reduction of human life to the mere pursuit of material goods.

This strand of reaction found clearest expression in mainland European thinking, a diverse group of thinkers came to reject the crude materialism of the positivists (utility) and their equally simple mechanic-formal styles of argument (self-regulating systems) in favour of a reaffirmation of the nature of human beings as irreducibly social, routinely creative and practical (thus reasoning worked within received traditions and involved moral, aesthetic and practical reasoning, as well as the narrow sub-set of rational calculation favoured by newly influential neo-classical economists). One novel departure included, in particular, the rise of the idea of the unconscious and the irrational in human life. In sum, the late nineteenth century produced romanticism: it was available in varieties, progressive and reactionary (approval/disapproval): in politics, a reaffirmation both of the role of culture as carried by tradition and the contrasting novelty of urban life; in society, a reaffirmation of the notion of inherited patterns of community and the contrasting possibilities of new forms of living; and in culture, experimentation, in particular, in the arts, modernism, celebrations of design along with affirmation of the appropriateness of new arts to the realms of ordinary life.

All this work can be summed up under two headings: first, the idea of tradition and, second, the notion of a conceptual vocabulary. In the former case the work constituted a tradition of enquiry, a body of sophisticated work, running debates internally at the same time as intellectual machineries were put to work to read the social world. The tradition has not been fixed. It is not a settled canon of great names. Work shifts as issues internal to scholarship and external to it in the wider social world are addressed. In the second case, attention is directed to the quotidian realm of this tradition, that is, to a rich conceptual vocabulary, the basic vocabulary of the contemporary social sciences.

As this work spilled into the twentieth century it was increasingly ordered in terms of disciplines, and the intellectual endeavours of the scholars of the Enlightenment, which had ranged freely across the territories of today's social sciences, were increasingly channelled into discrete areas of enquiry. Each discipline claimed an area of expertise and these areas were to be kept separate in the knowledge marketplace. Thus key disciplinary concerns, methods and results were all created and deployed within a burgeoning institutionally ordered knowledge marketplace.

The process can be summed up in these terms:

- expansion, fragmentation and consolidation – the work of social scientists grows as more people are involved and more topics pursued – but questions once pursued freely become the restricted concern of one or other delimited professional group – as disciplines take shape more attention is paid to this sort of work – it feeds into state, corporate and public spheres;
- institutionalization and professionalization – disciplines are consolidated within the confines of new institutions – universities, research centres and so on – and in these environments they build up their particular stocks of knowledge — associations, journals, degree schemes and so on – thereafter they lay claim to exclusive control – to accredited professional expertise.

Divisions of intellectual labour

As the nineteenth century advanced the analyses of change informed by the debates of the Enlightenment (and criticized by theorists of romanticism) slowly gave way to the spread of specialist disciplines, which now order the social sciences. This process took place during the period from – roughly – the 1870s marginal revolution through to the outbreak of the Great War, a period of around forty or so years. The first moves to reform were made in the sphere of what is now economics.

First moves towards change

One starting point was found amongst English theorists where the broad prospective work of political economy produced a reaction, a narrowly politico-intellectual reaction as theorists objected to its apparent generality (holistic work embracing many issues), its moral engagement (questions of distribution) and its technical inability to resolve the issue of value and market price. The rise of marginalist economics addressed these problems: value was expressed as price, determined by supply and demand in the competitive marketplace; labour was one more commodity which had its price, determined by the labour market (so worrying about distribution was not necessary as the logic of the marketplace determined price); and, finally, the work could be unpacked in a technical fashion using mathematics. In England, Stanley Jevons was a key figure. Other work was done in Austria, where around the turn of the twentieth century Vienna was a major intellectual centre; again, theorists, including the influential Carl Menger, were concerned with analyses of individual-based market activity and again the individual came to the fore.

The marginalist revolution displaced political economy. In place of the complexities of the political economy, with its multiple classes, inequalities and inherent conflicts, neo-classical economics offered a model of an individual-based self-regulating system – the market – and the concerns of political economists were simply by-passed.

In England, as political economy was overtaken by new concerns (for markets and the price mechanism), neo-classical economics took shape and so too did sociology. The former claimed the status of a hard social science, that is, sought the status and utility of the natural sciences, whilst the latter was left to deal with the realms of subjective social interactions, implicitly, a lower status activity. Similar debates took place in France, where sociology was established early as a core social science discipline – Emile Durkheim – and in Germany, where the divisions of labour were somewhat different but overall the process of creating discrete disciplines continued.

The process was facilitated by the growth of the modern university system. The social sciences found new homes in new faculties in the new universities. A key here was the development of the American university system and the related emergence of distinct professional bodies serving particular disciplines. A number of influential professional bodies emerged: German Economic Society (1873); American Economic Association (1885); Royal/British Economic Society (1890); American Political Science Association (1903); American Sociological Association (1905); German Sociological Association (1909); French Economic Association (1950); British Sociological Association (1951); International Studies Association (1959); and British International Studies Association (1975). These associations with various local inflections were copied in many other countries and, in the years following the Second World War and the rise to prominence of the USA, it was, unsurprisingly, the American pattern of learned societies that was copied in other places.

It should be noted that there were other strategies of institutionalization. All societies have ways of reflecting upon their logics and legitimations. Scholars of the humanities along with historians are able to identify what have been tagged Great Traditions, complex sets of ideas carried in the work of formalized cultural machineries such as religion and the arts (the realms of the powerful and their ritual modes of display). These same scholars can also identify Little Traditions – the sets of ideas carried in routine ordinary social life. The shift to the modern world impacted these received forms of thinking around the planet.

The historical trajectory of the Europeans took the shape of the creation of state-empires and modernity was presented to a global, albeit mostly elite, audience in the guise of European colonial rule. Local scholars and political agents had to read and react to these novel circumstances: in China, an early response to the arrival of the modern world in the guise of rapacious foreigners was called 'self-strengthening'; in Japan, the Meiji reformers organized study missions to Europe and America; and, of course, many political figures travelled. The ideas carried in the very notions of modernity could be transferred, notwithstanding the deceits and cruelties of the colonial environment, thus colonial pilgrimages: Ghandi and Nehru travel to Britain; Lee Kuan Yew travels to Britain; Ho Chi Minh travels to France; and Mao Zedong travels to the USSR. In the Soviet Union and the People's Republic of China the social sciences were gathered under the heading of Marxism – represented as a counter-tradition to the social sciences of the Western capitalist societies.

Once again, ideas travel – the pattern of social science disciplines finds further instances – further ways in which the impulse to understand the unfolding modern world could be expressed.

The current spread of disciplines described

Conventionally, there is a quartet of disciplines. (1) Economics – the positive study of individual behaviour in the marketplace – has its roots in nineteenth-century political economy and has developed along multiple tracks (schematically – political economy, mainstream neo-classical market economics and institutional economics). (2) Sociology – the interpretive study of the ways in which individuals dwell within communities – has its roots in early twentieth-century divisions of labour and is available in diverse strands (abstract theory (various) and applied social policy (various)). (3) Political science – the positive study of individual behaviour in the political realm – has its roots in the early twentieth-century division of labour and is available in a variety of forms (institutional, behavioural and rational choice). (4) International relations – the study of exchanges between sovereign states – has its roots in early twentieth-century divisions of labour and is typically focused on the institutional machineries of the state (domestic and international).

In addition, there are sister discipline areas dealing with cultural analysis: the work of arts and humanities, notably philosophy (dealing with nature of knowledge in natural and social sciences, ethics and political philosophy), narrative history (unpacking details of historical trajectories of political communities), cultural studies (unpacking the ways in which historically carried demands of the elite find wide expression throughout society) and law (the business of using formal texts to buttress order).

In respect of the two areas of political science and international studies, Colin Hay reviews contemporary approaches and argues for a critical political analysis that is alert to the role of ideas, sensitive to the balance between structures and agents and always attentive to the open-ended contingency of economic, social and political systems. Hay offers a summary of the available traditions, detailing in particular the influence of the post-war rise of the USA and the spread of its English-language vehicle influence is evident. Thus, political science in its current form can be characterized as in significant measure an American discipline, narrowly focused and professionalized. In contrast, the classical European tradition offers different pictures of the nature of political life: not the mechanisms of party competition and institutional power, rather the historical dynamic of complex change.

In the discipline of political science, three strands can be distinguished. First, institutionalism: early on this focused on the study of formal institutions of government taking the standard descriptions of the functions of each part (ministry, legislature, committees and so on) as given; it fell out of favour during the 1950s and 1960, but has since revived and new institutionalism looks in more detail at the processes animating the machineries of the state. Second, behaviourism: in the post-Second World War period social scientific work was often characterized by a preoccupation with natural science style empirical analysis. Scholars favoured quantification, studying that which could be readily quantified; such enquiry was presented as atheoretical, and its domain assumptions militated against interpretive and critical work. Third, rational choice theory: this developed in the post-war period and argued from a neo-classical economic analysis of individual choice making within a competitive marketplace to the analogous analysis of individual choice making in a competitive political environment.

In the discipline of international relations, there are three strands. First, idealism/liberalism: the work of early twentieth-century idealists conventionally associated with President Wilson and the League of Nations argued that enlightened self interest favours peace; similarly, post-Second World War liberalism argued that international trade favoured cooperation so once again enlightened self interest was invoked. Second, realism/neo-realism: realism has its roots in the 1930s, as E.H. Carr argued that states act in the light of their interests; they are pragmatic, amoral and calculative. So idealism was rejected. Post-Second World War neo-realism offered a similar analysis cast in structural terms; the global system was unregulated and this environment shaped state realist behaviour. Third, constructivism: an interpretive approach (various strands) that calls attention to agency; the global system is animated by persons and persons act in the light of their understandings; consequently states come to hold institutionally secured opinions of themselves and others; so ideas shape global exchanges.

Mainstream work is intellectually rich and so too the classical tradition; it is these materials that are available to social scientists as they deal with their particular research questions.

Putting it to work

Social theorizing is an active and prospective business as sets of ideas are taken from the materials of available tradition and put to work in order to produce substantive analyses; in this way, theoretical machineries are enhanced or modified or abandoned. The intellectual tradition shapes enquiry and is reaffirmed and reshaped in its turn.

Argument making – formal and substantive

Mills argued that the scholarly imagination begins with the contingent intersection of private concerns and public issues; this intersection prompts intellectual curiosity, in turn shaped into a specific question, which can be pursued using the intellectual machineries of the social sciences.

The business can be summarized in the form of two diagrams: one diagram addresses the formal relationship of the elements involved in making an argument; the other addresses the substantive phases of a simple research process.

Formally, the elements of an enquiry can be thought of in terms of four windows: the first window, the largest, sitting in the front of the computer screen, contains the question to be pursued or the problem to be investigated; the second window, sitting behind the first, contains all the intellectual machineries of the social sciences; the third window, sitting behind the second, contains all the intellectual machineries of the philosophy of social science; and the fourth window, siting behind the third and encompassing the run of windows, contains the materials of history, the widest social context within which all enquiry takes place.

And substantively, the process of making enquiry can be thought of as an iterative process: it all starts with curiosity > intellectual tradition > theory > questions that can be asked > specific question > methods of answering > results > discussion > presentation to audience.

Argument making – change and development

The review of available theory plus the focus of this text on change and development in East Asia results in a number of broad scholarly concerns. Each informs an aspect of the overall enquiry: (1) historical analysis – turned to the task of detailing the unfolding trajectories of polities in the unfolding shift to the modern world; (2) critical analysis – turned to the business of the elucidation of the collective understandings of these processes as presented in official texts, scholarly analyses and ordinary life; (3) forms of life – a concern for the contingent patterns of social life within any community; (4) a focus on the business of complex change – this is a domain assumption of the European tradition of social theorizing that specifies a core concern; (5) the idea of development, created in the relationship of sometime metropolitan cores to earlier now independent peripheries, which points to the nominally engineered historical development trajectories.

Theorizing change and development in East Asia

In brief, from the discussions made in Chapter 1, the idea can be taken that any work made within or with reference to the classical European tradition will be philosophically interpretive, critical and dialogic. In brief, from the survey work presented in this chapter, the strategies of historical institutionalism supplemented by culture-critical work can be taken. And from survey work done by numerous development theorists, their discussions of the business of grasping and ordering complex change can be taken. These three areas of reflection will feed into the substance of the discussions presented in this text – a comparative discussion of complex change and development in East Asia.

In sum: this text is lodged within the classical European tradition and will offer an interpretive and critical analysis of the historical development trajectories of the present collection of countries that together are familiarly taken to comprise the macro region of East Asia – the shift to the modern world will be noted as it impacted extant civilizations, the absorption of the region into European state-systems will be discussed, so too the disintegration of these systems and the creation of novel states, which, thereafter, have pursued nation building and development – the text will endeavour to attend both to system logics and life-worlds.

3
GRASPING THE CORE LOGICS OF FORMS OF LIFE

The materials of the European tradition of social theorizing revolve around a core preoccupation with the elucidation of the dynamics of complex change in the unfolding shift to the modern world. Within this tradition the historical trajectories of discrete polities can be described and their animating logics unpacked where such enquiries would typically embrace a range of work from the social sciences and humanities. A central aspect of the logics of these polities will be the fundamental issue of material and social welfare for these concerns lie at the heart of human communities. It is here that the business of the social production of livelihood can be found. This chapter reviews social scientific approaches to the analysis of the social production of livelihood and offers an agenda for the analysis of the historical trajectories of the extant polities of East Asia.

An agenda for East Asia

The earlier discussions of the nature of social theorizing, both formal and substantive, demonstrated the richness and cultural context-bound nature of the classical tradition of European social theorizing – the tradition, in general, is interpretive, critical and dialogic and is turned to the analysis of complex change. A number of key ideas were identified as more directly useful for the current text, which is oriented towards the issue of change and development in East Asia and these were summarized as follows: first, there were strategies of analysis, then there were some deeper assumptions of enquiry.

First, in regard to strategies of enquiry this text uses two strategies. The first is historical analysis: the business of tracking the historical trajectories of discrete communities, their domestic and international patterns; the phases in their trajectories along with the breaks in their trajectories; and the institutional machineries created plus the ideological legitimations affirmed. This work is supplemented with culture-critical analysis: here enquiry is turned directly to the ways in which social order and their accompanying institutional machineries are understood; elite understandings and legitimations and mass understandings where one area of functional overlap is found in the claims comprising the national past. Then, a third idea can be added, that is, forms of life: the overall pattern of life of the community in question, its discrete characteristics; in brief, culture-as-praxis.

Second, in regard to deeper assumptions, the European tradition is concerned with complex change, the intermingled processes of economic, social, cultural and political change that run through and enfold any discrete community; change is central to the collective social life of communities. Orderly coherence is bestowed after the fact with elite-sponsored top-down understandings intermingling with popular understandings. At a macro scale, the present global pattern is merely the sum total of all available historical trajectories and like the individual trajectories it is contingent. Then finally there is the idea of development. Rooted in Enlightenment ideas of progress, the notion expressed the intention of departing colonial powers to maintain links with former territories but has subsequently come to mean any willed programme of economic, social, cultural or political construction.

The first set of ideas point to analytical strategies, that is, ways of making sense, the latter point to domain assumption of the classical European tradition, that is, its concern for complex change. In all this the issue of livelihood is crucial: it points to the social production of human material and social welfare and it acknowledges the multiplicity of factors involved in complex change as all economic life is always and everywhere embedded with wider social systems. The notion also carries an explicit intellectual rejection. Talking about livelihood is not the same as talking about the economy or economics: this particular discipline-bound area of enquiry has come to revolve around the positivistic examination of a putative self-regulating market system, but the approach is flawed procedurally – as social science is not the same as natural science – and substantively – as the object of enquiry does not exist: there is no free market, and never has been, for all economic activity is always and everywhere lodged within complex social rules, that is, societies, and they in turn are ordered and understood in terms of received cultural traditions. The key for this text is the business of the social pursuit of livelihood – the ensemble of ideas and actions that secure the material and social well-being of discrete communities.

Theorizing the issue of human livelihood

Here, first, is an overview organized in formal terms: a spread of approaches ranging from the more or less interpretive through to the more or less positivist. Ordinarily the running order would be reversed, first the positivistic claims of mainstream liberal market economics and then the other forms of analysis, but this implicitly grants the status claims of the mainstream; however, there is no reason to do this and indeed many reasons to simply reject these claims. Hence the running order given here:

- interpretive analyses;
- historical institutionalism;

- institutional economics;
- political economy;
- mainstream neo-liberal economics.

Here, second, a note on the argument strategies used by the various schools of thought. Thus there are several ways of grasping the business of human livelihood and here five key strategies have been mooted. They offer different packages, telling different tales and proposing different sorts of actions. These strategies can be unpacked by considering: (1) the model of human livelihood affirmed/implied in the work; (2) the concepts used; (3) the procedures of enquiry adopted; (4) the data sources used; and (5) the policy advice offered. The various approaches tell different tales; they do not simply describe an equally simply given reality, rather they are highly selective ways of reading the social world within which their advocates operate.

Interpretive analyses

A number of streams of analysis are available which turn their attention directly to the business of elucidating the social logic of discrete forms of economic life, the ways in which people secure their livelihoods. In some work, this is presented in a systematic fashion, in others examples are accumulated piecemeal, but whatever the style of work, the core is the presentation of interpretive elucidations of the dynamics of discrete ways in which humans organize the business of livelihood.

The early twentieth century saw the creation of an economic sociology, but this was eclipsed by the influence of mainstream economics, neo-classical and later Keynes. However, the work has recently been revived. It is a specialist tradition of enquiry that picks up the work of turn-of-the-twentieth-century figures such as Max Weber (*The Protestant Ethic and the Spirit of Capitalism* or the earlier analyses of peasant migration in the eastern areas of Germany), and Georg Simmel or Karl Polanyi. This sort of work looks at economic activity in its social context: thus, with Weber, economic activity can be informed by non-economic motives, respectively, here, religion and politics; or with Polanyi, who presented the notion of embeddedness: all economic activity is lodged in a social world, but capitalism has been concerned to dis-embed the sphere of profit-driven activity. In recent years the tradition has been reanimated by various scholars, including, recently, Richard Swedberg, Fred Block and Wolfgang Streeck. This type of work offers a rejection of mainstream economics as either inadequate to its chosen field (incapable of elucidating the nature of the pursuit of livelihood), or ideologically obfuscatory (serving the status quo, whether inadvertently or intentionally), or both. Streeck, in particular, has urged sociologists not to vacate the sphere of the economic but to address it directly.

A parallel stream of work is available in economic anthropology. In one early form anthropologists and colonial administrator scholars turned their attention to the task of elucidating the logic of livelihood in pre-industrial colonial territories.

In today's world equivalent enquiries are turned to development style issues; thus the logic of the informal sector or the logic of rural to urban migration. And in today's world the work can be turned to the task of unpacking the economic logics of particular sectors within the territories of the rich countries of the global system. Thus Stephen Gudeman presents a discussion of economics as culture and makes a distinction between universal and local models of economic life, with the former, for example, neo-classical work, tagged as one more local model (in this case, deluded as to its scope). Thereafter, relatedly, economic critical journalism: thus Gillian Tett's examination of the tribalism of the market players in New York and London that contributed to the 2008–10 Anglo-Saxon financial crisis; thus Alexander Briants' report on corporate responsibility trip to Nigeria; thus James Meek's report on the players involved in dismantling the British operations of Cadbury's; and thus, in the context of a polemical treatment of the recent euro crisis, Yanis Varoufakis's anecdote about the banker embarrassed at his 'predatory lending', that is, his role in pushing insecure loans onto his customers, the European equivalent to Wall Street's sub-prime fiasco. All this work cuts against mainstream concerns with scientific status and unpacks directly instances of the social construction of livelihood. Advice offered: attend to the detail of forms of life.

Historical institutionalism

Historical institutionalism is grounded in ideas taken from sociology and anthropology; in particular, the idea that human beings make their social world in ordinary social interaction and that such activities must confront the central task of securing livelihood, that is, material and social reproduction. Thereafter the approach lodges these activities within the unfolding flow of time, substantively, history; any community will have its own particular history and the overall record can be summed up as a development trajectory. It records the way in which the community in question has handled the issue of livelihood, accumulating a distinct set of understandings, creating a discrete culture and building a distinctive set of institutions, the organizational means to ordering the pursuit of livelihood.

So, historical institutionalism as an analytic strategy draws on the work of historians to sketch out a territory's development trajectory, it draws on the work of institutional analysts in economics and political science to spell out the ways in which machineries of governance have been constructed and it draws on the work of cultural analysts to unpack the intellectual and popular ways in which the resultant track and machinery are understood and legitimated. It is thus interpretive, critical and dialogic.

Historical institutionalism focuses on the long-term trajectories of communities within the global system. It attends to the dynamics of structures and agents (routine social interaction) and to the institutional machineries that are constructed to order the resultant social world. Such communities are taken to have their own discrete logics. The approach favours case studies, historical studies of long-term changes, comparative analysis of different trajectories sketched out by different communities.

The approach looks to path dependency, episodes of change and at long-term change in terms of an idea of punctuated equilibrium.

Advice to state elite is that change can be managed probably for progress; advice to masses is similar. However, for both, the expectation is of continuity – change does occur but it is neither predictable nor is it necessarily for the better.

Institutional economics

Institutional economics begins from the claim that economic activity is always and everywhere embedded within social relations, and that these are always and everywhere embedded within political relations, and these in turn are always and everywhere understood with reference to particular cultural traditions, and this ensemble of characteristics is in turn always and everywhere embedded in discrete historical trajectories.

The approach has its roots in late nineteenth-century critical reactions to the claims of neo-classical economics, claims about self-regulating systems maximizing human welfare. Against these claims, institutionalists pointed to the intellectually impoverished nature of neo-classical work and to the real world problems of industrial capitalism. A tradition of enquiry was created: thus Thorstein Veblen, Gunnar Myrdal, Karl Polanyi, J.K. Galbraith and so on. In substantive terms, the work of institutionalists found expression in the policy work of the New Deal, itself a precursor of the settled mixed economy of the post-war period European welfare state.

In sum, the approach reads economic activity as a thoroughly social activity and it looks to the mechanisms of reproduction, the ways in which particular economic practices sustain themselves. Stability is expected, so too change, but this is likely to be piecemeal, for if economic systems are social systems, then they are likely to be resilient, and able to absorb shocks to the systems. And – more generally – as economic activity is read as a social activity it can be analysed using all the available resources of the social sciences.

With institutional work the fundamental claim is that economies are always lodged within societies that are always understood with reference to distinct cultural traditions. The keys to advance are found in technology, the make-up of firms and the pursuit of growth. Institutional analysis can be used to grasp the social nature of economic life. Analysts can use government, private and scholarly data to grasp the logics of economic activity. Change is on-going and the state can and must participate.

Advice to elite and masses is that change can be managed for the collective good.

Political economy

As the European world developed the beginnings of industry and became richer social theorists sought an explanation. Political economy developed in the eighteenth century from discussions about organizing agricultural production when powerful landowners sought to 'improve' their operations – better crop management, better use of labour, better marketing and so on. It was a practical task. As the shift to the modern world of science and industry continued, political economy grew up as a more systematic study of the pursuit of livelihood but it retains its practical concerns. The first key albeit pre-modern figure is Adam Smith. Others follow in the nineteenth century, including David Ricardo, Thomas Malthus, Karl Marx and John Stuart Mill. They offered general theories about how human society organizes its livelihood. Later in the century and in the twentieth century further other work of a political economic character was produced, including Paul Sweezy and Paul Baran.

Theorists using these traditions have engaged in multiple debates; in the developed world these ideas have been pushed aside by neo-classical economics, but they retain their influence, thus the work of J.M. Keynes, or more recently work associated with Susan Strange tagged international political economy; in developing countries, institutional and political economy approaches retain influence. More recently, Latin American dependency theorists have produced an entirely new school of political economy work; and most recently great interest has been shown in international political economy. It might be said that political economy retains its interest precisely because it addresses the nature of human livelihood in a holistic and engaged fashion. In making an argument it considers all relevant aspects, thus, economic, social, cultural and political, and thereafter proposes ethically grounded political action.

Classical political economy developed in Britain in the nineteenth century. It was concerned with understanding the production, distribution and consumption of material wealth. The focus was substantive. The political economists began with factors of production – land, labour and capital – and asked how they could be combined to produce goods, how these factors of production were rewarded, and how ownership of factors of production shaped social and political thinking; and they asked how these interactions shaped the system, facilitated its growth and rewarded its participants.

They also asked how group interests fed into distinct political agendas:

- land – landowners – rent – interest in laws protecting land ownership – interested in policies protecting domestic markets – uneasy with capitalist industrialists/financiers – hostile to agricultural unions – conservative in outlook;
- labour – labouring classes – wages – interested in laws protecting working people – interested in agricultural free trade (reduces price of food) – uneasy with land owners (conservative) – hostile to capitalists (low wages, poor conditions, factory discipline) – radical in outlook; and
- capital – industrialists/financiers – profit – interested in laws that protect business – interested in laws that encourage/assist domestic traders – somewhat suspicious of landowners – hostile to workers unions – progressive in outlook.

The business of securing a livelihood was taken to be social. The social world was made up of groups and groups pursue their interests which are shaped by social power relationships. Political economy insisted that economics and politics were closely linked: they were two sides of the same coin and so it did not make much sense to speak about them separately.

As with other strategies within the social sciences, political economic argument can do certain sorts of jobs. It can make structural analyses of the domestic circumstances of an economy, its international context and its general line of development. It can raise issues of the fairness of the system: do the factors of production get a fair share of the overall product? It can consider the governance of the economy: who is in charge, running what policies? Classical political economy has a central concern with the idea of value, asking where does value come from (air has no value, diamonds do, yet the former is vital to human life, the latter are not); the answer offered mentioned the amount of creative human labour embodied in a product. The labour theory of value placed creative labour at the centre of the system; and by implication mere landowning or the manipulation of finance was not so central.

Debates in political economy became very abstract and politically inconvenient to the key customers, the newly powerful financial and industrial capitalists and political economy failed to offer plausible answers to some important technical questions, in particular, the business of setting market prices. In the 1870s in Austria and Britain, a new approach became influential and it started a new discourse; now here was no particular concern with classes, interests and the like, instead neo-classical economics focused on behaviour in the marketplace and thus opened up a new conceptualization of economic analysis.

As noted, for political economy economics and politics are two sides of the same coin – it is not sensible to try to analyse one side rather than the other – there is no self-regulating system, rather patterns of politico-economic life unfold as contested contingent balances. Markets represent the surface of economic activity, beneath there are differences in technology, there are different economic sectors, there are different social groups (classes) and these factors come together to shape social group understanding, interests and action. Structural and historical models can be used to grasp the dynamics of technological and politico-economic change and thus inform action. The state elite and corporate world can use state and corporate world data in order to identify sectors and groups and their inherent dynamics.

Advice to the elite is that change in inevitable and it must be managed (probably for progress). Advice to the masses is that change is inevitable and that a preferred direction can be sought (probably for progress) but securing that line of advance is not automatic.

Mainstream neo-classical economics

In the late nineteenth century, political economy was criticized comprehensively as too general, too political and too technically ineffective. In a reaction in the 1870s tagged the marginalist revolution, the foundations of contemporary professional liberal neo-classical economics were established and the focus of enquiry shifted from the social production of livelihood to the ways in which producers and consumers buy and sell in an ideal marketplace. It was a very different intellectual and political agenda. It was the theory of liberal market economics. The key idea was that of supply and demand in the marketplace. A series of interrelated markets set prices which are signals helping to match up supply and demand: there was a market for finished goods; there was a market for intermediate goods; and there were markets for the basic factors of production. If buyers and sellers could meet in these markets they could make contracts and markets would clear (that is, all available materials would eventually sell at some agreed price). The system as a whole would operate automatically: it would maximize wealth (automatically clearing markets are necessarily efficient) and it would also maximize human freedom (individuals choose to make or not make contracts). It is the theory of a liberal capitalist market, which offers a quite different tale to that of political economy. The arguments do different jobs, they address different audiences. In the event, the neo-classical approach has informed the mainstream of contemporary economics.

Mainstream neo-classical economics aspires to the status of a natural science and it offers a particular model of the economic system. The system is grounded in the choices made by individuals within a competitive market environment. The choices arise within the person and they are subjective (advertising addresses this contrived model – thus 'because you are worth it'). The system is said to secure maximum benefits for all those involved and neo-classical economists identify four areas where the market system maximizes benefits:

- socially – as action and responsibility reside with the individual a market system acts to maximize human moral responsibility;
- materially – as free markets are efficient then they operate to maximize human material welfare;
- politically – as market systems restrict the state to minimum activity they facilitate the maximization of human freedom;
- intellectually – as economics is the science informing market systems then human social knowledge is maximized.

Critics of neo-classical work make three broad criticisms. First, the positivistic treatment of the business of human livelihood is misconceived, for the social world cannot plausibly be modelled as though it was a natural system; it is, whatever neo-classical theorists might wish, a social system. Second, after J.K. Galbraith, there is no abstract-general market and unpacking this idea produces nonsense; however, there are specific markets of all kinds, each a local model, each embedded within its own social environment. The liberal market is one such local model turned to the requirements of the corporate world and finance in particular. And third, the justification of the real-world system offered by neo-classical theorists, that is, the four maximizing claims, cannot be sustained.

Neo-classical economics affirms the idea of the self-regulating market system; markets fix prices and link supply and demand and firms and consumers; the market ensures economic efficiency. Practitioners use aggregate statistics and formal mathematical models in order to grasp and predict market dynamics. The work is used in state and corporate world to measure the market.

Advice offered to the state elite is to leave the market well alone and it will ensure progress. Advice offered to the corporate world is to anticipate short-term shifts in market sentiment and prosper. Advice to the masses is to adapt, power is out of your reach.

Argument strategies compared

In sum, each theoretical package is a way of making sense of livelihood: they work differently, they offer different tales and they are addressed to different audiences:

- interpretive analyses – concerned to spell out the multiple logics of discrete forms of life – ideas flow into the public sphere;
- historical institutionalism – concerned to spell out the business of creating the institutional forms necessary to sustain forms of life;
- institutional economics – concerned to unpack multiple layers of agency;
- political economy – concerned to unpack the interactions and agendas of the multiple agents involved;
- mainstream neo-liberal economics – concerned to spell out the causal logic of the putatively self-organizing system.

Running through these particular approaches and their mutual interactions (or not) are a number of broader questions: agency, the role of the state and the business of elite projects.

Agency and the liberal market: theoretical debates

Three interrelated ideas lie at the heart of the intellectual apparatus of mainstream neo-classical economic argument; they are the basic building blocks of a way of characterizing the world: first, an idea about human reason; second, an idea of how the social world is made; and third, an idea about the nature and role of markets.

Mainstream economic argument centres its explanations on a notion of instrumental rational behaviour or means-ends rationality – the idea of rational economic man; when mainstream economic argument seeks to explain behaviour it takes this form of reasoning to be the key to grasping human behaviour. People can be understood as egoistic calculators and the social world can be understood as the outcome of a multiplicity of individual exercises in calculation. Thus mainstream economic argument collapses all human reasoning into one form – instrumental rational calculation. Critics say that this is not sustainable as reasoning is diverse, for example, aesthetic/reflective, ethical/critical, social/pragmatic and technical/scientific. Critics say it is absurd to reduce the subtlety of human reasoning to simple egoistic utilitarian calculation.

Behind these ideas about rational calculation there is an idea about how the social world is constituted. Mainstream economics takes individuals as the basic building blocks of society; they are autonomous calculating agents who contract with other individuals in order to make society – it is a liberal theory. Critics mention two lines of objection. First, work in anthropology and sociology insists that social relationships are the starting point for thinking about society. Second, from language philosophy where it is argued that language is social (a system of trans-individual rules) and that any speech depends upon these rules; so too with society – social relationships establish the social world and individuals are located within that social world. Both lines of argument suggest that it makes no sense to speak of autonomous individuals; individuals are constituted via their involvement in wide networks of social relations.

Having cast the pursuit of livelihood in individual rational calculative terms, mainstream economic argument must explain how all these individual actions are organized, for clearly the social world is ordered. In mainstream economic argument it is the market that aggregates individual decisions so as to maximize individual and collective welfare. Mainstream economic argument and popular discourse, along with the styles of writing of commentators, often represent the market as if it were both an automatic machine and (somewhat paradoxically) an agent with concerns of its own. Critics make two objections: first, reification and, second, the imputation of agency.

Reification makes a social arrangement thing-like, it can represent a historically contingent pattern of social relationships as if it were a natural given or a machine. Critics say that the mainstream's market is not a natural given and it is not a machine, because when we talk about markets we are talking about human social practices; elaborate sets of social rules constitute the practices making up the pursuit of livelihood. Around the planet markets come in a multiplicity of forms (because so do human societies) and within the rich industrialized countries markets also come in a variety of forms (all are constituted/regulated by social/juridical rules – in one formulation, there are varieties of capitalism).

Agency is imputed to the market in mainstream economic argument and commentary. The market is said to have its own logic and to make demands, but critics say this is a poor way of arguing, for markets are sets of social relationships constituted through elaborate sets of rules; markets are not agents, people are.

So, to sum up, critics respond to mainstream arguments by saying:

- the liberal market is not a machine with a will of its own;
- actual marketplaces are social institutions, established via social/juridical rules, and they are diverse in their nature;
- the use of the term 'the market' is often just a political metaphor, it serves to persuade people about some course of action – thus one popular argument

today is that 'the market is becoming increasingly globalized' and the political/policy consequence is suggested to be 'we should adjust and compete harder' – but critics say that globalization is not a natural given – nor is it a machine with a mind of its own – it is a distinctive political project focused on the particular requirements of the corporate world generally and the financial world in particular – it can be supported – or ignored – or resisted – but it is certainly not inevitable.

The notion of a self-regulating liberal market is a fiction. The liberal markets that do exist are social constructs, they work the way they do because that is how they have developed over time, that is how they have become institutionalized, and now these arrangements are protected by an elaborate apparatus of legitimation (from TINA ('there is not alternative') to 'because you are worth it'); liberal markets reflect patterns of social rules and power; thereafter, critics add, the state can and should participate in curbing, regulating and perhaps directing these activities in the interests of the community as a whole.

Agency and the state: theoretical debates

Mainstream liberal market economic arguments advance a particular view of the state. The state is a mechanism with a restricted function: it serves to secure social order (simple control, deployment of legitimate violence as necessary), property rights (bodies of law and mechanisms to secure their recognition) and contracts (core deals between individuals, supported in law and secured as a matter of social order); these are the minimum requirements of autonomous individuals interacting with other equally autonomous human beings in order to pursue their several projects. This activity lies at the heart of a social world that exists only as a sphere of multiple agreed contracts. So egoistic rational economic man dwells in a contractual utilitarian network world.

In mainstream liberal market economic argument, in respect of policy issues, the state is viewed as a potential problem. It has a clear minimum function but tends to expand beyond this minimum function and becomes involved in a range of activities; for example, business activity, health, welfare, the arts, leisure provision and so on, which are really none of its concern. Mainstream economic argument can be presented more aggressively; it is not just that the state gets involved where it is not necessary but the involvement damages the functioning of the market, thus business leaders complain of red tape, whilst free market ideologists speak of rolling back the state.

Critics of these views see the state quite differently, in brief:

- as an interlinked set of institutions;
- lodged within trans-state structures of power;
- where each institution has power/authority over a restricted sphere;
- and each centre of power/authority is contested;

- and the set of institutions, the state, is the key to elite political projects, both international and domestic;
- and, moreover, critics add, the proponents of liberal market characterizations of the state know this full well, making their pronouncements ideological in the pejorative sense, designed to serve the sectional interests of the corporate sector in general and the financial sector more particularly.

The state is not a machine; it does not have a designated minimum function. The state is not an agent; it does not have intrinsic interests. The state is a crucial arena of political interaction; an arena for resolving debates about the direction society should take and the vehicle for translating into practice the political projects of the elite. The point is made differently in the various intellectual traditions.

Thus in the tradition of historical institutionalism the creation of institutions is key to social life. In the modern world this has meant in particular the creation of states (lodged within a system of states and sovereign over their respective territories (Treaty of Westphalia)) and to suppose that they are not central to modernity is foolish. Then, second, in institutional economics, the state is a key player; the idea that it should restrict its activities to the provision of basic order within which a liberal market can then function is regarded as wrong, as states are everywhere involved and the real questions are how and on whose behalf. Anthropologists have also considered the state unpacking the ways in which politically contingent institutions have been represented as inevitable and given. And, finally, in political economic argument the social world does not comprise autonomous individuals freely making contracts but instead multiple contending social groups/classes; they seek power and an elite in control of the machineries of the state can pursue a distinctive project, follow an idea about how the country should develop. It will use the machineries of the state to explain/legitimate this vision.

Structures, agents and projects – the logics of discrete communities

The tradition of political economy has routinely been consigned to the status of historical curiosity, part of the pre-scientific history of the contemporary social sciences; however, one curiosity about political economy is that its holistic approach to the business of social construction of human livelihood continues to attract attention, most recently in the guise of international political economy. Here familiar themes are represented and produce a holistic, engaged macro analysis – reading the business of complex change.

Susan Strange has written about structures of power in the global system and how state agents must react. Strange offers a discussion of the relations of structures and agents cast in terms of the necessity for states (the key agent considered) to read and react to a number of structures of power within the global system; the pattern of response indicates the preferred direction of development of the polity, implicit in this action is an ideal design for the polity, a model of how it might/ought to be. The agents that concern Strange, with her background in international relations, are states. But these are not the only agents, for the pursuit of development involves multiple agents; it is a fluid, contingent process and local elites have been crucial in East Asia.

The analysis approach can be explained in a number of steps. First, the base line for this approach is an idea of ordinary social interaction; we make up the world through our social interactions. We inhabit structures (the sum total of what everyone else does, the way in which the social world presents itself to us as a given) and we can act, we are agents thus we formulate projects; we have ideas about where we would like to be tomorrow or the day after. The process is an on-going interaction. This idea can be used at a micro scale (individual or small group interaction) or meso scale (interaction between organizations) or a macro scale (interactions between states). Second, at the macro level of the state the process sketches out a path, a historical trajectory. The state marks out this trajectory over time. The trajectory records how the state has dealt with the surrounding structures; how key agents have formulated projects, Third, the global system has many states and their trajectories are intermingled in the on-going shift to the modern industrial world. Fourth, there are phases in these trajectories and in each phase structures shape the activities of agents; each phase will be relatively stable and the change from one phase to another will likely be difficult with un-clarity, tension and maybe violence.

These ideas enable analysts to map the international situation of the elite: these elites must read and react to enfolding structural circumstances and they must do this day by day, the realm of diplomacy and international relations. These ideas also enable analysts to map the internal structure of the polity: which agents hold power, how the power holders are related to the masses. These ideas allow analysts to investigate how elites understand themselves; and how they explain themselves to the masses, matters of claims to legitimacy. These ideas also allow analysts to access the fundamental models built into political arrangements, the ways in which communities have solved basic human questions about order/legitimacy:

- in mainland Europe (we could argue that) the model of political life seems to revolve around the ideal of a rational consensus secured by dialogue in the public sphere (an ideal of reason/progress);
- in Japan (we could argue that) the ideal seems to be of elite-centred consensus secured via extensive private consultation amongst bureaucracy, business and politicians with popular acquiescence (an ideal of familial harmony);
- in Singapore (we could argue that) the ideal seems to be a rational technocratic consensus amongst elite participants secured by state/party coordination and requiring popular obedience (an ideal of top-down order/progress).

In brief, international political economy can be presented as focused upon the ordinary processes of human social life. The approach grants that the pursuit of livelihood is central to human social life. The approach notes that ordinary social practices give rise to structures, which in turn shape subsequent social life.

These ordered social practices embody more formal models of social life (ethics/politics) and these structures endure. These structures condition the activities of the elite as they organize projects for the future and thus communities sketch out a trajectory over time. The domestic situation of the elite is mirrored by its international situation; elites must read and react to given enfolding structures and plot a route to the future; the intermingled trajectories of many state-elites creates the overall global pattern. There is no system, and so the current situation is the contingent out-turn of these intermingled trajectories.

The approach can be used to track intermingled trajectories of polities of East Asia; the approach can compare their changing structural circumstances, identify the changing agents involved and describe the various projects; it can uncover the basic political logic of a given community; the approach is qualitative; the approach attends to quantitative material; the approach is sensitive to theory and to substance (the detail).

A strategy of analysis outlined

This text draws on the resources of the classical European tradition of social theorizing, with its central concern to elucidate the dynamics of change in the unfolding shift to the modern world. It tracks the historical development trajectory and contemporary circumstances of the countries of the region. The analysis adopts a cross-disciplinary approach drawing on the work of scholars in the social sciences and humanities:

- the overall focus is on the historical trajectories and contemporary forms of life of the countries and peoples of the region;
- the formal strategy of enquiry is interpretive and critical;
- the approach to substantive analysis centres on historical institutionalism;
- the style of the text embraces materials from historians, social scientists and scholars in the arts and humanities.

In the case of East Asia an overall tale could be sketched:

- extant civilizations;
- impacts of incoming colonialism and initial local responses;
- colonialism (exploitation/development and the shift to the modern world);
- general crisis as the empires collapse;
- the subsequent pursuit of projects determined by replacement local elites;
- the establishment of local variants of the modern world (an unfolding process);
- the emergence of an interlinked region in East Asia.

Thereafter, the detail of individual countries could be presented. These will be discrete historical trajectories built around elite dominated projects, embodying core logics and developing both domestically and within wider international structural circumstances. However, as noted, there is one caveat: the work is interpretive-critical in form and it is lodged within a distinct tradition; European assumptions might or might not fit with those underpinning other cultures; so, finally, the work is offered as one move in a broader dialogue, that carried by various communities of scholarship. Neat, tidy definitive answers would be convenient, but they are not on offer or in prospect.

Human livelihood: the European tradition and 'other cultures'

The European tradition is concerned with making sense of the on-going shift to the modern world and the approach contains crucial domain assumptions, which can be noted.

A cluster of assumptions revolve around an affirmation of the core role of reason: reason in natural science; reason in material production; reason in social and political life; reason in aesthetics; reason in ethics; and reason in pragmatics – otherwise, the disenchantment of the world, the long shift from theistic schemes to materialist schemes. These ideas would be widely accepted as the success of the natural sciences offers a routine informal practical confirmation and these assumptions have been investigated in the philosophy of social science sketched out above.

A cluster of assumptions revolves around the notion of modernity (thus modern, modernism and (unhappily) modernization). The notion points to a characteristic of contemporary culture; an engaged scepticism about received ideas informing an inclination to look optimistically to the future.

A further cluster of assumptions revolves around the social production of human livelihood: humans are read as social and they are read as creative; they are read as working together in order to make the societies that they inhabit. The key to these activities is the business of human livelihood, sustaining life. These assumptions are more awkward and they are more readily challenged and so – as noted above – they are more readily presented in different, perhaps incompatible, guises.

In this text, these are read as domain assumptions; read as a philosophical anthropology, that is, an abstract argument offering a characterization of the essential nature of humankind. Humans are active and creative and they create their social environment. So, the key issue is livelihood. It lets us access the core logics of contemporary modern forms of life and, as noted later, it provides the basis for offering characterizations of other forms of life.

The classical European tradition has roots in the pre-Enlightenment work of English philosophers, and thereafter in the work of Scottish, French, German and other European thinkers. A concern for livelihood figured in the earliest formulations made within the tradition – thus, political economy: concerned with the social production of human wealth; concerned with the contributions of particular production factors (land, labour and capital); concerned for the practical interests of the people animating these factors, thus classes; and concerned for the interaction of these social classes. In brief, a holistic analysis of the dynamics of change

As an intellectual approach, political economy was set to one side in the late nineteenth century. Critics charged that it was vague, moralistic and unscientific. A new scheme found favour. It focused on the marginal analysis of prices within a nominally self-regulating market system. At roughly the same time the familiar spread of social science concerns came to have institutional form; they became discrete disciplines in new universities. Nonetheless this style of argument making keeps recurring: in the socialist tradition (as the basis of class analysis) and in development theory (as a way to read change holistically) and recently in the guise of international political economy (concerned to access the logic of trading relationships and their regulation). The approach endures precisely because it addresses a core concern, namely, the social production of human livelihood.

Characterizing discrete forms of life (cultures/countries)

The social production of human livelihood assumes many forms. In the metropolitan heartlands of the modern world that form has been industrial capitalism. But there are also many other ways in which livelihood can be secured and in recent years these enquiries have typically been the province of historians (past civilizations) or anthropologists (forms of life outside the modern world) or development theorists (forms of life in process of change as they are drawn into the modern world). These enquiries have revealed that there are many ways of organizing the social production of human livelihood, which have their own logics and their own historical trajectories; in brief, there are multiple discrete forms of life.

Cast in terms of the intellectual resources of the classical European tradition – the resources informing this text – these forms of life can be grasped in terms of a series of areas of enquiry: their history; their productive activities; their social structures; their political structures; and their cultural ideas and products. Much could be said and has been by the discipline specialists noted above. To simplify, each form of life will evidence a discrete mix of agents, ideas and institutions, each will have a discrete logic, a way of sustaining and reproducing itself down through time and each will evidence a discrete historical trajectory

So, routine questions are:

- in politics – mapping the social distribution of power between elite and mass;
- in society – detailing social distinctions and related social hierarchies;
- in production – detailing core activities, domestic patterns and external links;
- in culture – unpacking the available legitimating theories associated with discrete forms of life.

In this way some sort of access to the logic of a form of life can be secured.

The classical European tradition provides the environment within which particular lines of argument can be constructed. Such work is shaped by domain assumptions and three clusters have been mentioned: reason, modernity and livelihood. A further cluster of assumptions revolves around what is taken to be a concern for democracy, which is lodged in the very nature of language itself; speaking accurately implies an environment that permits such accuracy – ideas from Jürgen Habermas – and this means, in brief, that European tradition work is ethically engaged, it judges but it does so in a reflexive fashion, alert to its own assumptions and granting that other cultures might affirm other ethics.

All this issues in a double move: first, characterize the success/failure of the form of life in its own terms – the ideas against which it claims it would be judged – thereafter, the form of life can be judged against the ethics embedded within received European tradition.

An agenda: forms of life in East Asia

The discussion presented here will look at the historical trajectories and contemporary logics of forms of life in East Asia. It will work at the level of countries. The general overall tale is easy, whilst the detail is both difficult and absorbingly interesting.

So, in brief, pre-modern East Asia was home to a number of long-established distinctive and successful civilizations. The historical centre of the region was China, but there were distinctive sub-regions in Northeast Asia (China, Korea and Japan), Southeast Asia (the Malay archipelago) and Indo-China (Thailand, Vietnam, Laos and Cambodia). Yet the route to the modern world taken by all East Asian countries includes the nineteenth-century experience of colonial absorption within primarily Europe-centred state-empire systems. The accidental invention of industrial capitalism in Europe opened the way to domestic intensification and external expansion. European countries moved to create global empires and trade was the key. Other civilizations were more or less completely remade, often with the help of violence as a system of state-empires was made. Pre-existing civilizations were absorbed within these systems. The state-empires were multi-ethnic, underpinned by trade and ordered as a hierarchy of cores and peripheries. Elite competition in the cores and resistance in the peripheries led to the collapse of the state-empire system; East Asia experienced severe general crisis in the earlier parts of the twentieth century in the form of multiple overlapping conflicts. As the state-empires dissolved successor elites looked to the construction of sovereign states, the creation of nations and the elite-dominated pursuit of national development. The currently available pattern of states and their associated domestic forms of life are the outturn of these historical processes; the past has bequeathed discrete forms of life to the denizens of today's pattern of countries.

PART II
The shift to the modern world in East Asia

The shift to the modern world has its origins in Europe as the structural dynamic of natural science-based industrial capitalism overwhelmed existing agrarian-based economic, social and political systems. Domestic forms of life were remade and thereafter elites embraced the opportunities offered by the disparities in power between their own metropolitan territories and those overseas that were home to other cultures, and so domestic intensification was supplemented by external expansion. The process of expansion overbore local forms of life creating state-empires comprising a hierarchy of cores and peripheries and embracing large geographical territories and multiple distinct ethnic groups. They were implausible systems. However, for a period, they functioned, but they were rife with tensions as metropolitan elites competed and peripheral populations rebelled. The system moved into general crisis and from 1911 onwards the state-empire system was in crisis and decline. In the late 1940s and early 1950s they disappeared; replacement elites sought power, built states, invented nations and pursued national development, creating over the next half century the outlines of the contemporary global system.

4
COLONIALISM AND MODERNITY
The overall trajectory

The East Asian world in the early seventeenth century was rich. It was home to highly developed agrarian and trading economies. It was home to well ordered societies. It was home to sophisticated polities. It was also home to highly developed arts. In brief, the region was home to highly sophisticated civilizations. There were a number of centres: China, the territories of Northeast Asia, Japan and Korea, mainland Southeast Asia and the multiple kingdoms scattered through the islands of the archipelago. The region was an object of respectful fascination for early European travellers and writers. Early travellers' tales offered an exotic picture of places and peoples. Early trade goods offered similarly exotic products with spices, silks and the like. Around this time, Europeans produced an unusually dynamic form of life, natural science-based industrial capitalism, and a period of domestic reform and external expansion began. Change swept through the European heartlands, remaking long-established agrarian societies, and thereafter commercial trading activities turned outwards in the search for new markets. At first Europeans became regular participants in Asian networks of economic activity and over time they slowly came to dominate and remake these networks of activity. The most obvious political expression of the period of European and American dominance was the creation of the distinctive colonial world. Here local interactions of peoples, typically ordered in terms of race and class hierarchies, fitted these areas into the wider global system. The colonial period was brief but the experience drew the peoples of East Asia into the modern world (economic, social, political and cultural). Today, commentators speak of the economic advance of East Asia as a process of re-establishing global power.

The shift to the modern world: Europe and East Asia

The shift to the modern world is usually taken to have its initial centre in Europe where a network of trading cities linked northern parts of Italy, through parts of Germany, on into the Low Countries and thence into northern France and southern England. But trade was only a part of the tale, for what was contrived along this geographical track was a novel form of life and this system displaced the extant agrarian feudal systems. It was a slow process of displacement, with initially an agrarian capitalism but eventually a wholly novel political economy, society, polity and culture: natural science-based industrial capitalism: in Karl Marx's terms, a mode of production; and it was this system, which for a historically brief period, offered these Europeans the opportunity to export their form of life around the planet. This they did, creating trading networks, factory bases and, in time, formal colonial territories. However, European pre-eminence did not last long, reaching an apogee in the years before the Great War, and the system dissolved away during the middle years of that same century.

Industrial capitalism: Europe as heartland, East Asia as periphery

The modern world revolves around natural science-based industrial capitalism; a distinctively energetic form of life originating in Europe where a concatenation of circumstances permitted its emergence; it has spread around the globe and it now includes most parts of the world. But the modern world is not all of a piece. There is no single integrated global system, for the route to the modern world taken by discrete polities shapes the manner in which the demands of modernity have been grasped. Different routes imply different modern polities. But in all this, the essence of this form of life is change as natural science continually produces new knowledge and this in turn informs new ideas, practices and technologies. The ideas can invite changes in self-perceptions (evolution/race), ideas can inform new practice (germ theory/hygiene), and in the commercial sphere producers generate new goods (electricity/consumer electronics) and in the marketplace groups prosper or fall by the wayside (DVD/VHS). Individuals and communities work within these received structures to secure their livelihoods.

1 Europe and East Asia relations – reasons debated

The reasons or occasion of European pre-eminence – albeit brief – have been debated by historians and others. In the nineteenth century claims to the superiority of Europe were familiar: thus knowledge or social organization or race (and so on). Such essentialist claims are not made these days. A more plausible line of analysis points to natural science-based technology – thus Carlo Cipolla pointed to guns and sails – where advances in these technologies allowed the Europeans to construct far-flung trading networks as other trading networks were overwhelmed and absorbed.

A broader analysis from Kenneth Pomeranz pointed to the resources available to Europeans, both domestic, that is, advances towards modernity, and international, that is, their linkages with other successful parts of the world. Europe's success in this perspective depends on local and international factors. In a similar vein, Christopher Bayly has argued that during the eighteenth century the global system as a whole was experiencing an upturn in economic activity. As the European countries began to

FIGURE 4.1 A tea warehouse in Canton, 1790.

Source: British Library, no original source given.

FIGURE 4.2 A view of Batavia.

Source: British Library, described as 'An aquatint by Wells after a drawing by Drumond', no date given.

Shift to the modern world in East Asia

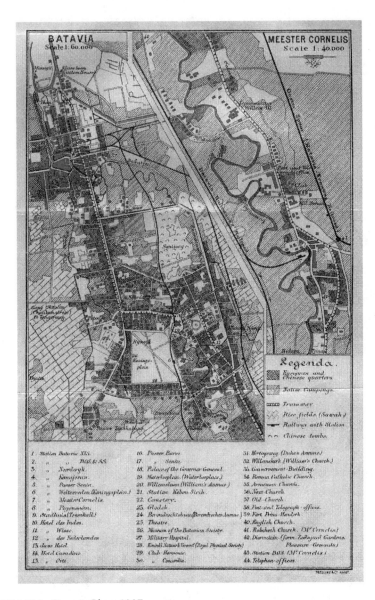

FIGURE 4.2(a) Batavia Plan, 1897.

Source: Perry-Casteneda Library, *Guide to the Dutch East Indies* by Dr. J.F. Bammelen and G.B. Hoover, Luzac and Co., London, 1897.

accumulate domestic wealth along with overseas possessions they were in fact only one amongst many sophisticated civilizations. In Northeast Asia, the principal country was China: it was an economic, cultural and political power. Domestically, it was ordered as a species of bureaucratic feudalism with an elaborate state machinery centred upon the emperor and reaching down via a series of administrative cores and

FIGURE 4.3 Singapore: view from Government Hill, 1830.

Source: British Library, no original source given.

peripheries to the most local levels of peasant agriculture. Internationally the country sat at the heart of a network of tributary states, together the Sino-centric system, which embraced both trade and culture. Japan, Korea and Vietnam all had elites that looked to China, embraced the cultural models on offer and traded with that country. These were sophisticated cultures. In the particular realm of the arts, the work brought back to Europe – silks, ceramics, paintings and the like – provoked widespread admiration. And the same was true of the no less sophisticated cultures of Southeast Asia. Here there were numerous polities or country powers: the local sultanates whose borders changed as they gained or lost status within the wider networks of the archipelago – thus, for example, Mataram or Srivijaya or Johor-Riau – plus those who made their bases in the river basins of mainland Southeast Asia, thus, the Cham or Thai or Khymer – all of whom were long-established.

A.G. Frank argued that before the rise of modern Europe, the whole lengthy process from early trading networks, to state-empires and thence via collapse to the situation at the start of the twenty-first century, the centre of the global economy was in Asia where circuits of trade and money linked the countries of South, Southeast and East Asia. Frank argues that these areas were integrated by trade and money flows and that the Europeans joined in these flows and by doing so slowly became prosperous, later aggressive and later still colonial powers. In brief, the Europeans became rich by participating in these existing Asian flows of trade and money; lines of enquiry pursued by Angus Maddison who has reconstructed relative economic positions and concludes that Asia was indeed wealthy long before the Europeans arrived. So, as these processes unfold, East Asia enters the modern industrial capitalist world via this exchange with European, American and Japanese colonialism.

The work of A.G. Frank (like that of Immanuel Wallerstein) has been criticized by political economists for confusing trading links (systems of exchange) with systems of production. Thus liberal market capitalism does indeed stress trade, but the society is shaped by system demands for ever-increasing productive efficiency and expansion (in short, profits from production); that system, as Robert Brenner, following Marx, put it, is a mode of production: a mix of economic, social, political and cultural elements where the drive for accumulation is built-in, that is, intensification and expansion are system givens.

2 States and state-empires

At a macro scale the world of industrial capitalism was first configured as a Eurocentric system of states, then for a multiplicity of reasons European states acquired overseas territories. These territories accumulated and fed into the creation of state-empire systems; complex systems of metropolitan cores, networks of subsidiary centres and wide multi-ethnic territories. However, these arrangements proved to be historically transient and from the late nineteenth century onwards state-empires were beset by tensions. There was routine competition between states at the core (commercial and military) and there was resistance from groups within the peripheral holdings (low-level opposition plus elite calls for independence). In the event the breakdown of the European state-empire system was violent. The Pacific War fatally undermined European colonial holdings in East Asia and territories acquired over centuries dissolved away in a few post-war decades; in its stead the current pattern of nation-states took shape.

The system of natural science-based industrial capitalism came under pressure as independence leaders sought better lives for the their peoples; there was talk of socialism and non-alignment, but in the event the basic system survived. New successor elites sought development: the benefits of modernity and alternatives to the forms of life created during the colonial era – local variant forms of modernity – proved difficult to change. However, politically, as new nation-states took shape, the system in East Asia slowly turned into an America-centred system. Now in the early twenty-first century it seems to be in the process of reconfiguring once again and within the region China is quickly emerging as a key power, whilst on a wider scale East Asia now seems to be one region amongst others; part of a tri-regional system, with powerful cores in North America, Europe and East Asia.

The political economy of empire

After the Spanish and Portuguese moved into Central and Latin America in the sixteenth century there was more money available in Europe as silver was exported back to Europe, which underpinned credit. All this funded excess consumption, and some investment in Spain and Europe; it also funded further colonial expansion across the Pacific as the Spanish colonized the Philippines in the sixteenth century. The Spanish joined in the Asian circuits of trade and money. Other European powers slowly joined in. At first they were just one more group of unimportant traders, working within well-established multi-ethnic networks.

The Spanish and Dutch were the early European traders and specialist products were sought: silks, ceramics and spices. The existing patterns of East Asian trade could accommodate these demands. At first the traders came in small numbers and eventually they set up trading bases, or factories, with a few dozen people. These exchanges could be accommodated within existing patterns of trade. It was the rise of industrial capitalism that caused changes. The Europeans were more powerful militarily and now they had a wider schedule of demands: (1) from output of traditional producers to the output of mines and plantations; and (2) they sought larger markets for their manufactures. As their economic impact deepened so did their political demands: factories turned into treaty ports; seasonal trading (monsoon winds) turned into all year trading; and they began to change the local economy with new imports and new exports and new trading partners. The European trade was organized via large trading companies: for example, the East India Company (EIC) and the Dutch East India Company (VOC). They organized trade, signed treaties and organized armies. By the mid-nineteenth century they had been superseded by direct British and Dutch state involvement; at this time the French state also became involved and at the turn of the century US involvement began. All this marked the start of formal colonial empires and the economies were then organized according to the policy decisions of the metropolitan elites – a core and periphery relationship – creating an ambiguous mix of exploitation and development.

Colonial economies served multiple interests: in the first place, the interests of metropolitan capital, but, thereafter, opportunities were opened up to local groups and sub-regional migrants. Colonial port cities typically attracted significant inflows of people and elaborate social structures were created with distinctions of ethnicity, economic function, duration of residence, membership or not of a settled community and, thereafter, all the sociological detail of particular cultures in respect of gender, age, marital status and so on.

Once up and running a series of changes took place. And whilst the colonial systems were not all of a piece, cast in general terms the changes included the following matters. European commercial law was introduced. European style landownership was introduced. European systems of taxation were established to pay for the apparatus of colonial rule. Commercial agriculture in the form of plantations was established. Mines were established. Roads and railways were built. Colonial port cities were built. There was inward migration from surrounding areas. Populations within an area could comprise multiple ethnic groups – sojourners, traders, migrants, locals and so on – and relationships within and between these groups were complex. In the cities there was residential segregation of races, matters underscored where residential segregation was supplemented by a parallel economic specialization. All these distinctions were marked and commentators spoke of plural societies.

The confused pattern led to subtle exchanges between various agent groups; simple stories of Westerners overcoming the passive East or alternatively of the harmonious stable East being overcome by aggressive outsiders are false. The expansion of state-empire systems and the formation of colonies was an exchange involving multiple agents; forms of life were impacted and remade and there were winners as well as losers, but given the expansionary logic of the industrial capitalists system, the key, as ever, was the business of economic exchange.

In colonial Malaya, for example, economic behaviour could be segregated according to ethnic group (here schematically):

- British financial institutions;
- British trading houses;
- British owned plantations;
- Chinese petty traders in towns;
- Chinese tin miners in rural areas;
- Indian plantation labour;
- Malay small holders in rural areas;
- Chinese merchants and financiers;
- Indian professionals; and
- Malay landlords.

Such economic differentiation could provide seeds for social/political conflicts and the political exchanges were also subtle:

- British were focused on trade sectors;
- British used local people as traders and labourers;
- Chinese controlled the opium retail trade in colonial Singapore;
- Chinese traders controlled the inflow of labourers from Southern China;
- Straits Chinese were a privileged group;
- Indians became a privileged group;
- Malay Royals were co-opted into the Empire, receiving pensions; and
- Malay peasantry remained rural.

Amitav Acharya has argued that the colonial powers organized economic activity in a fashion that cut across the established patterns of economic activity in Southeast Asia. A regional trade network was disrupted by colonial mercantile spheres of interest: Dutch, British, French and American. In place of an integrated sub-regional pattern of trade amongst the archipelago and mainland Southeast Asia, the incoming powers took care to order their activities along mercantile lines and so spheres of influence were created; any novel local forms of economic activity were constrained by these mercantilist arrangements.

The impact of the newcomers generated a complex pattern of economic activity; it can be thought of as a series of layers of economic and trade activity; from the local, to regional and thence to global system levels:

- the lowest layer would be traditional products for local consumption;

FIGURE 4.4 Rangoon: storming the principal stockades, 1824.

Source: British Library, no original source given.

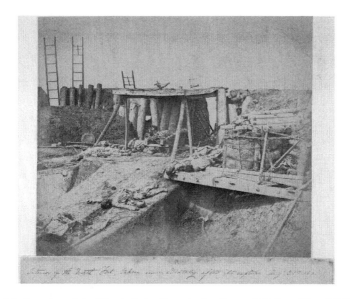

FIGURE 4.5 Interior of the North Taku Fort during Second Opium War, 1860.

Source: British Library, described as 'This is print 13 in the published catalogue of Beato's China Views…'.

FIGURE 4.6 Pu Yi.

Source: British Library, described as 'Image taken from The Daily Mirror'.

- the next layer traditional products still traded across colonial boundaries along old established regional trade routes;
- the next layer would bring people and goods into the region from the surrounding areas; and
- the final layer linked the colonial sphere to the global economy through colonial port cities to the metropolitan core.

By the turn of the twentieth century these local economies were deeply impacted; for example, in Southeast Asia, from around 1900 Singapore was embedded in the global industrial capitalist system by virtue of trading links with metropolitan Britain and the USA (tin and rubber for new industries of cars and canning). This sort of process of involvement was repeated across East Asia. By the time of the Pacific War the economies of East Asia were deeply involved in the modern global industrial capitalist system and they had been changed from the pre-colonial forms forever. The war caused extensive destruction and amongst Western experts there was pessimism about the chances of the area advancing and a future of agriculture plus low-tech manufactures was envisaged. This was the starting point for the leaders of the new nations. It was the legacy of their colonial route to the modern world. It was the structural pattern they had to deal with once they took power.

The politics of empire

Economic historians have argued that in the seventeenth century, Europe, East Asia, South Asia and parts of Africa, the Middle East and Latin America were all roughly on the same material economic level; in various forms they had sophisticated agriculture, craft-based manufacturing, functioning credit systems and extensive trading networks.

Their political systems differed, put very roughly: European feudalism; East Asian bureaucratic empires; Southeast Asian maritime empires; South Asian princely kingdoms; African kingdoms, Middle Eastern theocratic/princely states; and Latin American landed oligarchic feudalism. None of them were democratic. None of them were liberal. None of them were liberal-democratic. Most of these communities seem to have been energetic, stable and prosperous. Hence the arguments of the economic historians that – at this time in the pre-modern world – the major economic, cultural and political region within the global system was East Asia, with China at the core.

Yet the political and economic system being created around this time by Europeans was powerful. The political economy was or was becoming industrial capitalist. The polities were or were becoming liberal, a process that took some time. The mixture of natural science, industry and market competition underpinned these nascent liberal polities. In England liberal polities were theorized by Thomas Hobbes and John Locke who argued that the keys to the polity are individuals (or families) and the multiplicity of private contracts that they make. The state secures order and is the minimum rule-setter. In all this, standard theological explanations about the polity (for example, the divine right of kings to rule) were cast aside. The system was very dynamic. It continually increased its demands on its domestic population (efficiency and discipline). It expanded overseas (new markets, new resources). And it overwhelmed East Asia in a series of waves of expansion coupled with deepening involvement in local forms of life: the Spanish, the Portuguese, the Dutch, the British, the French, the Russians, the Americans, the Germans and the

Japanese all carved out colonial spheres. The key motive for its players was economic, a concern for markets or raw materials, supplemented by ideologies of ethnic superiority, responsibility or whatever and a defensive concern for the activities of other colonizing powers. Thereafter foreign political structures were imposed on local existing structures which created the distinctive political world of the colony: multi-ethnic, hierarchical and turned to the business of making its hinterland available to the wider global system.

The Europeans and Americans slowly created a series of empire spheres in East Asia: formal empires in insular and mainland Southeast Asia coupled with informal empires in China. Only two countries escaped formal colonization, though both were strongly influenced by outsiders: Thailand and Japan. In the context of this system, each colonial elite had to deal with the local polities/cultures and with the demands of its metropolitan core – each colonial sphere developed its own style of colonial polity.

In all this there were common political themes:

- rhetorics of expansion – the politics of trade and progress;
- rhetorics of superiority and inferiority – claims about reason and unreason – claims about behaviour (rational and reliable versus irrational and unreliable) – claims about race – establishment of race hierarchies – formation of intermediate groups;
- rhetorics of responsibility – caring for the people – caring for development – holding the ring between competing local groups – establishing direct and indirect rule – co-option;
- colonial pilgrimages – the successful colonial citizens travelled to the metropolitan heartlands – they discovered the gap between colonial rhetoric of freedom and development and the reality of discrimination – the seeds of independence movements were sown – the political rhetoric of rulers were turned back upon them; and
- nationalist movements – independence movements – religious and secular.

In time, the empires came under various sorts of pressure; there were local reformers and metropolitan reformers and there was also inter-state conflict. It was an episode of the latter which finally destroyed foreign empires in East Asia. The Pacific War marked the shift from one historical phase to another. The war was extremely destructive with some 20 million killed, millions more injured and millions displaced. There was extensive damage to infrastructure. The war destroyed the empires, economically, socially and politically. Crucially the idea of empire was overthrown: local nationalists opposed it, the military victor in East Asia was the USA and they would not support it; fairly quickly a series of new nation-states emerged and some older polities were reconstituted.

Managing this dissolution of empires was difficult. It was made more difficult by the start of the Cold War. American anxieties in respect of the shape of the postwar world prompted them to intervene in the Korean peninsular where they helped

TABLE 4.1 Wars of colonial expansion[1]

1795–96	British occupation of Malacca
1810–11	Anglo Dutch Java War
1811	British occupation of Java
1824–26	First Anglo-Burmese War
1825	Dutch conquest of Palembang
1825–30	Great Java War
1837	British campaign against piracy off Malaysia
1846–49	Dutch expeditions against Bali
1852	Second Anglo-Burmese War
1857–65	Dutch Bandjermasin War
1858–62	French War against Annnam
1867	French consolidate Cochin China
1872–96	Dutch Batak War
1873	First Dutch Aceh War
1874	Pangkor Engagement allows British into Malay peninsular
1874–1880	Second Dutch Aceh War
1883–85	Sino-French War consolidates control of Indo-China
1884–96	Third Dutch Aceh War
1885–87	Third Anglo-Burmese War
1893	Franco-Siamese War
1898–1900	American invasion of the Philippines
1905–08	Dutch Expedition against Southern Celebes
Casualties	Unknown

Note
1 The list is taken from P.W. Preston, 2010, *National Pasts in Europe and East Asia*, London, Routledge; the information is culled from websites, see in particular World History at KMLA: History of Warfare at www.zum.de/whkmla/military.

TABLE 4.2 The career of Imperial Japan

1855–1905	Sakhalin/Kuriles
1879	Annexation of Ryukyu Islands
1886	Hokkaido Agency established
1894–95	Sino-Japanese War
1895	Acquisition of Taiwan
1904–05	Russo-Japanese War
1911	Annexation of Korea
1915	The 21/15 Demands
1931–32	Advances into Manchuria
1933–45	Invasion of China
1941–45	Invasion of Southeast Asia
1945–50s	Collapse and occupation of Home Islands
Casualties	Unknown

a reactionary nationalist into power in the southern zone who thereafter provoked aggressive exchanges with the leadership of the northern zone. Open war broke out in 1950 and this, plus the suppression of labour movements in occupied Japan, plus the victory of the CCP (Chinese Communist Party) in the civil war, prompted American intervention on a larger scale. The US government and it successors sponsored anti-communist movements throughout the region, fostering, thereby, civil wars and a range of covert actions that cost the lives of many tens of thousands. More broadly, this meant that the economic, social and political advance attendant upon the dissolution of foreign-controlled empires and the creation of new states was accompanied by significant violence; some of the political legacies of the period persist in state structures and official ideology and popular memory.

The culture of empire

The structure of state-empires was a hierarchical network of cores and peripheries, with the metropolitan capital city as the highest-level core. The empires reflected these arrangements: nationality, social class, ethnicity and perhaps religion all fed into the interactions of everyday life and these interactions would vary between empire systems, but always it was the local expatriate elite that set the tone for peripheral areas and thereafter they looked to the core in their respective homelands.

1 In the metropolitan cores

In regard to the peoples whose territories they controlled there were claims to superiority and these could cover a spread of areas: most obviously, technical, where the sciences and technologies of the core metropolitan state-empires were more advanced (in particular in weapons and certain mass produced goods, thus early textiles); more generally, civilizational, where argument moved from certain technologies to a wider claim to general superiority (technical advance signalled progress, the metropolitan core peoples were thus more advanced); and bluntly, racial, where these comparisons were inflected by a social reading of the work of Darwin (thus competition between races was inevitable, so European colonial holdings signalled their race superiority); thereafter, more narrowly, professional, where the colonies offered core citizens career opportunities closed to other residents (and perhaps to themselves at home) and which they justified on the basis of their reliability as compared with locals. All these assumptions, in various mixes, disposed metropolitan elites and other agents to regard colonial holdings instrumentally (and perhaps paternalistically); in particular their economic value or their strategic value or their symbolic value.

In regard to the activities of other metropolitan core elites, the early relationships were antagonistic with economic competition for markets and resources, strategic competition for bases and territories and symbolic competition for status. At the extreme these attitudes could unpack as local-level warfare (thus, in East Asia, in the early years of expansion, the Dutch, British and French competed) but such exchanges moderated as the state-empire system became established over the period of the nineteenth century and sharp conflicts were fewer, cooperation more likely.

2 In the peripheral territories

In regard to the expression of these attitudes within colonial holdings where there were mixed populations of foreigners including administrators, soldiers, missionaries, traders and miscellaneous adventurers, or in total, sojourners, these could find multiple expressions: in routine administrative decision making oriented towards concerns of sojourners; in routine commercial exploitation of labourers; in routine claims to superiority in every day interactions; and, conversely, in paternalistic concerns for the welfare of the natives, in scholarly concern for studying the forms of life of the inhabitants of colonial territories (thus colonial scholarship) and sometimes, later, in participation in reform and independence movements opposing colonial rule.

The end of empire: violence and the search for new directions

The state-empire system was beset by tensions, both within each of the state-empire systems as actors within peripheral territories pushed against the restrictive frameworks of colonial rule, and between state-empires where core interests could conflict, even though by the later phases of the system cooperation was more likely. In the event these tensions came to overwhelm the system in the 1930s. The various problems came to a head in East Asia. The impact of the Great Depression on Japan brought to power a military government and conflicts with Nationalist China intensified, eventually leading to outright invasion. Opposition to Japanese activities in China came from the USA, and through the late 1930s Tokyo's diplomatic conflicts with the USA intensified, eventually leading to open warfare. The early phases of the Pacific War saw Imperial Japanese forces capture most European and American colonial holdings within the region of East Asia and, although Japanese occupation was in the event relatively brief, it did serve to open a political space for local nationalists for now their voices could be heard both within the colonial territories and within the metropolitan core countries. The idea of empire was undermined. These systems were no longer sustainable and the process of dissolution began and new nation-states were created.

In East Asia we can point to a series of interrelated wars: the Chinese Revolution and Warlords (1911–26); the Chinese Civil War (1928–49); the Japanese invasion of Manchuria (1931–33); the Japanese invasion of China (1937–45); the Second World War (1939–45); and the Pacific War (1941–45). There was extensive war damage: approximately 24 million people were killed; cities in Japan, China, Indo-China and Southeast Asia were destroyed or damaged; a large part of the economic base of the countries was thus destroyed, including plant, machinery, workers, workers housing, government offices and infrastructure. However, the crucial economic problem seems to have been the disruption, not the simple physical destruction.

There was disruption of hitherto established economic linkages built up over time: firms establish networks in order to pursue their business, including finance, plant and machinery, staff, distribution systems and final customers; social groups establish patterns of working; factories and offices are built and tax revenues raised to fund local/national government; individuals find employment and earn wages and thus secure livelihoods. All these linkages are built up over time and they are very subtle as everyone finds a place within the economic order. The episode of war disrupts all these established linkages; both domestic and international, as in war, established patterns were subject to dramatic change. Conquest means new rulers with new laws, new regulation, new currency, new factory owners, new patterns of labour and new customers; it also means all the demands of collaboration.

There was consequent social and political disruption. The effects of military actions were not simply economic and there were wider implications. As the damage accumulated, established social and political organization broke down. As the established patterns broke down new ones were formed. The survivors had to deal with their circumstances: some negative, with crime, looting, black markets and so on, and some positive, with spontaneous self-help and new social/political movements. As the open warfare subsided, the domestic and international linkages were difficult to re-establish.

A summary statement: the Pacific War had four main areas of impact:

- great loss of life;
- destruction of plant and infrastructure;
- dislocation of domestic economic organization and linkages;
- dislocation of international economic organization and linkages; and
- with consequent social and political disruption and thereafter advance.

In terms of political life by the 1930s East Asia was changing. The foreign elites tended to be complacent and did not expect change, but the local people were beginning to look towards a different future: sometimes the impulse to change was expressed in religion, sometimes in everyday resistance and most importantly in growing nationalism. In the wider region there was growing conflict and, in particular, the Imperial Japanese had begun to advance into China. The Americans objected and when eventually the Japanese launched all-out war in China the USA imposed trade sanctions on Japan. This in turn precipitated war. The Pacific War 1941–45 had severe impacts upon East Asia: the Imperial Japanese armed forces swept into China, Indo-China and Southeast Asia and there was political upheaval, economic damage and social dislocation, as well as millions of casualties, mostly civilian.

In politics the confusions of the Pacific War gave the nationalist political groups their chance: they did not emerge out of nowhere, clues to expectations of change

TABLE 4.3 Overlapping wars: multiple participants, experiences and memories

1916–28	Warlord era
1928–49	Chinese Civil War
1931–32	Imperial Japanese invasion of Manchuria
1932–37	Imperial Japanese invasion of Northern China
1931–34/35	Jiangxi Soviet and Long March
1937–45	Sino-Japanese War
1941–45	Pacific War
Casualties[1]	
Warlords and civil war	4,000,000
Chinese Civil War	2,500,000
Sino-Japanese and Pacific War	12,600,000
Southeast Asia Occupations	5,000,000
Total	24,100,000

Note
1 Estimate made from information on various websites; indicative of scale only.

had been accumulating for some time. Some encouragement had been given to them in the years before the war by political reformers in Europe and America. Some encouragement had been given to them by the record of Japan, in particular its effective embrace of the modern world along with later Imperial Japanese authorities (who had spoken of Pan Asian ideals and a Great East Asia Co-Prosperity Sphere). A number of nationalist elite members made colonial pilgrimages where they learned their nationalism from the colonial rulers. They put these ideas to work in the confusions of the end of the Pacific War, advocating independence and development and seeking the support of local populations for their political projects in return for promises of better lives for all.

Creating new units: states, nations and development

The end of the Pacific War meant the end of colonialism, but the end of colonialism was never going to be simple – rather it was confused and more often than not violent. As the large multi-ethnic territories of the now failing state elites dissolved away, new political arrangements had to be made – power relations established and ordered (otherwise, what had been called warlordism, lately termed failed states) – new elites had to coalesce – these elites had to make states, invent nations and pursue development. As state-empires dissolved away, new replacement elites had to pursue political security, order and development.

In respect of security, aspiring replacement elites had to lay claim to an area of territory (a part of the wider territories of the now disintegrating colonial empires) and a population (a section of the population of the now disintegrating empire). These were the keys to any claim to statehood: place and people. So, inevitably, there were many aspiring elites. There were conflicts amongst these aspirants for control of territories and peoples; and there were conflicts between these elites over the same issues. Once in power the replacement elites faced difficult tasks of defining borders. Thus the elites had to define citizenship, that is, membership of the new state, and so elites had to reach agreements with resident non-citizens and long-established minority communities (and all these people had status positions within empires, now perhaps in question) – when these matters are settled it provides the bedrock of the political project of building a new state – territorial boundaries and citizens.

States are legal units with sovereignty over a specific territory and population; they are recognized by other states within the international system, at the present time there around 200 states. The key issues in state making revolve around recognition and constitution. In the first place, the new state has to be accepted within the international system of states via diplomatic mutual recognition; this is not straightforward, for the creation of new states is unusual and typically follows some wider social upheaval, thus warfare opened the way to the creation of new states within the territories of failing state-empires or, recently, the dissolution of the Soviet Union opened the way to the creation of new states (each of which, deploying nationalist rhetoric, promptly claimed a long-suppressed virtual existence). In the second place, the new state has to establish a basic law, and here the constitution gives politico-juridical expression to the intention to establish a state.

The process of establishing a state is difficult. Aspirant elites must come together, formulate a claim to statehood (often invoking the idea of a nation), lodge the idea within the international community of extant states and then have them accept the claim. Thereafter, the business is practical, giving practical form to the aspiration (again, often a violently contested business and again often legitimated in terms of the re-establishment of a suppressed nationhood).

In East Asia there were problems of mutual recognition between competing elites holding different parts of dissolving empires (for example, Indonesia's claims on the territory of Malaysia) and there were conflicts between domestic class groups, ethnic groups and minority groups. The process of state making has often involved violence.

In respect of order, replacement elites must organize the territory internally, so there must be effective lines of political control and exchange, that is, an institutional structure that binds elite and mass together. The newly empowered elite must be able to access the lives of the masses and the newly created citizens have to be brought into effective dialogue with the elite: the whole business of domestic politics. The institutional forms vary as local colonial inheritances are turned to new tasks; a coherent organized community has to be created as the colonial system fades into history and it often also involved making a nation: in sum, the creation of legitimate authority and social order.

Nations are different from states, as they have to be made in the minds of citizens. The idea of 'nation' can be considered in two ways. First, there is the nationalist understanding of nation. Nationalists think that their nation has always existed; it is primordial. The origins of the nation may be lost in the mists of time but it has always existed and is grounded in the given facts of race or ethnicity or language or culture. The key questions for nationalists revolve around finding a home for the nation (a state) and maintaining the nation in the face of threats. Second, there is the social scientific understanding of nation. In the shift to the modern world, the rise of science-based industrial capitalism, a new political structure emerged, the system of states. States then constructed nations and the invention of a nation allowed the elite to legitimate their rule, helped them to maintain order within the territory and gave the people who lived there a sense of belonging, membership of an imagined community. The nation is therefore a social construct.

The process of constructing a nation is difficult. It is an imagined community, a community of similar people or people persuaded that they are similar. There is an elite element and there are also popular elements (ideas of elite plus grass-roots elements). The resultant elite-sponsored web of understanding might involve statements about national identity, national goals or the national past (where everyone is supposed to have come from). It might mention people from history or myth whose actions exemplify the national identity. These claims will be read into popular understandings. These, in turn, will be supplemented by the collective memory of past events running through ordinary life: maybe popular figures in the arts or sports world (popular heroes) or claims to typical practices (food or social mores) and so on. It is through these symbols – official and popular – and their routine repetition that members of a community learn and relearn and thereby sustain a national identity.

Then came development, the fundamental political agreement, explicit or implicit, made between replacement elites and masses and involving the exchange of political support for the promise of better lives in the future. This was understood in material terms, and later the United Nations would cast the matter in terms of four Basic Needs; this deal meant that the elite had to deliver on economic growth and social welfare. Development came to be a key idea in the years following the end of the Pacific War, as new elites were anxious to create material prosperity with economic growth and social welfare. East Asia had many poor people, so raising levels of living was crucial to the success of new states and the region. But the pursuit of development is difficult. At first there were two broad strategies: liberal market style organized within the America-centred sphere, paradoxically the key invention of the countries of the region in this sphere was the developmental state; and then in contrast, state socialist planned development organized within the China-centred sphere where early success gave way to doubts and then market-oriented reforms as the country embraced a variant form of the developmental state.

In sum, new successor elites had to make states, invent nations and thereafter had to pursue development (focused on economic growth and social welfare).

The new states

The European and American colonial powers did return at the end of the Pacific War but the political system of colonial empire was discredited. The colonial systems dissolved into a series of new or reconstituted states. In East Asia modern nations had to be made where they had not previously existed except as nationalist aspirations.

1 Sometime European spheres

As the British sought to manage their inevitable withdrawal they confronted inter-ethnic tensions (Chinese/Malay) and a cross-cutting problem of communist rebellion. The British ordered a constitutional settlement and fought successfully against the communist guerrillas so that by the end of the 1950s Malaysia was independent; later in 1965 Singapore was independent and, later still, Brunei. Thus the British Empire dissolved into Burma, Malaysia along with Singapore, plus the tiny Sultanate of Brunei and, for a period, the residual holding of Hong Kong. In Malaysia anti-colonialism plus ethnic tension led to assertion of Malay priority; the idea of the *bumiputeras* plus NEP (New Economic Policy) – an idea of 'Malaysian' was constructed which embraced ethnic sub-sets (Malay, Chinese and Indian). In Singapore anti-colonialism plus ethnic tension led to assertion of a muted Chinese priority, veiled through a pragmatic ideology of meritocratic multicultural development. Singaporeans were invented and they came to have different officially recognized ethnic roots.

The French Indo-China Empire dissolved in violence into Vietnam, Cambodia and Laos. In Vietnam anti-colonial leaders take power but they are characterized as communist and resisted; similar situations obtain in Laos and Cambodia (which later has its own variant of activist peasant nationalism with Pol Pot). The key territory was Vietnam. The French returned to Indo-China to be greeted by Vietnamese nationalists and, after a year of negotiations, war began; however, by the mid-1950s it was clear to the French that they could not win and they withdrew. The Americans took over until they too withdrew in 1973. The war ran on until 1975, at which point Vietnam was independent and the country ordered as a party-state.

The Dutch tried to re-establish their control in what had been the Dutch East Indies but they were resisted by Soekarno and Hatta who declared the existence of an Indonesian Republic. The Dutch fought two small wars against the Indonesians and they tried to get American support by speaking of the Indonesian nationalists as communists, but they failed and withdrew. Indonesia was established: anti-colonialism, a popular memory of revolution plus the ideology of *pancasila*, the creation of national language plus an elite concern for development slowly drew a multiplicity of ethnic groups into a coherent nation-state.

The Portuguese kept East Timor until the mid-1960s; thereafter the Portuguese empire dissolved into East Timor (later absorbed for a period in Indonesia) and Macau (later absorbed into China).

2 Sometime American sphere

The American empire dissolved into the Philippines plus a number of smaller island dependencies. In the Philippines a mixture of elite pragmatism, the overwhelming influences of Spanish and American colonial rule plus, in particular, the Catholic Church created a version of liberal democratic nationalism.

Siam became Thailand and was drawn into the post-war American sphere. In Thailand recovery from wartime quasi fascism was accomplished by military rule; the territory plus monarchy plus Buddhism are keys to the idea of Thai identity.

3 Sometime Japanese sphere

In Japan the military defeat meant Japanese nationalism was suppressed. A somewhat confused amalgam emerged: an economic nationalism, plus peace constitution plus residual influential cultural nationalists plus the influence of the American occupation authorities. In the empire holdings the Imperial Japanese armies withdrew. Korea was divided into the Democratic People's Republic of Korea (DPRK) and the Republic of Korea (ROK). Taiwan became the Republic of China (ROC). Sakhalin and some northern islands were taken over by the USSR. Thus the Japanese empire dissolved into Japan, North Korea, South Korea and Taiwan. In Korea the DPRK looked to a Korean history of anti-colonialism plus Confucianism plus state socialism and the elite stressed self-reliance, the centrality of the army and the core role of the elite Kim family. South of the 39th parallel in the ROK, anti-colonialism plus Confucianism plus state-sponsored development summed up as the ideal of renovation moved to the foreground – in brief, Korean nationalism plus pride in national achievement.

4 China

China ended its civil war as the People's Republic of China plus Taiwan. In China (1) the civil war continued until 1949 when Mao declared the PRC; (2) the nationalists withdrew to Taiwan as ROC where they were sustained by the USA; and (3) Hong Kong and Macau returned to China in 1997 and 1999 respectively. In China Mao took the resources of Chinese culture, the modernism of the 1911 Republic and the materials of Marxism-Leninism and fashioned a distinctive revolutionary ideal centred on the moral energy and action of the peasantry, hence Maoism. In Taiwan, the defeated Kuomintang (KMT) offer an authoritarian dictatorial celebration of the legacy of Sun Yat Sen.

In East Asia elites made states, made (or remade) nations and pursued development, both nominally liberal market-oriented and variant forms of state-socialism. The elites had one further complication, that is, outside powers brought the Cold War to the region. In the American sphere, Cold War expenditures fostered growth and this in turn helped create the developmental state. In the state socialist sphere, there was early success in China as Mao unified the country, later a lack of growth, then dramatic reforms such that China is now a major economic power. The record thus shows a number of crucial turning points and the first such was the coming of the Cold War to Asia.

The Cold War in East Asia

By the end of the Pacific War anti-communism in American politics was more or less routine. The hostility of the elites in Moscow and Beijing quickly followed. American anti-communism was deployed worldwide; it was deployed in particular in Europe and in East Asia. The key idea was containment: the USA announced that it would act to contain the expansion of global communism. The Cold War developed slowly but eventually involved diplomatic, economic, military and ideological competition. There are competing explanations of the Cold War. The USSR tended to speak in terms of American aggression. China tended to speak, and still does to some extent, in terms of American aspirations to hegemony or hegemonism. Americans spoke of resisting expansionist international communism. Once the Cold War had begun it quickly developed a life of its own. It dominated global politics from the late 1940s up until 1989–91.

The Cold War saw the world divided politically into two blocks; one was in theory liberal market-based with liberal-democratic political systems with a centre in Washington (the free world), whilst the other was made up of socialist party-state political systems with an uneasy double centre in Moscow and Beijing (the socialist world). Many of the nations that had just emerged from colonial empires had no great desire to join either block and founded the non-aligned movement in Bandung in 1955. They tried to stay neutral, to plot a distinctive route to the future, but this meant that both camps looked at them suspiciously and competed for influence. In East Asia the Cold War began in Northeast Asia. The period 1945–50 is crucial. Three interweaving strands can be identified: SCAP (Supreme Commander for the Allied Powers), Korea and China.

In August 1945 the Americans occupied Japan (SCAP) and began an optimistic reform programme that aimed to rework Japan as a species of liberal democracy. Amongst a wide spread of reforms was the establishment of trade union rights, and local people resentful of the chaos the elite had brought upon the country used these rights. There were many unions and some strikes, eventually suppressed by SCAP. This marked the end of the first phase of occupation. A second phase began, the change noted as the 1947 reverse course, and popular aspirations were suppressed as Japan was reworked as an economic cum military regional ally of the USA.

In the Korean peninsular two wartime allies struck a deal over the heads of the local population that resulted in the sometime Japanese colony being divided into two new states, but the circumstances were difficult. A state-socialist regime took shape in the North whilst the Americans installed an émigré nationalist in the South who proceeded to inflame relations with the North. In 1950 the North invaded the South, first the Americans and then the Chinese joined in. After three years of war the original division was still in place but the country had by then been devastated; both North and South ruling elites had to rebuild in very difficult circumstances.

In October 1949 the Chinese Civil War (1928–49) came to an effective end with the defeat of the Nationalist armies. The remnants of the Kuomintang forces that had received extensive aid from the USA fled to Taiwan, creating a new state. The reaction of politicians in Washington was severe and commentators spoke of 'losing China'. When the Chinese armies became involved in Korea, any inhibitions on the part of Washington to the pursuit of Cold War were swept away.

The complete division of East Asia rapidly followed. In the US bloc the official goal was liberal markets, individualistic societies and liberal democracies (modernization), whilst in the socialist bloc the official goal was a socialist economy, society and polity – a socialist country. The Cold War was organized systematically; that is, there were networks of diplomatic alliances, trade links, military alliances whereby overt and covert assistance was given to local actors, and there were also two severe regional wars, in Korea and in Vietnam.

War and memory: collective memory and the national past

In the middle period of the twentieth century there was a series of wars which helped to shape modern East Asia: these wars involved different peoples, they took place in different places, they lasted different times and they are remembered today in different ways.

These conflicts have left contemporary residues in official and popular memory. Such residues help shape contemporary ideas – patterns of understanding that help shape current attitudes and actions, both official (the national past) and popular (collective memory).

TABLE 4.4 Wars of colonial withdrawal, 1945–75

1945–50	Partitian of Korea
1950–53	Korean War
1945–46	Colonial Reoccupation of Vietnam
1946–54	First Indo China War
1944–46	Colonial Reconquest of Philippines
1946–54	Huk Rebellion
1945–46	Colonial Reoccupation of Dutch East Indies
1945	Colonial Reoccupation of Malaya
1947	First Dutch Police Action
1948–49	Second Dutch Police Action
1948–58	Malayan Emergency
1955–75	Second Indo-China War
1963–65	Konfrontasi
1965	Indonesia Coup
1975	Reunification of Vietnam

The wars took various forms: some of them were major inter-state wars, some of them were civil wars, some of them were major Cold War conflicts and some of them were smaller-scale wars associated directly with colonial withdrawal and the choice of replacement regimes. Together, these conflicts cost the lives of upwards of 20 million people with their impact further extended by the injured, the bereaved and the displaced, along with all the attendant material destruction.

There were major inter-state wars:

- 1931–45 the war(s) as the Chinese remember;
- 1931–45 the war(s) as the Japanese remember;
- 1939–45 the war(s) as the Europeans remember;
- 1941–45 the war(s) as the Americans remember.

There were major Cold War conflicts:

- 1950–53 the war(s) as the Koreans remember;
- 1946–54 and 1960–75 the war(s) as the Vietnamese remember.

There were also a number of smaller wars associated with the dissolution of empire:

- 1947–49 Dutch police actions in Indonesia;
- 1948–58 Malayan Emergency;
- 1963–65 Konfrontasi.

There was also one major civil war:

- 1928–49 Chinese Civil War.

These episodes have been read into popular and elite memory: in the former case via collective memory, individual, family, group or community; and in the latter case via the national past, a formal memory of events of warfare. The past is thus extensively constructed and malleable: collective memory is fallible given its nature and multiple participants, and the national past is self-consciously contrived as it encompasses elite-level memory and the ways in which the elite wishes these matters to be presented, both to their domestic audience and to an international audience.

Tony Judt has argued that the familiar business of memory is the outcome of two processes: active remembering and equally active forgetting; the resultant agreed story might have only a tangential relationship to the record established by scholarly historians, who will be professionally committed to getting the story straight, but they will feed elite and popular understandings. For local elites and masses, the past is available in the form of a number of stereotypical events and these come to stand for the wars in general. The detail is lost as scholarly history takes a back seat.

For example:

- China/Japan – Yasakuni – apologies/reparations – Nanking/Manchuria – textbooks;
- Korea/Japan – Yasakuni – apologies/reparations – comfort women – textbooks;
- USA/Japan – Pearl Harbour – Hiroshima – Nagasaki – Smithsonian;
- Europeans/Japan – memories of European survivors of Pacific War;
- Japan/Japan – right-wing versus (left-wing) peace movement – Yasakuni – textbooks – flag – constitution – national masochism/normality;
- Vietnam/USA – revolutionary victory – punishing Vietnam – popular memory;
- Cambodia – ASEAN (Association of Southeast Asian Nations) plus PRC plus EU (European Union) plus American support for Pol Pot regime;
- China – the official memories of civil war – CCP and KMT – slow movements to mutual acknowledgement – in China the overarching theme is that of a century of humiliation.

Modernity: diverse trajectories within the unfolding modern world

It was the impact of European state-empires that began the process of the shift to the modern world in East Asia; traders, soldiers, missionaries and assorted adventurers rode the wave of natural science-based industrial capitalism and overwhelmed extant long-established sophisticated civilizations in East Asia. The fullest extent of this unequal exchange was realized in the creation of elaborate state-empire systems where core and peripheral territories were acknowledged in formal institutional machineries. In the peripheral realms distinctive forms of colonial life took shape, multi-ethnic, hierarchical and fissured with tensions. These tensions fuelled nascent nationalist sentiment and minority groups of nationalists were given their chance when the core countries of the system of state-empires opted for a species of civil war. The long period from 1911 to 1945 was one of crisis and warfare of various sorts which killed millions and rendered the state-empire system unsustainable. It duly collapsed, although not without precipitating a further round of wars of colonial withdrawal.

Thereafter the disintegrating territories of the former empires were reworked by successor elites as states were created, nations invented and development pursued. In the event, in general, with very great success: first, in the area of Northeast Asia as a rebuilt Japan offered a model to that group of states that came to be tagged the Four Tigers; later, in Southeast Asia, with the countries of ASEAN; and then, later still, in the heartland of the region, China. Overall, in recent years, the area has emerged as a more or less coherent region notwithstanding difficult historical legacies and on-going diplomatic tensions, and it is now one of three powerful regions within the contemporary global system.

5
COLONIALISM AND MODERNITY
Disentangling the issues

The shift to the modern world in East Asia was routed through the experience of subordinate incorporation within metropolitan European, American and Japanese state-empire systems. The record of both cores and peripheries within these systems has been much debated. Here, three issues can be explored, each internally complex. First, in respect of the construction and character of empires, where two polar opposite positions are readily identifiable and have shaped much debate: (1) colonialism brought enlightened civilization to traditional societies; (2) colonialism violently overthrew existing civilizations in the pursuit of profit – in the one case, development, in the other, the development of underdevelopment. Second, in respect of the process of the collapse of state-empires in general crisis, both events and residues have been extensively debated. And third, in reset of the role of state-empires in the process of the shift to the modern world in East Asia, the mixture of external and internal social dynamics have been discussed.

The construction and character of state-empires

The episode of colonial rule has been widely debated and two polar positions are readily identifiable: first, that Europeans and Americans brought civilization to territories whose forms of life were pre-modern (available in multiple varieties, from aggressive through to apologetic); second, in contrast, Europeans and America overwhelmed otherwise well-established civilizations, hitching their fate to that of the metropolitan core and costing such territories dearly until they were able to throw off foreign control (again, available in varieties, more or less aggressive). Yet against these two positions, it is clear that the detail is more revealing; thus the route to the modern world for the current set of sovereign states in East Asia lay through the experience of peripheral incorporation within state-empire systems, and so colonialism offered a mixture of exploitation, learning and development.

Questions: the time lines of empires

Within the intellectual space sketched out by these positions there are a number of questions that can be pursued in regard to the creation and dissolution of empire.

1. *Structures and agents*
   The mix of structural and agential factors: with the former, analysis points to the changing logic of the wider system, an expansionist industrial capitalism, which constituted the environment within which individuals and groups operated; and with the latter, analysis points to the actions of individuals or groups, where these are taken, in principle, to be considered and willed actions (a line that does not ignore circumstances or rule out unintended consequences but does focus on the self-conscious actions of individuals).
2. *Violence*
   The role of violence, where the issue is whether or not such violence is necessary or contingent to the creation and maintenance of empires, and where, noting the familiar narrative histories of East Asia, such violence seems to have been intrinsic, routine and asymmetric.
3. *Agendas*
   Metropolitan agendas and the nature of arguments made at the time legitimating the exercise, where there were a number of arguments legitimating the expansion of empires and where also, it might be noted, there were both critics of empire and more paternalistically those who sought either to mitigate its impact or learn about other cultures (thus the issue of the role of anthropology in the colonial world).

FIGURE 5.1 Chinese snipers, 1894.

Source: British Library, 'Chinese snipers attack Japanese Officers by Yosai (Watanabe) Nobukazu 1893'.

FIGURE 5.2 Japanese Navy, 1894.

Source: British Library, 'The Japanese Navy sinks Chinese battleships at Haiyang Island off Dagu Mountain by Shinsai Toshimitsu 1894'.

4   *Reparations*
    The status of contemporary arguments in favour of reparations, where arguments are made to the effect that contemporary Third World countries or residual groups of pre-contact indigenous peoples (for example, Native Australians) should be compensated for the various impacts of colonial rule.

5   *Memory*
    As the episode is historically recent much remains to be dis-interred and debated there are important issues of collective memory and the national past, where, in regard to both areas, there is much to be discussed about the process of empire dissolution and new nation construction (thus, for example, two recent films by Joshua Oppenheimer dealing with the Indonesian army coup of 1965 and the associated mass killings).

Structures and agents: modernity and the creation of European state-empire systems

There is some debate in regard to the creation of the European state-empire systems about the use of structural or agent-centred argument: thus whether the business was a matter of contingent politics shaped by structural circumstances, or, alternatively, whether the business was the outcome of choices, made, finally, by individuals (state or corporate or organizational, thus, for example, churches/missionaries, or perhaps individual adventurers).

The structural line of reflection calls attention to the environment within which agents operated and so enquiry turns to the logic of the system and the ways in which it informed and shaped the activities of discrete agents. Industrial capitalism was a dynamic system, evidenced in both intensification and expansion; metropolitan populations were required to become ever more efficient at the same time that new peripheral populations were drawn into the system. Both populations were subject to these system demands and it created a complex hierarchy of elites and masses throughout the state-empire territory. This type of argument implies at a macro level that the state-empires were the extraordinary out-turn of otherwise ordinary politics within a peculiarly dynamic system. In regard to individual agents, their behaviour was shaped by the system: ordinary politics, contingent, short-term and pragmatic.

Agent-centred argument offers a rather different take and here attention turns to the activities of individuals, persons or organizations. It begins from an assumption that they knew what they were doing: they appreciated their situation, operated instrumentally in pursuit of explicit goals and understood that their actions would have a spread of consequences, direct and indirect, and such consequences were, for them, acceptable. A softened formulation could also be made and understandings, strategies and consequences could be seen in outline, not detail, and so the actual pattern of activity would have a contingent element as untoward events occasioned rejigging unfolding projects, or, in brief, things did not always go according to plan. But there was still a plan and thus a direct responsibility embraced by those agents and this implies that later generations can judge directly; actions could be read as acceptable or unacceptable.

It might be noted that such debates are not new, indeed they are quite familiar within the realms of the social sciences and humanities; thus one recent and ongoing debate concerns the nature of the process of the mid-twentieth-century destruction of European Jewry. It can be read as either contingent, a by-product of the mad logic of warfare, or intentional, an extreme modern expression of an otherwise familiar anti-Semitism. Cast in terms of contemporary social science, if one wants an overview of events then it is surely a false choice, as from Marx through to Anthony Giddens or Susan Strange the dynamic of structures and agents is general to social life – including empire building.

Thus, for example, in regard to the British Empire scholars have advanced both structural and agential arguments: Linda Colley and John Darwin.

Colley's argued to the effect that the local elite was stymied in both North America (having lost the War of Independence) and in mainland Europe (with the rise of republican politics, the French Revolution and later Napoleonic Wars) and was perforce obliged to look elsewhere for trading opportunities; thus the elite turned outwards and, on the basis of nascent industrial capitalism and contingent success in warfare, went on to create a global empire. The elite made the British Empire and they made Britons at the same time: an enduring outcome shaped initially by contingent circumstances.

Hence the superficially apposite nature of the comment associated with Robert Seeley according to which the empire was accumulated in a fit of absent-mindedness, that is, there was no grand design and territories were acquired in a random fashion. A parallel argument is offered by Bernard Porter who argues that the domestic population were never that bothered about empire, and so here the core elite is excused and the consequences of the global collection of territories disregarded.

A further more direct argument is available from John Darwin who writes about the empire project: there may not have ever been a grand plan but there was a systematic drive to accumulate trading opportunities and later to accumulate territory; this last because there was competition between core elites both for position within Europe and in regard to the accumulation and possession of peripheral territories. Thus, for example, debates in respect of – say – Japan and Germany, both latecomers to the business of acquiring colonial empires.

In regard to Japan, a faction of the elite organized a conservative revolution from above and the country was self-consciously remade; study missions were sent to Europe and America in order to learn the lessons of the modern industrial capitalist system. Ideas current at the time included: Social Darwinism (the notion that relationships between groups – including races – were competitive); Malthusianism (scarcity was inevitable, thus securing supplies was vital); and mercantilism (development had a zero sum aspect, thus securing territory was vital). One further aspect of elite thinking was expressed as Pan-Asianism: as the historical core of the region had seemingly been overwhelmed by foreign powers it was the business of the Japanese to respond, to assert the collective interests of East Asian peoples. All these ways of reading the circumstances of late nineteenth- and early twentieth-century politics in Northeast Asia pointed the elite in the direction of the acquisition of empire; thus the process of expansion in Hokkaido, Sakhalin, the Ryukyu Islands, Korea and Manchuria.

In the case of Germany, similar arguments apply. In 1871 the country was unified under the leadership of Prussia and rapid economic advance followed, so that by the late nineteenth century the country was clearly a rising power within Europe. The elite sought to compete with the British and one aspect was stressed by key figures in the elite, that of naval power. A naval arms race ensued. And over this same period the elite determined that a powerful country should also have overseas possessions, the motive seems to have been status. The territories that were acquired in Shandong and in the South Pacific (and also East and Southwest Africa) seem to have held little economic value, although Shandong gave access to China. Later discussions have revolved around the responsibility or not of the German elite for the outbreak of the Great War and here historians do fall into distinct camps; agent-centred work points to direct German elite responsibility, whilst structural-centred work points to shifting concatenations of circumstances and thus Europe sleep walking into war.

The mixture of structural pressures and elite-level choices is evident in these histories. The expansion of the British Empire was secured in conflict with the Dutch and the French in particular, plus later the Americans (acquiescing in the declaration of the Open Door), Imperial Germany (where competition tipped over into a naval arms race, one occasion for the subsequent Great War) and Imperial Japan (where the British signed treaties of amity).

In respect of the British, the arguments to contingent political actions seem far-fetched. The British elite did not accumulate overseas territories by accident, they sought them and they sought them in particular circumstances. They fought other European powers to claim them; they fought local political elites to secure them and they went to great lengths (force and persuasion) to sustain them; Darwin is correct to write of an empire project.

Similar remarks could be presented for other empire builders. Thus the Dutch in what is now Indonesia fought a series of wars over a period of 100-plus years in order to control the bulk of the archipelago. Thus the French in mainland Southeast Asia fought three wars against the local state to secure these territories. Thus also the Americans: routinely self-presented as anti-imperialist but fighting numerous wars against Native Americans to seize territory and expand the country so that it was a continental power (legitimated by the idea of manifest destiny); making claims about regional pre-eminence (Monroe Doctrine); making claims in the Pacific, hence Commodore Perry in Japan; fighting wars against Spain to seize territory in the American Southwest and Caribbean along with the invasion of the Philippines and the annexation of Hawaii; plus, finally, their extensive involvement in China coupled with the promulgation of the doctrine of the Open Door.

All that said, in hindsight, structural argument seems the more plausible; thus, industrial capitalism was a dynamic system, increasing its demands on its home population whilst seeking new opportunities overseas through a process of intensification and expansion. Metropolitan elites sought overseas territories on the back of these structural pressures. Elites could have acted otherwise, they did not; instead they embraced system pressures and built state-empires and the key elements were trade and violence.

The role of violence in state-empires

The state-empires were built on the dynamism of the industrial-capitalist form of life, with its intensification and expansion; the latter process entailed the practical business of interaction with diverse other forms of life. One familiar characterization of such forms of life is 'traditional' but this is misleading, implying a common pre-modern non-progressive stability – there were many forms of life and they ranged in scale from great civilizations to small tribal societies which had it in common that they functioned, that is, they worked, they were coherent forms of life. They also had it in common that agents lodged within these forms of life had to read and react to the actions of the incomers.

These exchanges were always local and particular, as one small group of European agents interacted with small groups of local people; incoming traders were minorities within their new host communities. These exchanges then developed and whilst there were varied motives on the part of the Europeans, the core preoccupation was with trade and the available ideology of trade stressed its benefits to all those involved. These trade links were accumulated in a variety of ways. Agreements could be made with local authorities, contracts made and treaties signed, but violence was always available. Historians have recorded many wars of colonial expansion. There were also colonial wars of pacification or control. And, more recently, there were a number of wars of colonial withdrawal. At which point it might have been thought that matters of control were settled, but thereafter there have been post-empire wars, in particular overt and covert Cold War-period proxy wars and recently a number of ill-considered destructive humanitarian liberal interventionist wars in the Arab world.

By way of illustration, the major episodes of violence included: (1) the Dutch advance into the archipelago, with a series of wars against local sultanates; (2) the British advance into the region, with conflicts with the French in South Asia and the Dutch in Southeast Asia and crucially against the Qing Empire in the Opium Wars; (3) the French wars of conquest in mainland Southeast Asia, the creation of Indo-China; (4) American exchanges with Japanese elites, the invasion of the Philippines and the declaration of the 'Open Door', securing access to China. Cast in descriptive terms, in simple narrative history, the use of violence to advance the business of territorial expansion was familiar, and this is demonstrated by the list of wars; however, simple description does not get at the central role of violence in the creation of empires. It is appropriate to treat the violence as intrinsic to the business of state-empire. This is clear in three areas: expansion, maintenance and dissolution.

In respect of the expansion of the system, non-European forms of life were overborne and mechanisms included treaties, trade and migration, and, as necessary, violence. Carlo Cipolla has argued that the technology of sails and cannons helped the early traders deal with local opposition.

In respect of the maintenance of the assorted peripheral territories acquired by the metropolitan core powers, here the mechanisms included colonial administrative apparatus (regulation and co-option), colonial police forces (official, corporate and societal) and, finally, armed forces (corporate, thus in the early period, the trading companies ran armies and later the state provided standard modern armed forces garrisons). All these machineries were available as necessary.

In respect of the dissolution of state-empire systems, the violence was multiple in form: (1) there were local groups (with various programmes – preservation of status quo, independence or, later in the war period, collaboration and resistance), (2) territorially oriented groups (with various agendas – warlords, participants in civil wars), (3) those involved in wider warfare (again with various agendas as allies with or against Axis Powers). And in this last noted section, individuals or groups could be caught up in multiple levels of violence (thus local villagers in China obliged to collaborate with the locally ascendant armies of warlords, civil war enemies or the Japanese).

The dissolution of state-empires in the years following the Second World War saw these large geographical, multi-ethnic territories, which were ruled from physically remote metropolitan cores via a hierarchy of subordinate cores, dissolve away. Metropolitan elites in Europe did not have the political, moral or material resources to re-establish and sustain these systems and these vast territories had to be reworked in a difficult shift from state-empires to nation-states. The process involved local elites seeking to control territory, invent nations and mobilize the populations they controlled for national development. It was not a simple process and nor one that is compete (thus, say, problems of borders and populations in parts of Africa and the Middle East, with Israel as a useful instance of the sometimes ambiguous nature of success).

The issue of violence has been addressed by numerous historians, with past records noted, and so too the ways in which empire has been read into the collective memory of both new nation-states and residual states of former core territories of state-empires. First, in respect of the sometime metropolitan core territories, local elites have had to deal with reduced territorial holdings, lost wars and the demands of their local populations for new political directions, in particular, welfare states of one sort or another. The empires have been reimagined as belonging to the past, maybe never really that important: thus, for example, Vienna, capital of Hapsburg Empire, now capital of Austria, or London, once capital of a global empire, now merely one more European capital city – and so on. Second, in respect of peripheral territories it is clear that the violence was routine. The wars were routine. These wars involved various participants; they were played out in various locations and are today variously remembered: multiple wars, multiple participants and multiple memories, but in many cases a national past has been created that celebrates the struggle for independence, that designates certain political players as fathers of the nation and that offers a stylized history of the active achievement of a thoroughly justified independence.

All this makes writing the histories difficult. Recording the history of violence is not straightforward for there is no single narrative, as there were multiple wars with multiple participants in various places at various times with a spread of subsequent collective memories and national pasts.

Metropolitan agendas, legitimations and the nature of the peripheral territories they created

Once again there are a mixture of issues to pursue: first, metropolitan elite concerns (roughly, as in Chapter 4, some mix of trade, security and status); second, the legitimations offered by core figures for the process of expansion (the impact upon other cultures was known, the issue was how to justify these impacts); and, third, the particular nature of the forms of life created in the peripheral colonial holdings.

And once again, in respect of Europeans and Americans in East Asia, whilst they all followed a similar basic path – asserting their control and concerns – there were also significant differences in their approaches: the ways they understood themselves in relation to colonial subjects, the ways in which these subjects were acknowledged in law and then the ways in which colonial cadres dealt with colonial subjects on a day-to-day level.

1 Metropolitan elite concerns

There was trade and political elites sought to facilitate trade linkages, routinely cast in mercantilist terms, thus controlling trade spheres. The expansion of trade was justified in terms of an ideology of trade such that trade was held to be beneficial to all concerned. Its expansion was sought in treaties with local rulers and such treaties could be secured through involvement in local politics (thus British expansion in South Asia and Malay Peninsular or the many-sided manoeuvring amongst incoming and local groups that secured Singapore) or such treaties could also be secured by the use of violence (hence, paradigmatically, the Opium Wars and the construction of the Treaty Port system in China).

There was also inter-elite competition. Thus (1) mercantilist competition for trade linkages outside the metropolitan core entailed routine conflict. In the early modern era this took the form of wars (hence a series of Anglo-Dutch wars and a series of Anglo-French wars), whilst in the later nineteenth century these conflicts were moderated: at Fashoda 1898 the British and French chose not to fight and again at Agadir 1911 the French and German authorities chose not to fight. And (2) a related aspect was straightforwardly military competition, thus the accumulation of the means of violence, in particular armies and navies (air power figures more in the period of the dissolution of state-empires). The British, later joined by other European powers, deployed naval power in their conflicts with Qing authorities; the latter had supposed that it was not possible for the British to deploy forces at such a distance from their home bases, but by the mid-nineteenth century the British had both ships and a network of bases, these last being links in a chain oriented towards securing access to China. And (3) there was status competition between elites, claims to national prestige, with ships used for showing the flag (thus Spithead Review) and armies used for flags, parades and inspections; the latter, in particular, aimed not only at other empire powers but at the local inhabitants of those territories already drawn into the empire system (hence say, Queen Victoria in India).

There were also administrative issues. As the early modern era engagements (distant, via particular persons) gave way to more familiarly rational bureaucratic engagements, large machineries of colonial administration were constructed: ministries based in the metropolitan capital, cadres of administrators and networks of subordinate centres in a hierarchy spreading downwards. European systems differed in design but all were perforce variations on this theme as distances, communications and lack of local knowledge prevented any closer top-down control. One key concern was with the funding of local colonial administrations as the machineries had to be paid for, and core authorities preferred not to subsidize them, funds had to be raised locally.

And elites also turned their attention to popular aspects of empire: encouraging exchanges or temporary settlement (administrative, business, social or cultural); encouraging migration so as to settle permanently newly acquired territory (Australia, New Zealand, South Africa and, on a larger scale, the American West); offering legitimations of the whole enterprise and inviting domestic core populations to enjoy the success.

2 Legitimations: trade and civilization and race

There were several strands of legitimation offered by key figures in the metropolitan cores. These figures included government and state functionaries, corporate world spokespersons, assorted commentators and contemporary social scientists. All their claims revolved one way or another around assertions of the benefits of trade, which, in turn, it was said, was best organized for the benefit of all concerned by the denizens of the more superior civilizations.

First, government figures looked to the high politics of relations with other nation-states in the European system of state-empires and thus an element of competition; hence the argument that expansion was necessary to counter the expansion of others. So there was inter-governmental competition amongst the metropolitan core countries: for example, at a low level, thus, as noted, the Fashoda 1898 episode, or at a high level, thus Franco-German exchange over Agadir 1911.

Plus, there were the activities of state-functionaries, less high politics, more nuts and bolts: agreements about spheres of influence and joint activity within peripheral territories; drawing demarcation lines (Dutch and British spheres in Southeast Asia) or establishing areas of control (Anglo-American and French Concessions in Shanghai); or establishing common rules (thus American declaration in regard to China of the Open Door); or establishing rules in regard to local law/custom and metropolitan law/custom (thus in Malaya, status of local Sultanates within British Empire systems).

Also there were the activities of the corporate world with their focus on trade; hence the concern with accessing peripheral territories; hence the concern with the assertion of property rights to facilitate trade; and hence agreements with local powers for territorial access (thus the Treaty Port system in China or the manoeuvring to set up Singapore and so on). Then there were agreements with local powers and peoples, which established locally relevant machineries of law securing property (for example, in Fiji land ownership surveys, or in Hong Kong parcelling out land in Victoria).

There were many commentators involved in these activities. They typically read the expansionary activity in optimistic terms and a number of themes appeared in various writings. There were claims about civilization, that is, that the Europeans offered a model for other groups. There were claims about technology, that is, European natural science and technology (thus in industry) showed the rest of the world their future. There were claims about race, that is, empire was read culturally downstream from Charles Darwin – this produced an explicit statement in the work of Herbert Spencer with Social Darwinism, thus there were distinct races, competition was inevitable and clearly the European race had come out on top. These lines of argument could be given various slants; there were claims to superiority, claims to responsibility or alternatively claims to the worthlessness of those dispossessed by the relentless expansion of the system of state-empires.

Social scientists, concerned to read the unfolding shift to the modern world, took empire as a given and images of non-European peoples shifted from optimistic characterizations (denizens of other cultures undamaged by modernity, hence at the clichéd extreme, the noble savage) to more pessimistic schemes (variations on the theme of traditional or uncivilized or moribund societies). One group of social scientists were closely involved, thus the rise of anthropology is bound up with the expansion of colonial holdings. The expansion occasioned debates and, whilst some objected to the expansion, others tagged it as inevitable in Social Darwinist terms, with competition between races read as a given, it was best to be on the winning side.

These debates had many strands (as indicated) and the overall concerns of these debates shifted and changed as the excitement of early so-called voyages of discovery with their reports on exotic peoples gave way to the more detailed and comparatively mundane concerns of established state-empires with trade, communications and flows of goods and people. In summary, briefly, two strands can be mentioned: first, the claim that trade was beneficial to all concerned; and second, the claim that the more advanced countries had a responsibility towards those less developed, or in contemporary French terms, a civilizing mission.

3 Forms of life in peripheral (colonial) territories

The domestic organization of colonial settlements was quite distinctive. They created distinctive forms of life. These settlements were home to mixed ethnicities, with social segregation between ethnicities and social hierarchies within these groups. There was also marked economic segmentation as sectors of the economy became associated with particular ethnicities. And there was both cultural separation (as discrete communities maintained their own customs) and cultural intermixing (as discrete communities interacted within these territories).

In regard to policy making there would be differences between incoming metropolitan groups and local groups as they would all have different expectations of their circumstances and prospects within the colony. But one crucial factor would be that the colonial authorities were always in a position to deploy violence to buttress their positions and, whilst the use of violence marked administrative failure or social or economic breakdown, it was always available.

Thereafter, it can be noted that colonial territories evidenced not merely domestic arrangements but they were subject – quite directly – to wider contextual pressures. They were not sovereign states, but local elites were, like other elites, obliged to read and react to structural pressures; for colonial elites this meant not merely the usual spread of demands but also those flowing from the relevant metropolitan centre – the demands of the home government (relations varied – thus the British colonial authorities left much to the man on the spot).

Arguments for reparations to be made by former core countries to former peripheries

Commentators have argued that, as the expansion of state-empires disrupted hitherto settled communities, compensation should be paid by sometime cores to sometime peripheries. Here one example of the argument would relate to the situation of those groups involved in the slave trade: stripping West Africa of people and depositing them in the Caribbean, at high cost to those enslaved and with great profits to those running the slaving business, the plantation owners in the Caribbean and their downstream customers in the product importing cities of England. Many grew rich on the back of the slave trade and commentators suggest this be acknowledged and recompense made.

These types of arguments are familiar in Europe, in particular regarding two episodes: first, the episode of the Second World War with multiple aspects, in particular the return of looted material property (arts, buildings, businesses, land and so on) and the return of looted financial property (thus bank accounts); and second, the episode of the end of the Cold War and the reunification of Europe when some of those persons and families expelled or who had fled in 1945 sought the return of property in Eastern Europe, typically, German citizens asking for property in Poland, Czech Republic (ex-Sudetenland) or Hungary.

In regard to this matter, in general, a particular issue has been reparations paid to the relatives of Jewish victims of the war. The West German state transfers of monies to Israel and West German corporate transfers of money to former slave labourers and their relatives, plus the return of properties, as noted.

Several issues emerge: first, the current generation's responsibilities for the actions of earlier generations as moral responsibility attaches to individuals not to nations (Germany and its past and Israel); second, the passage of time and claims of remote descendants of those killed in the war years or in the period of the division of Europe into eastern and western halves (Gustav Klimt's painting of Adele Bloch Bauer has gone to the USA; and newspaper reports suggest a remote relative is now seeking ownership of the Beethoven Frieze) (commentators have suggest that these claims can be dubious); third, the nature and details of international law (what does it say, when was it written) and relatedly the nature and details of agreements on the return of stolen property (what does it say, when was it written); and fourth, there are important distinctions to acknowledge – reparations or restitution or compensation.

Collective memory and the national past

Tony Judt has argued, in regard to the twentieth-century history of Europe, in particular the episode of the Second World War, that memory is a matter of active remembering and active forgetting; memory is thus a creative business. Scholars have written about two variant forms with one running through ordinary life and the other found primarily in the realms of official life: in the first place, collective memory running down through multiple social channels into the present day – it is informal memory, found in family, community, organizations and the like; in the second place, the national past, that is, an official memory constructed over time in a dialogue of elite and popular memory. The 'national past' offers an agreed public version of the nature of a political community, recording where it has come from, who is now embraced within its borders and where in principle its logic implies that it will be going. The national past fits a political community into the unfolding flow of time: yesterday, today and tomorrow.

The long episode of the expansion, maintenance and collapse of the state-empire system has been read into collective memory in a multiplicity of ways, with local-level memories in all those parts of the world impacted by these systems. It means that most peoples in the modern world of today have some sort of memory of the state-empire period. There is also an elite-level memory, aspects of the national past, that makes claims about the nature of the system and the manner of its eventual demise. The versions found in sometime core territories and those found in sometime peripheral territories would of course differ, perhaps quite sharply (Britain/India, Britain/Myanmar or France/Indo-China or France/Algeria or Netherlands/Indonesia or, more awkwardly, Britain/Hong Kong, and so on).

By way of a more detailed example, as indicated, the state-empire systems have been read into informal and formal memory in a multiplicity of ways; thus, for example, British official memory contrasted with that of the Chinese state. Here British official memory – the national past – records a generally benign process of expansion, perhaps coloured here and there by particular episodes or persons, which produced an empire that gathered widespread popular support before the territories

FIGURE 5.3 Combined Japanese and British attack on the German naval base at Ching Tao, China, August–November 1914.

Source: Imperial War Museum, 'Crowds in Tokyo wait to welcome the Japanese and British troops after the successful attack on Tsingtau 12 December 1914'.

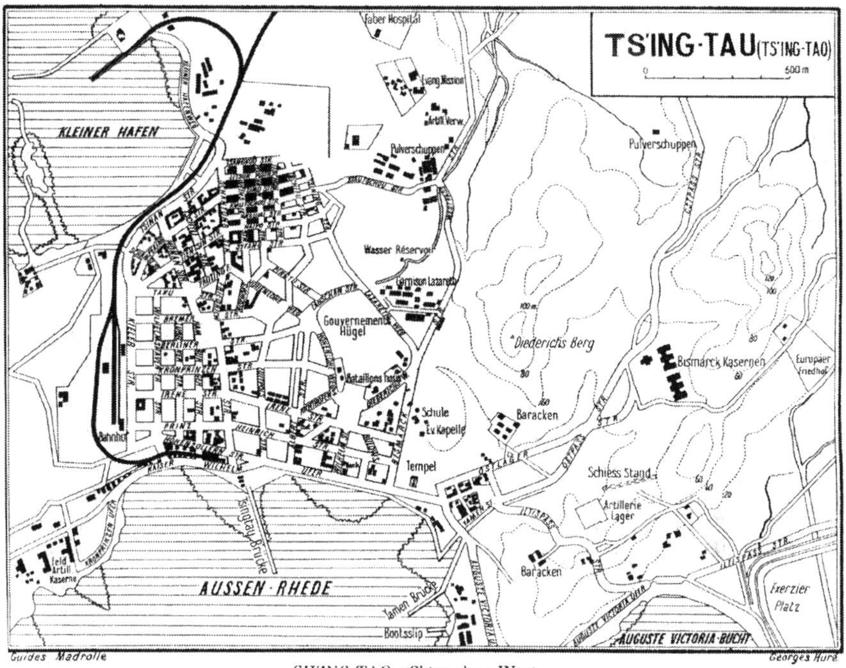

Disentangling the issues 89

FIGURE 5.3(a)   Ching Tao Plan, 1912.

Source: Perry-Casteneda Library, *Madrolle's Guide Books: Northern China, The Valley of the Blue River, Korea*, Hachette and Company, 1912.

achieved a level of development that provided the basis for their independence and membership of the Commonwealth of Nations – the process was not without its difficulties but overall worked to the benefit of all those involved. However, in sharp contrast, Chinese official memory – the national past – records a process of thuggish incomers undermining local authorities, industries and customs such that the country entered a period best recalled as a century of humiliation, a situation that endured until the National Revolution of 1911 began a process of resistance that led in time to the formation of the People's Republic of China, at which point the people had recovered their independence.

These examples and the stark contrasts they reveal could be multiplied many times over. The process of the shift to the modern world embraced most of the planet and reconstructions of extant forms of life were routine and extensive. The heartland territories of Europe were the first to undertake this shift and to read events into collective memory; the changes were variously experienced and variously read into memory (at the extreme, as a celebration of all the new symptoms of modernity or, in contrast, the defensive reactions of romanticism, celebrating the past or nature, symbols of deeper continuity) and, thereafter, of course, the experience with its associated patterns of memory was repeated in the peripheral territories of empire as these territories were absorbed into state-empire systems thus feeding into historical memory and the national pasts of eventually new nations.

Modernity, crisis and national development

These new nations emerged from the dissolution of the state-empire system; large, multi-ethnic territories dissolved away and replacement political structures had to be found (otherwise domestic anarchy conjoined to external perceptions of lawlessness – in contemporary terminology, failed states). The available model was that of the nation-state. As state-empires collapsed, many new nation-states were created, forming over time the contemporary global system, the contingent pattern of today. It is the cumulative pattern of the diverse routes to the modern world of extant polities, unfolding and on-going.

The creation of new states

Three issues can be pursued under this heading: elite competition, crisis and the collapse couple with emergence of independent states.

Metropolitan elite competition was routine. The state-empire system comprised a number of discrete state-empires and throughout the early modern period their relationships were understood to be competitive in a zero-sum sense – what one gained, the other, necessarily, lost: in economic terms, notions of mercantile competition for exclusive trading spheres; in social terms, notions of race-based struggles for survival; and in political terms, notions of the inevitable nature of competitions for power. The European-centred system of state-empires prospered through the nineteenth century, that is, it expanded; however the latter decades of that century saw new competitive tensions introduced with the increasing economic strengths of hitherto relatively secondary players, thus the United States, Imperial Germany and Imperial Japan. The system was plagued by these new competitive exchanges. These tensions were not resolved, rather they grew more difficult to manage and they were accompanied by the build-up of military machines. Eventually, these tensions found expression in the Balkan states with nationalism plus assassinations and the upshot was the Great War 1914–18. That, however, was not the end of it, even though it ended the empire ambitions of Austria-Hungary, Imperial Germany and Czarist Russia, and a further round of metropolitan warfare followed in the late 1930s and early 1940s, but by this point the European system of state-empires was in disarray. It was not reassembled: in part because war-damaged core elites lacked the power; and in part because the denizens of peripheral territories were not disposed to acquiesce.

Peripheral tensions were significant. The shift to the modern world was accomplished in many areas via the historically relatively brief episode of colonial rule and such rule entailed exploitation, development and learning; this last, an appreciation of the economic, social and political logics of the modern world, in particular, ideas of nation and democracy and development. In China these were embraced by Sun Yat Sen and his colleagues and these ideas, plus other local resentments and conflicts, fuelled the 1911 Nationalist Revolution. The Qing were rejected, so too was foreign influence. This pattern of turning modern ideas back against the agents of metropolitan power was replicated throughout the peripheral territories: in South Asia, Ghandi and Nehru; in Burma/Myanmar, Aung San; in Singapore, Lee Kuan Yew, and his allies; in Siam, a military coup abolished the absolute monarchy in favour of modern ideas; and so on. Throughout the peripheral territories, local elites sought statehood, nationhood and thus the possibility of development.

The European system of state-empires collapsed in general crisis as a result of metropolitan and peripheral conflicts during the early part of the twentieth century. The earlier collapse of Spanish and Portuguese holdings in Latin America and the earlier still collapse of British holdings in North America belonged – at best – to the earliest phases of the shift to the modern world. What was now in process of remaking was a new system of natural science-based industrial capitalism. The collapse saw extensive warfare involving various participants and later various memories.

A sequence can be identified: collapse, independent nation-states and the invention of development. The final period of collapse took place after the Second World War. Dutch, British and French powers sought to re-establish their holdings in Southeast and East Asia but were unable to secure former territories; however, withdrawal was not straightforward and was marked by wars of colonial withdrawal. These episodes were further coloured by the way in which the American government, which was virulently anti-communist from the 1940s onwards, read nationalism as communist, and intervened to prop up various unsavoury regimes. Thus Cold War proxy wars, overt and covert. However, the Dutch, French and British were largely gone by the late 1950s, whilst the Americans remained militarily engaged until the early 1970s, and thereafter further warfare continued in mainland Southeast Asia until the late 1980s.

The role of state-empires in the shift to the modern world in East Asia

In East Asia the route to the modern world lay through the experience of foreign colonial rule and so the transition was neither voluntary, nor was it smooth. Metropolitan elites manoeuvred against each other and sought allies amongst country powers, and they made and remade treaties. Alliances were always shifting and violence was always in play (thus necessary). However, by the period of the high tide of empire, say the early 1930s, relations between metropolitan powers were settled, patterns of overseas possessions were generally stable and the relations of colonial powers with their colonial subjects also seemed in the main to be stable.

Over a lengthy period, most of Southeast Asia was absorbed as peripheral territories of state-empire systems with their metropolitan cores in Europe and America. The activities of foreigners further east, in mainland Indo-China and China itself were extensive and one estimate records around 150 foreign concessions in Qing

China. In the process of expansion, the crucial players in this process were traders, later soldiers, administrators, missionaries and the wider spread of sojourners who made up expatriate colonial society. The colonies were novel communities: they were typically multi-ethnic, home to sojourners, migrants and native inhabitants; they were typically hierarchical in organization and distinctions would be made between foreign elite and ethnically diverse masses, and the locally based ruling elites would belong to the metropolitan power and their numbers might be quite low in comparison to the numbers within the colonial territory. As the colonies became more established, their population profiles changed – less dependent upon readily available trade and violence, more able to work as settled communities.

Notwithstanding internal complexities the process of absorption into the modern world went ahead – some groups thrived – others did not. In this fashion most of mainland Southeast Asia was remade; so too the territories of mainland Indo-China. Further north – at the limit of European and later American lines of trade, China was remade, not this time by direct colonization, but rather by the spread of numerous concessions, each a micro-colonial holding. Once again the shift to the modern world advanced, this time slowly as a long-established highly advanced civilization was overborne.

State-empire systems: inherently weak

All that said, the state-empires were intrinsically weak, and competition in the core and learning-cum-resistance in the peripheries worked to undermine the system. The system dissolved. The tensions evident in the core produced the Great War and, although empire holdings continued for a while (and in some areas were supplemented by the collapse of the pre-modern Ottoman Empire), the seeds had been sown for the system's demise. Peripheral resistance can be dated to the 1911 nationalist revolution that overthrew the Qing dynasty – the revolutionaries looked to build a republic, a political vehicle for the reconstruction and progress of China – such resistance was evident albeit on a much less obvious scale throughout the holdings of colonial powers. The Second World War and the Pacific War signalled the end of empire. East Asia was in the process of radical remaking from this time onwards, so that at the end of the Pacific War, notwithstanding the efforts of foreigners to resume control, it was clear that the empires were finished and what now unfolded was a process of territorial dissolution and the creation of a number of new states, whose elites proceeded to invent nations and pursue development.

PART III
Successor elites and the pursuit of national development

After the Pacific War, foreign controlled state-empires in the region dissolved away and this left an organizational void; given the nature of the wider international system this void could only be filled by states. The international system was made up of states; other forms of political organization were not acceptable. The process of creating these states was anything but straightforward and elite manoeuvring, popular mobilization, local civil conflict and outright foreign-inflected warfare all contributed to the final shape of post-empire East Asia. Patterns of reordering varied across the region: European holdings, mostly in Southeast Asia, were evacuated in short order as nationalist successor elites moved into place and a number of new states took shape: Japanese holdings were dissolved, the Japanese restored to their home islands, with two Koreas and Taiwan emerging from violent upheavals as new states. These events reflected changing American fortunes; their holdings in the Philippine were let go, but hostility towards communism led them to involvement in drawn out, disastrous and eventually lost wars in Indo-China. Meanwhile, in China, the sometime core of the region, now free of foreigners, the dynamics of civil war played out to be followed by experiments with utopian socialism. In all, it was a tangled, and uneasy period. It is these complex post-empire processes that have given rise to the current pattern of sovereign nation-states.

6
THE DISSOLUTION OF STATE-EMPIRES

The dissolution of European, Japanese and American state-empire systems in East Asia took place over a relatively short period. Prior to the start of the Second World War the global system comprised – in the main – state-empires controlling far-flung territories with ethnically mixed populations, which were ordered in terms of a series of cores and peripheries with the metropolitan capital cities standing at the hearts of these systems. By the end of the war – 1945 – none of these state-empire systems were sustainable, for the upheavals of war, metropolitan exhaustion and doubts coupled with the bids for power made by peripheral elites, combined to fatally undermine these systems. They collapsed in relatively short order and, unfortunately for many local populations, these last few years of empire were anything but orderly; after the disruptions of the Pacific War a number of wars of colonial succession took place before successor nation-states were consolidated and able to turn to the matter of national development.

The collapse of empire

The state-empire system dissolved away in a relatively few years, roughly, from the late 1940s through to the mid-1960s, and thereafter only fragments of empire were left: a few islands, a few military bases and other anomalous holdings. All this gave rise to a major task of political reorganization. State-empire holdings had been geographically dispersed and their populations multi-ethnic; now both places and populations had to be reworked and the available model was the nation-state, as other options, such as UN trusteeship or federations of colonial holdings were rejected; however, establishing these new units was no easy task.

FIGURE 6.1   Battle of Shanghai, 28 January–3 March 1932.
Source: Imperial War Museum, 'Chinese soldiers man a barricade in a factory'.

The problems of dissolution and reconstruction

In general terms, the collapse of state-empires left large multi-ethnic geographical territories without familiar systems of order. State-empires had been organized as a hierarchy of cores and peripheries, centred eventually on the metropolitan core capital city – London, Paris, The Hague, Washington, Tokyo or wherever – but as empires dissolved, new political structures had to be created and within the international system the available model centred on sovereign states. These, formally, were a creation of the Treaty of Westphalia, the institutional mechanism that had ordered the early phases of the unfolding shift to the modern world; however, it is worth noting that as the state-empires dissolved away, the early meetings of the United Nations had only around forty members. The reordering of the broad territories of empire was thus no small task. Today, in the early twenty-first century, there are around 200 members of that body. The whole process is fraught with difficulties: local elites must form, lodge claims to statehood and secure these claims against opponents and legitimate these claims in the eyes of their population.

As the sometime state-empire territories reconfigured, each new state would have to secure a delimited territory, assert its authority over this territory and its population, the whole exercise resting upon the agreement or acquiescence of both the elites of other states, in particular those controlling neighbouring states, and the

FIGURE 6.2 HMS Prince of Wales and HMS Repulse 1941.

Source: Naval History and Heritage Command, USA, NH 60566, 'Japanese high-level bombing attack on HMS Prince of Wales and HMS Repulse on 10 December 1941'.

people within the territory itself. In neither case was this guarantied. Externally, neighbouring states could and did challenge borders and could and did challenge the creation of the state itself (thus the Indonesian elite and its opposition to the creation of Malaysia), plus departing metropolitan powers sought to protect their commercial and social interests (businesses and settlers/sojourners). And internally, given the multi-ethnic nature of empires and the difficulties of demarcating boundaries (thus including and excluding groups of people), the support of local populations was anything but a foregone conclusion (particular groups could experience impacts on legal status and social status; thus, for example, recently, ethnic Russians in the newly created Baltic States).

The overall pattern of change sketched

The Pacific War fatally undermined the system of state-empires. The related intertwined conflict in China, that is, the civil war, ensured that all quasi-colonial holdings were dissolved. The entire region was reconfigured via complex processes attended by war, civil war and later Cold War proxy conflicts. It could be said that the process of reconfiguration did not really end until the 1975 reunification of Vietnam; an overall period of some thirty years or, perhaps, recalling the issue of a divided Korea and an ambiguous one China policy, that there are still matters outstanding.

The dissolution ran through a series of discrete phases. The earliest moves were made in Northeast Asia at the behest of the American occupation authorities in Japan. The bulk of Japanese empire holdings were dissolved and so most of the territories that the Japanese state had acquired in the years following the Meiji Restoration were forfeited: territory was transferred to Korean groups, to the Soviet Union, to Chinese groups and to Taiwanese groups; Hokkaido was retained; and the Ryukyu Islands were administered by the Americans. These withdrawals were neither smooth nor simple. Japanese troops and settlers were repatriated from China, albeit with difficulties and losses. There was conflict in Taiwan where retreating Nationalist armies clashed with and then suppressed local popular opposition. The withdrawal from Korea saw the sometime colony divided by outsiders before contending groups precipitated a civil war that saw foreign allies drawn back in with the USA in the south and the Chinese in the north. The success of the CCP and the involvement of the People's Liberation Army (PLA) in events in Korea meant that by the early 1950s the Americans read the politics of the whole of East Asia and not just the Northeast in Cold War terms, and Japan, having been an object of a New Deal style reform programme, became instead a conservative ally, political and military.

Moves were made in Southeast Asia around the same time – the late 1940s – but here the situation was quite different, because where the American occupation authorities could simply require the Japanese state to relinquish control of its acquired territories, there was no equivalent supervising authority in the south. Here European and American sometime colonial powers sought to reoccupy territory that had been militarily conquered in the early phases of the war by the Japanese: the Americans invaded the Philippines (and caused great casualties in Manila); the British, French and Dutch deployed forces in their sometime colonies after the wider war had ended, consequently they did not have to fight their way ashore (but there were notable disasters, thus the British army helping the Dutch in Surabaya).

The British returned to the Malay peninsular in late 1945. The local economy was in a parlous state, as might be expected, but so too inter-ethnic relations. The Japanese occupation authorities had dealt with sections of the population in quite different ways, and where Malays and Indians were encouraged to advance their national aspirations, local Chinese were harshly treated. The legacies ran on into the post-war period, in particular, the British fought a decade-long

FIGURE 6.3 Admiral of the Fleet Earl Mountbatten of Burma with General Chiang Kai Shek and Dr. T.V. Soong.

Source: Imperial War Museum, 'Supreme Allied Commander Southeast Asia: Mountbatten with General Chiang Kai Shek (left) and Dr. T.V. Soong (right). In the background are Captain R.V. Brockman, Lt Gen F.A.M. Browning and General Carton de Wiart VC at Chungking'.

counter-insurgency war against their erstwhile wartime allies in the Malayan communist party (a predominantly ethnic Chinese organization). Thereafter, the British helped both Dutch and French armed forces and administrators to return to their respective colonial territories. This was not a success. The sometime territories of the Dutch East Indies saw extensive violence as the Dutch tried and failed to resume control. And the returning French found themselves embroiled in a war of independence that ran on until 1954 (before being fuelled by American involvement, sustaining the war until 1975). Finally, whilst state-empire presence in China had been curtailed by the advance of the Japanese, their defeat was not the end of warfare, as the Chinese Civil War ran on, with continuing external involvement, for another four years.

The fraught process of state-empire dissolution produced over time the current pattern of sovereign states in East Asia. There were many differences in both processes and results. Some of these states were sometime pre-modern empires in a new guise (China), some were smaller monarchies that had perhaps unexpectedly survived the upheavals associated with the era of state-empires and were now re-presented as sovereign states (Thailand, Brunei), in one case the hitherto metropolitan core of a state-empire was reworked as a sovereign state (Japan). In most other cases, sometime peripheral elements of state-empires took their first shape as sovereign states (Indonesia, Singapore, Malaysia, Cambodia, Laos, Vietnam and the Philippines).

The emergence of new elites and the problems they confronted

As the empire territories dissolved away, local elites sought power and they did so in peculiarly difficult circumstances. The key empires were European but they were ruined by war; there was extensive destruction in Europe. East Asia was the other part of the world that had seen catastrophic war. Both sometime core and sometime periphery were in parlous states and there was no easy roadmap for the reconstruction of these geographically vast multi-ethic territories. In this daunting context, the first task for aspirant replacement elites was to formulate a project for the post-empire world and establish their claim to power against those of others, both local groups, representatives of departing colonial powers, sojourners and the players belonging to adjacent states (actual or prospective). Thereafter they had to secure their power, build the machineries of states, invent nations and thereafter secure their rule through the pursuit of national development.

In the early phases of the dissolution process, aspirant replacement elites comprised diverse individuals (and groups) and the ways in which these players understood their circumstances were different, so too their hopes, such as they were, for the future. There were many conflicts but it was through these that new elites were to take shape and thereafter take power.

The crystallization of new elites

The political dissolution of empire holdings was a drawn out and difficult business but the end point, that is, a species of independence for new states, allowed all concerned to reconstruct the process as inevitable and coherent. Yet it was neither, for there were multiple players involved in the process and they had, as might be expected, multiple, often conflicting, goals. The resultant pattern, the one familiar today early in the twenty-first century, is contingent. It could all have been otherwise. Cast in schematic terms and taking note of local and outside players it is possible to identify a number of groups: there were local groups of nationalists; there were citizens of the sometime state-empires anxious to maintain their positions; there were lobby groups within metropolitan core units with similar anxieties (in particular around economic interests); there were reformers in the metropolitan cores, those who took the view that empires were no longer sustainable (and metropolitan cores had public spheres, and here there were arguments for and against the creation of new states). And, finally, local peripheral cores had their own local presses and thus their own public spheres.

The process of the dissolution of multi-ethnic territorially extensive state-regimes took time and also saw intense political manoeuvring amongst all the local claimants for power, aspirant replacement elites, both conservative and reform minded, plus the continued active involvement of assorted outsiders.

Conservative groups (sojourners and indigenous) comprised those who had enjoyed relatively privileged positions within the state-empire systems, and they sought power in order to sustain a measure of continuity (domestic and international). Local groups with high social status sought to protect their positions, plus there were local groups with significant economic interests at stake.

Reform minded groups (sojourners and indigenous) included those who cast their ideas about the future in politically progressive terms: sojourners who looked for reforms; indigenous players who had made colonial pilgrimages to metropolitan cores. Both typically cast their goals in ambitious terms, looking to popular republics of one sort or another.

Outsiders had many interests and they were not shy of pursuing them. Thus there were departing colonial groups, state (diplomacy/security) and corporate (trade) plus incoming Cold War warriors – thus the activities of the CCP, sponsoring or aiding local CPs, and cutting against these actions the efforts of the USA supporting local elites/non-communists.

In brief, there were multiple players in the politics of securing replacement elites for territories that were themselves in process of crystallizing: thus new units, new elites and, in due course, new historical development trajectories. The process was anything but simple, with local groups, departing colonialists, neighbouring powers and, at a distance, contending great powers all playing a role in a process attended by open political manoeuvring, covert activities, public debate, policy planning and no little violence.

The creation of state machineries

As new elites crystallized, they built the machineries of the state. The institutional patterns created varied. The region saw drawn out fighting and so both elites and systems changed.

An overall indicative listing for this early period can be presented:

- parliamentary style systems (Malaysia, Singapore, Japan);
- presidential style systems (Philippines, Indonesia, Cambodia);
- absolute monarchy (Brunei);
- military dictatorships (Burma, Thailand, South Korea, Taiwan);
- party-state style systems (China, Vietnam, Laos).

As these processes of elite formation had typically been fraught and in many cases attended by fighting, the key to state making was possession of the means of violence; armed groups (hard security); newly created state armies; newly created security apparatus; and, finally, newly created state police.

Thereafter, the ordinary machinery of administration had to be created. This entailed a vast task: (1) remaking local colonial administrative structures (systems of law (constitutional, civil and criminal) and the infrastructure and personnel to run them); (2) creating systems of economic governance (along with requisite infrastructure and personnel); (3) making systems of social support (health, education, along with requisite infrastructure and personnel); and then (4) systems of external relations (diplomacy, treaty making and the like along with the requisite infrastructure and personnel). In most of these new states there was a legacy of colonial apparatus and these could be adapted with new local personnel employed, but all this took time, and as these institutions were built they had to begin their work amongst the population.

Establishing legitimate authority

The process of creating new nation-states involved a broad political deal between the incoming new elite and the local population; roughly, the deal was that the elite, in exchange for support during the process of state-empire dissolution and state formation, would turn its attention to the task of creating the conditions for better lives for the newly created citizens.

The task typically involved two aspects: the creation of a nation and the pursuit of development: matters of formal and substantive legitimacy.

1 Creating an imagined community

The creation of a nation, an imagined community, where this national community constituted an additional layer of identity for the relevant population, took some time and resources. In sociological terms, it was a matter of secondary socialization;

learning how to belong to a nation, and the process was handled by the machinery of the state:

- flags, parades and anthems – the symbols not merely of statehood but also nationhood;
- all buttressed by the mass media;
- the promulgation of a national past – a set of statements indicating where the nation had come from, how it was presently constituted and where, in principle, given its designated characteristics, it was going;
- all buttressed in the bureaucratic routines of the new state (currencies, letter heads, pictures of leaders, official celebrations (National Day) and so on).

Newly empowered elites typically cast their aspirations in terms of creating better material lives for their populations, those people who now fell within the bounds of the newly created state. As state-empires dissolved away there were competing ideas of the nature of the desired future and the ways in which it might be secured. As the post-war years unfolded and the Cold War assumed an institutionally buttressed form, that is, became an arena of regular competition, two ideas were presented: socialism, offered to both domestic and international audiences, and development, which was offered to international audiences. Other ideas such as non-alignment or dependency were presented and these ideas have continued down to the present day – they revolve around the issues of the historical legacies of colonial rule and the relations of the poor and rich countries.

2 The idea of development

The notion of development served (and serves) to offer new nation-states a route to the future: a way of catching up and joining in what was taken to be the mainstream of human life; that is, the form of life found in natural science-based industrial societies. The idea served (and serves) to run together the concerns of a number of discrete players (who otherwise have rather different concerns): first, the inhabitants of sometime metropolitan core government machineries, who sought to maintain some influence over former territories (for a variety of reasons – economic, security and nationalistic pride, in effect status claims); second, the business communities (in particular) of sometime colonial powers, who sought to maintain access to sometime peripheral areas of state-empire systems; third, groups of social reformers, who took the view that departing colonial powers had a responsibility to assist incoming replacement elites (the base of subsequent optimistic ideas of aid as disinterested or altruistic in nature) – communities of social scientists, located in cores and peripheries (recall, colonial pilgrimage journeys and thus learning), who theorized routes to the future around the idea of development (catching up and joining in); communities of experts and politicians in the institutional apparatus of the UN and its agencies where development was read as amenable to a technical treatment, thus eschewing the political aspects of the search for better lives for the denizens of the global south. The upshot of all these streams of thought was the imputation to replacement elites of the goal of development, where this was understood as effective nation-statehood; that is, joining in as one more nation-state, a formal truth to which all deferred.

Aid donor competition took off, that is, became familiar after the Soviet Union moved to offer the nationalist government of Egypt financial assistance in building the Aswan High Dam. The two Cold War competitors thereafter sought allies amongst the new nation-states of what came to be known as the Global South. The disbursement of aid became a major organizational activity. The UN and its agencies were crucial players, so too the states of former colonial powers coupled with a multiplicity of NGO groups, which were growing slowly in influence. The major Cold War powers also made grants and loans available, seeking to gather supporters to their cause in the context of the Cold War and both offered recipes, the one side offering modernization, the other socialism.

However, in practice, as all politics is local, replacement elites pursued a variety of projects and all revolved one way or another around the pursuit of national development. Sometimes these projects resembled the general pattern affirmed in international exchanges – the pursuit of effective nation-statehood – but often they did not, in particular, in East Asia, where the pursuit of national development took a distinctly state-led form subsequently to be tagged the developmental state.

What counts as development has always been contested; given that the task embraced is to read and react to enfolding sweeping change in order to build better lives for local populations this is hardly surprising. Answers have always been given by particular elites working in particular circumstances and formulating particular plans, ideas of routes to the future. The notion of development points to the creation of better lives for the inhabitants of particular territories and it can be unpacked in quasi-technical terms, thus the reports made each year by the World Bank and the United Nations Development Programme (UNDP), but, at base, the pursuit of development can only be a political project, and as noted all politics is local, thus any project will depend upon the ideas of local elites, local lobbyists, local media and local people.

The new states in the global system

The upshot of the process of state-empire dissolution was the creation of a number of new states plus in a couple of cases the remaking of extant states. The British withdrawal took around a decade or so, the French, the same and the Dutch, less; but in all cases the departing colonial power left behind struggles for power with varieties of political and ethnic violence.

The dissolution of state-empires entailed sweeping changes:

- the British sphere dissolved – a number of new states appeared;
- the French sphere dissolved – a number of new states appeared;
- the Dutch sphere dissolved – a number of new states appeared;

- the American sphere dissolved – a new state appeared;
- the Japanese sphere dissolved – a number of new states appeared;
- Thailand and China were reordered.

The British sphere

The British sphere in the wider East Asian region comprised territories in Southeast Asia, the crescent of territories running from the border of Imperial India down to the colonial port city of Singapore, plus adjacent areas of direct influence in Siam and amongst the peoples along the northern shore of Borneo, Sabah, Brunei and Sarawak. Plus, most importantly, a series of holdings in China, constituent parts of the Treaty Port System, whereby foreign interests, in this case those of the British, found practical expression in the form of small patches of territory, subject to British jurisdiction, that served as bases for trade, political and social linkages to their Chinese hinterlands.

The British advanced into Southeast Asia and thence to China and later Japan, from bases in South Asia. Initially these were controlled by the East India Company (EIC), then after what the British recorded as the Indian Mutiny 1857 these territories were directed by the machineries of the British state.

The British state advanced its interests through treaties and wars:

- the British seized Burma through three wars with the first Anglo-Burmese War in 1824–26, thereafter, 1852 and 1885–87;
- the British accumulation of power in Malaya began with the establishment of a base in Penang 1786 and later the Pangkor Engagement 1874 saw further inroads into local system of Sultanates;
- the British gained control of Singapore in 1817, extracting the territory from the wider Johor-Riau Sultanate;
- the British signed treaties with the Siamese monarchy in 1855;
- the British gained Hong Kong in 1842, thereafter accumulating further holdings in China.

But, as events unfolded, the British Empire in East Asia was swept away by the 1942 military advance of Imperial Japan; formal possessions in Hong Kong, Burma, Malaya, Sabah, Sarawak and Brunei were captured, concessions in China seized. During the Pacific War years there were tensions between the US government and the British in respect of these sometime colonial territories, but in the event the British determined to recover them, that is, reoccupy, save for the concessions in China, which were formally renounced. However, the recovery of these territories proved to be short-lived as metropolitan core doubts coupled to peripheral resistance pointed in the direction of change and the model embraced was that of independent nation-states.

Constructing such nation-states proved an awkward task. Multiple local elites sought power and did so with different maps and agendas in mind; a complex political process of withdrawal ensued and, as with the acquisition of these territories, withdrawal involved manoeuvring, treaties and no little violence (overt and covert).

In Malaya there was a privileged social elite (sultanates) and an influential popular religious organization (Islam – a part of what it was to be Malay and thus generally not available to Indian or Chinese residents). The ethnic division had been prompted, that is, made more significant, by the Japanese occupation authorities and a crucial split opened up between Malay organizations and the resident Chinese; these last noted had provided the bulk of forces working with British support against the Japanese, the Malayan People's Anti-Japanese Army (MPAJA), its membership overlapping with the Malayan Communist Party (MCP). The British also played a role in seeking to sustain economic links (tin and rubber in the early postwar era were key dollar earning export industries) and so the British looked to a conservative successor elite. The split with the MCP led to a drawn-out guerrilla war, the Emergency. The ethnic split in the territory also played a role in Singapore. The economic linkages of Malaya and Singapore were strong, as both were parts of the British state-empire, but they had somewhat different official status, and this plus political tensions between the eventually dominant Singaporean nationalists and the conservative Malay elite led to the formation of two elites and in time to two separate states, Malaysia and Singapore. In both cases, as the conflicts subsided, new and secure ruling elites pursued national development, arguably in a conservative fashion in Malaysia, and arguably in a robustly progressive fashion in Singapore.

In the other sometime British territories in the area, analogous tales unfolded. In Burma there was a quasi civil war as the central Burmese authorities fought to secure their control of border areas. These were home to a number of distinct groups: minorities within empire, now minorities within the independent state of Burma. These conflicts ran on for decades, with the central Burmese authorities ordered by a conservative military. The other territory in the region – Brunei – saw competition for post-empire leadership contested and the British helped to install another conservative figure, the local Sultan, in an absolute monarchy that endures to the present day.

Thus over a relatively few years the British holdings in East Asia resolved themselves into a number of new nation-states: Burma (later, Myanmar), Malaysia and Singapore; Brunei opted for independence; but Hong Kong remained an anomalous British possession until 1997 when control was handed to the Beijing government.

The French sphere

The French competed with the British in South Asia during the eighteenth century but were unsuccessful, and they turned their attention to the east where they sought holdings and influence in mainland Southeast Asia and from there, China. The French secured control of Indo-China through a series of wars and treaties in the late nineteenth century. The French asserted themselves against both local Vietnamese rulers but also against neighbouring China and Siam: Annam and Tonkin (1883–85); Cambodia (1863–1907); Cochin (1858–74); and Laos (1890–93).

Like the British, after the Pacific War, the French government determined to recover its colonial holdings in Indo-China, but in this case the situation was somewhat more complex: metropolitan France had been occupied, leaving the local political legacies of the Vichy regime; and against this De Gaulle was determined to reinvigorate the French state. One element of this project was the recovery of colonial territories.

In Southeast Asia peripheral French holdings had been occupied and the local government, loyal to Vichy, had had to accommodate the demands of the Imperial Japanese. In 1945 the French returned to these territories with the assistance of the British. Chinese Nationalist forces moved into the north. There were now multiple

FIGURE 6.4 Allied reoccupation of French Indo-China, 1945.

Source: Imperial War Museum, 'Japanese soldiers form a guard of honour at the quayside in Saigon as British warships come alongside to land troops of the occupation force'.

groups seeking to construct post-war states. In Vietnam, several nationalist groups faced each other along with the local communist party and an independent state was declared in August 1945. De Gaulle's authorities did not acquiesce. The result was a brief period of uneasy calm. A multiplicity of groups now sought power. In the highlands running down the length of the country, minority groups sought to manage their situation. The French attempted to suppress the independence movement and war began in late 1946 – part civil war and part colonial reconquest; a little later the war was read into the American sponsored Cold War and so was cast in terms of resisting communism.

After years of warfare the French determined to withdraw. The 1954 military campaign at Dien Bein Phu was intended to strengthen their hand in negotiations; however, they were militarily defeated and the dissolution of their colonial holdings began. A peace conference at Geneva 1954 produced an agreement. The territory was divided: the Democratic Republic of Vietnam (DRV), with its capital in Hanoi; South Vietnam (ASV/RV), with its capital in Saigon; Laos, with its capital in Phnom Pen; and Cambodia, with its capital in Vientiane. However, warfare continued and American forces arrived in the South. The French intervention, followed by the American Cold War inspired intervention, led to decades of civil war and conservative groups of one sort or another dominated South Vietnam whilst the communist party ruled North Vietnam. In Laos and Cambodia there was analogous manoeuvring and similar warfare and destruction. The Americans withdrew in 1973. Vietnam was reunited in 1975, but later there were further problems with Vietnam's neighbours and only in late 1980s, with the end of the Cold War in Europe and economic/diplomatic spill-over to East Asia, did wars finally subside.

The Dutch sphere

The Dutch turned their attention to the Southeast Asian archipelago in the sixteenth century; the area was the source of spices, hence Spice Islands. The Dutch competed for access with the British and slowly extended their trading interests within the archipelago over the next 300 or so years via a long series of exchanges with the many local Sultanates whose polities together ordered the entire area. The extent of integration of these sultanates is moot, but the existence of local sophisticated trading regimes is not, and it was here that the Dutch found a route to influence in the area: trade links, political manoeuvring and warfare led over time to the creation of a formal colonial territory, then the Dutch East Indies, now Indonesia.

Once again, as with the British and French, Dutch colonial holdings in the Southeast Asian archipelago were fatally undermined by their wartime occupation by the forces of Imperial Japan and once again the Dutch sought to recover their colonial holdings. The Dutch returned with the assistance of the British in late 1945 and found a self-declared Indonesian Republic. Once again, multiple groups manoeuvred for power.

There were local conflicts as groups vied for leadership; thus local Javanese, those from outlying islands, Dutch settlers, Islamic groups and a locally influential communist party; add to this ethnic divisions in a putative nation covering several thousand miles of islands. A period of intermittent warfare followed but the Dutch, unlike the French, could not secure American support, and were perforce obliged to acquiesce in the formation of Indonesia, which became an independent state in 1949.

The local elite pursued an erratic political course and, with the Cold War raging, matters came to a head in 1965 with an American-backed army coup that saw very many deaths. After this episode, the country was ruled by the army until changes in the early years of the twenty-first century.

The American sphere

The USA came late to overseas colonialism, an initiative it pursued with vigour. The mid-nineteenth century saw the country engulfed in civil war and thereafter through the late nineteenth century the country moved its borders westward, dispossessing Native Americans in a series of Indian Wars. Control of the continent provided further encouragement to expansion in wars against a decrepit pre-modern Spanish Empire: to the southwest of the content; and to the west, across the Pacific Ocean to the Philippines, which were seized in the 1898 invasion. The Hawaii Islands were annexed. And finally trading bases were created in China and Northeast Asia.

Like other colonial powers, the Americans were driven out of China by the advance of the Japanese in the late 1930s and early 1940s and their holdings in the Philippines were militarily captured in 1942. The islands were recovered in a series of destructive campaigns during 1944–45. There was great loss of life. Upon resuming control the colonial power confronted various difficulties: the local elite had collaborated with the Japanese; local resistance groups were associated with the communist party; a peasant movement was also active in the north. Nonetheless, the colony was reconstituted in order to be made independent. Once again local politics were complex; the anti-Japanese resistance movement was disabled, the peasant rebellion was suppressed and rebels in the south were contained. In post-war competitive liberal-democratic style elections, the communist party secured places but was excluded; the re-established elite now faced years of revolt, but with US help these local elites were kept in power. The islands passed into the emergent liberal trading sphere of the Americans and they did so as a sovereign nation-state.

The Japanese sphere

The Meiji Restoration of 1868 was a conservative revolution from above and brought a regime into power that was concerned to build a strong economy to underpin a strong state. They were successful, and a modern industrial economy was assembled with surprising speed and late development was followed by late imperial expansion. In this they followed the available European and American model. They expanded their sphere with claims to the Ryukyu Islands in the south and Hokkaido and Sakhalin in the north; the Japanese fought wars against Qing China 1894–95 and Czarist Russia 1904–05 for control of the Korean peninsular; thereafter, there were further advances into Manchuria and northern areas of China.

The impact of the Great Depression brought military rule to the country and warfare in China grew more severe. This occasioned tensions with the USA and eventually the military elite opted for war. This proved to be an error. The defeat of Imperial Japan at the hands of the American military was followed by the occupation of the home islands and the dissolution of all the territories gained since the wars against Qing China and Czarist Russia. The Japanese empire dissolved into a series of new nation-states: North Korea, South Korea and Taiwan; a number of island chains in the Pacific were passed to the Americans; island holdings to the north went to the USSR; and holdings in Manchuria and other parts of China were withdrawn. As the American occupation authorities remade domestic Japan, overseas possessions broke away and entered new development trajectories. The process was fraught with particular difficulties.

The withdrawal from Korea and Taiwan and the parallel creation of new states proved difficult. Korea had been annexed in 1911 and in the summer of 1945 a nominally independent government was formed, but outside players had their own agendas; in particular American Cold War players read local disputes in anti-communist terms and intervened. The division of Korea was accomplished. The émigré nationalist installed in the south by the USA offered numerous provocations to the north, which boasted its own more subtly installed figure, and civil war followed in 1950–53. The Korean peninsular was redivided and remains so to this day. South Korea was ruled by a succession of military dictators, North Korea by an analogous series of eccentric dictators drawn from the same family, namely Kim Il Sung, Kim Jong Il and currently Kim Jong Un. To the south, Taiwan became the refuge of the defeated Nationalists as the civil war ran down. It became the ROC and its diplomatic status is still contested.

Thailand and China

As the state-empire system expanded in the region, it suited the British and French to leave Siam as a buffer state between their respective holdings. That said, Siam was drawn into the British sphere in the late nineteenth century. The Siamese monarchy began a conservative modernization, implementing top-down reforms, but they were displaced in the early 1930s by an army coup, which deepened reforms and renamed the country Thailand.

The country was drawn into the Imperial Japanese sphere during the Pacific War. As with the Vichy regime in Indo-China they had relatively little choice, although the Thai elite did secure territorial advantages where the Thai border abutted French Indo-China. However, with the defeat of the Japanese and the return of colonial powers, in particular the Americans, the territorial gains of the war years were relinquished. Thailand attained its current shape on the map.

The country was also drawn into America's wars in Southeast Asia, the usual form of domestic regime being Royal/military governments interspersed with military coups. Post-war Thailand thus retained the essence of its politics and the bulk of its territory; thereafter the country continued with a slow-motion conservative dominated movement into the modern world.

China was also involved in these upheavals. The nineteenth century had seen the country slowly undermined by the activities of foreign powers, European and American. Domestic forces opposed the Qing authorities and in time an armed uprising took place. Yet the revolution of 1911 failed to establish a republic and a period dominated by regional warlords followed; the Kuomintang Nationalist regime sought to secure control of the country in the late 1920s and 1930s but it failed and civil war followed. The Kuomintang confronted the other progressive party, that is, the Communist Party. The civil war fighting was extensive. But from the late 1930s onwards both parties had to deal with the activities of the Imperial Japanese where limited incursions in the north of the country turned into outright invasion.

The civil war coupled with the Japanese invasion meant that foreign powers had withdrawn formal claims to the 150 or so concessions. The American forces were present in the far Southwest, supporting the Nationalists and using aircraft to attack the Japanese home islands; then a late Japanese advance into southern parts of China plus the success of the American naval attack across the Pacific meant that the military importance of China faded. American support for the Nationalists did continue in the form of money and materiel, but now those contending for power in China were as they had been since the 1920s the groups around the Kuomintang and those supporting the Communist Party. After the Pacific War ended, the civil war resumed its earlier intensity and there were major battles in the northeast of the country.

The business of war against Japan was clarified by the outbreak of the Pacific War (as both KMT and CCP took for granted the defeat of the Japanese). The defeat of the Japanese in 1945 at the hands of the Americans issued in a period of relative calm during which foreign backers introduced more war materials. The civil war resumed and the Nationalists moved armies into the northern parts of the country. In the event by 1949 the CCP had secured its military victory, although the fighting continued on a smaller scale as the CCP imposed its rule on more remote parts of the country; thereafter, like other successful post-empire elites, it turned to ordering the state and securing its legitimacy via the pursuit of development

The PRC was inaugurated in late 1949 and thereafter, as the Nationalists established themselves in Taiwan, the CCP undertook mopping up operations in China, established secure borders (more or less those of the Qing empire) and then turned to the business of reconstructing China after something like a century of intermittently violent change.

TABLE 6.1 China: the shift to the modern world, some costs[1]

1795–1806	Miao Revolt
1796–1805	White Lotus Rebellion
1813	Eight Trigrams Sect Revolt
1839–42	Opium War
1851–64	Taiping Rebellion
1856–60	Arrow War
1853–68	Nian Rebellion
1856–73	Muslim Yunnan Rebellion
1862–73	Tungan Rebellion
1864–85	Muslim Xinjiang Rebellion
1871–75	Czarist Invasion of Xinjiang
1884–85	Sino-French War
1894–95	Sino-Japanese War
1897–1900	Boxer Uprising
1911	Chinese Republic Revolution
1914–16	Yuan Shikai Interval
1916–26	Warlord Era
1918–41	Anti-Foreigner Sentiments
1926–28	Northern Expedition
1927–37	First Chinese Civil War
1931–34	Jiangxi Soviet
1931–32	Japanese invasion of Manchuria
1932–37	Japanese invasion of Northern China
1937–45	Sino-Japanese War
1941–45	Pacific War
1946–49	Second Chinese Civil War
1949–50s	People's Republic of China secured
Casualties	Unknown

Note
1 Information taken from various sources, see in particular Bruce Elleman, 2001, *Modern Chinese Warfare 1795–1989*, London, Routledge.

Timings

The dissolution of state-empires was neither straightforward nor easy, rather the reverse. It was difficult and it was hard, in particular, violent. The earliest moves were made in South Asia and adjacent areas of what is now dubbed Southeast Asia, specifically Burma. The 1948 independence of Burma was followed by civil war; these wars ran on until the early years of the twenty-first century. Nor was Burma unusual, for there were further conflicts: in the Malay peninsular, in the archipelago of Indonesia and in Indo-China. So, where Burma was the starting point, it was the reunification of Vietnam in 1975 that marked an end point of a sort, but it was only in 1989 that the fighting and diplomatic manoeuvring around the Cambodian Pol Pot regime finally came to an end. The business of securing independence from state-empires and settling new elites into new states took nigh on forty years.

East Asian in the post-empire world

In East Asia, after the Pacific War, foreign-controlled state-empires dissolved. They were succeeded by a number of new or reconstituted states with local elites in power, which were variously wedded to the goal of national development. These elites also had to manage a multiplicity of local tensions and conflict: in Burma (Myanmar) the Burmese government in Rangoon faced a spread of peripheral revolts; in Malaysia the government faced a full-blown communist insurgency; in Singapore the elite confronted popular forces with quite different ideas of the route to the future; in Indonesia multiple ethnic groups had to find common cause; in the Philippines elite collaborators confronted resistance and popular and religious groups; and in Vietnam and Korea, where such problems were also in evidence, the local problems precipitated civil wars. In Japan the elite were purged by the SCAP authorities and a conservative business-dominated regime installed. And in China, historically the core of the region, civil war gave way to the rule of a party-state oriented towards the creation of a peasant-based state socialism.

Add to all this problems with the major players in the global system: military concerns (Cold War), corporate concerns (access and rules) and more optimistically reformist concerns (development aid). At the end of the Pacific War outside commentators looked at East Asia – ruined, divided and poor – and held out little optimism for the future; they might be primary product economies, buying in advanced goods from the developed West.

In the event, local elites had other ideas.

7
THE FORMATION OF SUCCESSOR ELITES

As the dissolution of state-empires, foreign and local, ran its course, numerous locally based elites competed to seize territory, identify a population and claim for it the status of a nation, the basis of further claims to statehood and thus a role for aspirant replacement elites. The process was highly political; that is to say, it revolved around the power relations of discrete groupings and it was often violent, and this characteristic of the time marked the political lives of the first generation of post-colonial leaders. But in the event replacement elites, laying claim to discrete territories and the control of their populations, did emerge and these newly empowered elites thereafter had to articulate (if they hadn't already) a project for their newly established country; such projects were elite-determined and shaped by contingent circumstances. East Asia elites enjoyed success and some fifty years later these countries were cast in terms of a region, one of three powerful regions within the global system.

Successor elites: domestic and international projects

The elite pursuit of distinct projects involved several aspects; thus, reading and reacting to enfolding structural circumstances, determining upon a line of advance (oriented towards an ideal of where the country would be over the upcoming period of years or decades: an active utopia) and thereafter disciplining their population, that is, turning their collective efforts towards that elite-specified goal. As circumstances changed, so too would the goal; it was an orienting device, not a checklist, so the formulation of an elite goal coupled to the creation of a disciplined population were an on-going task; elites sought to mobilize their populations, typically for development.

The particular nature of any domestic project, typically a species of national development, was constrained by wider international contexts, and in the 1950s and thereafter this meant in particular the dynamic of the Cold War.

The first generation of independent leaders were shaped by war and civil conflicts and such conflicts could (and did) continue into the early decades of independence.

Many illustrative examples could be cited. Thus, Mao Zedong, caught up in the early civil war struggles of the party, then the Sino-Japanese War, later more civil war activity, then the dual demands of resistance to the USA (Korea and so on) plus continuing tasks of settling borders and asserting power of the party over domestic opponents – in all say, thirty years of war and conflict. Or Lee Kuan Yew, having to deal with the collapse of the British, occupation by Imperial Japan, later independence movement activities and finally the accidental invention of Singapore – in all say, twenty-five years of assorted conflict. These examples could be multiplied for Vietnam or Korea or Indonesia and so on.

Change came first to Northeast Asia where the collapse of the Japanese Empire and the occupation of the home islands by the Americans ensured rapid change was inaugurated. The overseas empire was dismantled, military and administrative personnel repatriated and settlers repatriated. Domestic reforms to politics and society were initiated and, where the repatriation of overseas personnel took some time, the domestic reforms ran on until the Cold War took hold, thereafter they stopped.

Change came later to Southeast Asia where attempts were made by sometime colonial powers to recover their territories, ensuring thereby another round of violence. Their final withdrawal was thus delayed for several years, running on into the 1950s, but it was never in doubt.

Change also came to China, as the civil war was resolved in 1949. The PRC established and foreigners removed (that is, outside military forces, traders, adventurers and so on). The new elite pursued a mix of utopian socialist experimentation coupled with more standard moves in pursuit of development (ILO (International Labour Organisation) rated performance of early years); but there were policy errors (GLF, Great Leap Forward) and political confusions (GPCR, Great Proletarian Cultural Revolution). The death of Mao enabled policy changes to be made and after 1978 policy was shaped by Deng Xiaoping. Now several generations shaped by conflict and ideological mobilization were invited to attend to their own immediate material concerns, to get rich. A sustained burst of energy plus policy changes began a dramatic and sometimes conflict inflected trajectory of growth that had one disaster in 1989 and a major celebratory moment in Beijing 2008.

Northeast Asia: Japan, South Korea and Taiwan

In the sometime Japanese sphere of Northeast Asia, the successor states came to be tagged the Asian Tiger economies. Local elites all ran state-directed national development projects – Japan, South Korea, Taiwan (and as an off-shoot Hong Kong): they expanded their economies within the broader expanding economy of the West; they were given extensive support by the USA; and they situated themselves within the Western bloc, which was anti-communist, free market, liberal democratic and so on. It might be noted that as events unfolded, there were considerable inconsistencies between the actualities of domestic elite-sponsored development strategies (state-led/nationalist), their wider environment (supportive/aid) and the public statements made for external consumption (anti-communism/liberalism).

1 Japan: the iron triangle, the LDP and the developmental state

Japan was occupied by the Americans in late 1945. The head of the American authorities was General Douglas MacArthur, sometime colonial ruler of the Philippines. The incoming US occupation authorities found the Imperial Japanese state intact. The military had been defeated, elite-level leaders had surrendered and the ordinary population were war-weary and blamed the elite for the disaster that had engulfed them and whose consequences they now confronted. But, in all this, the apparatus of the state remained intact. The American occupying forces worked with these machineries and it was through them that the occupying forces worked, with programmes of reform translated into practice via these machineries.

A political project for post-war Japan emerged via the exchange between incoming foreign occupiers whose initially dominant faction was determined upon a programme of reforms and a local state machinery whose thinking was the product of decades of nationalistic military rule. The upshot was a programme of reform. The constitution was rewritten (making the country into a form of liberal-democratic republic), the emperor system was abolished (the emperor became a liberal-democratic style head of state) and the armed forces were disbanded (and subsequent rearmament restricted by the constitution). The political structures of Imperial Japan were disbanded (and replaced with a nominally liberal-democratic party system), the established network of big business was broken up (in pursuit of a competitive liberal marketplace) and a land reform programme was undertaken. The official religion of state-Shinto was abolished and society was reordered (such that individuals in place of families became the basic social unit) and education was reordered (along American lines). All in all, it was an ambitious reform programme.

The programme ran until the start of the Cold War. American elite reactions to the defeat of the Nationalist forces in China and the establishment of the People's Republic of China were negative. American occupation policy was changed as a new faction within the occupation authorities gained influence; reforming Japan was no longer a priority, what now became important were the related tasks of the supply of war materials from local industry and the creation of Japan as an ally in the Cold War. At which point, the long-term Japanese elite concern for building a strong economy to buttress the nation's security re-emerged.

At this time a new elite took shape, with many figures from the war years retained. The system came to have three main players. First, the state bureaucracy: American reforms had abolished the military, purged politics and was in process of remaking big business, so the only group left were the technocrats in the state and, as they controlled access to foreign currency and raw materials, they had great power; hence MITI (Ministry of International Trade and Industry). Second, the remade political system: engineered by the Americans, it came to be known as the LDP (Liberal Democratic Party of Japan) system and was essentially a conservative corporatist political system where popular left-wing groups and trade unions were squeezed out. Third, the corporate world: here American enthusiasm for reform waned as the Cold War took hold and pre-war corporate players re-emerged.

Together the three elements formed the iron triangle and they engineered the dramatic post-war economic recovery of the country; in this they were aided by the Americans with finance, technology transfer and the local purchase of war materials for use in Korea. The drive for war material production and the wider rebuilding of the economy was handled by the institutional machineries of the Japanese state. With the old political elite and its business and military allies gone, the Japanese civil service came to the fore – later to be celebrated by Chalmers Johnson's work on MITI – and it became the directing force in the new iron triangle. The elite now pursued state-led national development, buttressed by the continuing presence of the emperor and more broadly sustained by a social ethic of harmony.

This model was to become known as the developmental state. In outline it was replicated in South Korea and Taiwan, albeit in rather different circumstances, as during the process of the dissolution of the Imperial Japanese state-empire system along with the Chinese Civil War and related Cold War, both territories were further scarred by warfare.

2 Korea: the military, the corporate world and the developmental state

In the summer of 1945 the Imperial Japanese government handed power to a local group of Korean political leaders who, as might be expected in the circumstances, were reform minded, whilst more conservative groups avoided these political movements. Nonetheless, the beginnings of a local state were constructed throughout the country. Unfortunately, outside powers, in particular the USA and Soviet Union, also became involved. The Potsdam Summit had left the peninsular to the Russians but now the Americans had second thoughts and the Russians agreed to divide the country along the 37th parallel. Both powers found local allies as they withdrew. In the North, the Communist Party led by Kim Il Sung gradually displaced co-parties and a party-state system took shape. In the South the situation was more difficult, as the Americans disregarded and then suppressed the local political groups that had emerged as the Japanese withdrew and instead parachuted in a right-wing nationalist émigré, Syngman Rhee. Rhee established an authoritarian quasi dictatorship and engaged in a series of provocations directed to the North, until in 1950 the North invaded and a civil war began. Foreign forces now returned; the Americans returned in force to the South whilst the USSR supplied materiel to the North and a little later, when the North was at risk of military defeat, the Chinese intervened with ground troops.

Of course, the immediate upshot of the fighting was catastrophic as the country and its people were devastated. Most areas of the peninsular saw armies moving back and forth – with attendant devastation – and the US air force bombed the North – again, with attendant devastation. The original partition was reaffirmed in 1953 along the same 37th parallel; it was an armistice, not a peace treaty, and with reunification no longer possible, two Korean states took shape: the Republic of Korea (ROK or South Korea) and the Democratic People's Republic of Korea (DPRK or North Korea).

The elite of the DPRK state have pursued an autarchic state socialism and two overarching policies have been affirmed: *juche*, or self-reliance, along with the military first. The country has been led by the Kim family: respectively, Kim Il Sung, Kim Jong Il and Kim Jong Un. The economy of the country is weak and there have been serious famines in recent years. The country is supported by China, in both material and diplomatic terms. However, the DPRK's foreign policy stance – in particular its pursuit of nuclear weapons – is not welcomed by its regional neighbours (including China) and is a point of serious if intermittent contention with the USA.

The elite of the ROK under the leadership of Syngman Rhee did not pursue any very coherent development policy. The country was very poor (agricultural, with most industrial areas, such as they were, located in the north) and for many years was bankrolled by the USA. In time Rhee was removed in a military coup that saw a sometime Japanese colonial official move into power in the Blue House, General Park Chung Hee. The new leadership invoked the notion of renovation and copied the Japanese model across to Korea; the country's now widely recognized success story began around this time. However, Park too was extra-constitutionally removed – his chief spook shot him – and further dictators followed. Roh Tae Woo was the first president chosen by popular liberal democratic style elections, this in the early 1990s. All these figures have pursued a top-down project of national development and political elites have cooperated with large family conglomerates in a variant form of the developmental state. The ROK, in terms of culture and society, evidences a distinctive form of life; picking up legacies of Korean tradition (family, lineage), Japanese occupation (first moves to development) and the demands of post-Korean War national development within the American sphere (electoral politics, business and security). The country now has a role as a key economic power within East Asia and wider.

3 Taiwan: dictatorship and the developmental state

In regard to Taiwan an analogous tale can be told. The territory entered the political modern period when it was formally made a part of the Qing Empire late in the nineteenth century – in 1887; however the peace settlement of the 1894–95 Sino-Japanese War transferred the island to the Japanese. It became a colony and was developed for around fifty years as an element of an integrated Japan-centred state-empire. As that empire was dismantled its status was unclear given the civil war in China. In the event it became a refuge for Nationalist Chinese forces after 1949 as the PLA were not able to mount a military attack across the Formosa Straights, particularly given American support for the Nationalists. In Taiwan a species of military dictatorship was installed and Chiang Kai Shek maintained an official state of emergency whilst laying claim to the rule of the whole of China. The government introduced a programme of state-led national development in which the interests of indigenous Taiwanese and now settled mainlanders were managed. The development programme was well regarded by commentators.

Chiang ruled the island until his death in the late 1970s and his son followed him into power, but thereafter there was a shift toward a liberal democratic style party plus competitive election system. In respect of culture and society the territory has developed a distinctive form of life: picking up elements of Chinese traditions (more clearly sustained than on the mainland where Maoism sought to update beliefs and practices) coupled with the demands of the creation of an authoritarian state machinery now democratized on the generic Western model but still oriented towards its relation with China.

Southeast Asia: the countries of today's ASEAN

As the Pacific War came to its abrupt end, with the Japanese surrender following the atomic bombing of two cities and the entry into the war by the Soviet Union, sometime colonial powers moved quickly to place their troops in relevant strategic locations in Southeast Asia, in particular the capitals and other large cities. The British had significant armed forces in Burma and they moved elements of these forces into Malaya, Singapore, Java and Vietnam. Many of the troops they used were ethnic South Asians and in places the still coherent Japanese forces were used as local police forces. These mixed and ad hoc military forces assisted the return of both Dutch and French. However, the period of Japanese occupation – 1942–45 – had irrevocably changed the possibilities for empire; in brief, where empires had seemed secure in pre-war days, now they were an impossibility and the only questions were the manner of colonial withdrawal, the make up of replacement elites and the nature of subsequent relations, if any, of sometime periphery with sometime core.

1 British sphere: violent and uneasy dynamics of withdrawal

In 1948 Burma (Myanmar) became independent and promptly turned inwards. The independence leader Aung San was assassinated by a figure from a minority ethnic group, allegedly armed by dissident factions within departing British authorities. The Burmese authorities had to deal with multiple pressing ethnic problems and so state building was crucial. The core areas of the country fell under military rule – thereafter a socialist/Buddhist approach to development – the country remained poor and inward looking for many decades – there were numerous armed conflicts with restive minority groups along the eastern border areas.

In Malaya the British had created a primary-product exporting economy and accepted inflows of migrants from southern China; this had created a society with a distinct split: geographic (east/west); settlement (urban/rural); ethnic (Chinese/Malay); and economic (rich urban, Chinese east and poor, rural Malay west). Add to this the episode of the Pacific War, where, to simplify, the Imperial Japanese had favoured the Malays, encouraging a nascent nationalism, and fought the mainly Chinese resistance (which had British support), and whose dynamics ran on into the post-war era in the form of a British/Malay campaign against the communists, mostly sometime resistance fighters.

The British withdrew, leaving Malaysia and Singapore as distinct units; both pursued state-directed national development, the former on the basis of a primary-product economy within a society split by an ethnic divide and the latter on the basis of a colonial era trading port, which was an established nexus in global flows of trade, and with a more homogeneous population, ethnically distinct from those of its near neighbours.

The conservative Malay elite, the group that inherited power from the British, was lead by Tunku Abdul Rahman. They assembled a coalition made up of UMNO (United Malays National Organisation) plus MCA (Malaysian Chinese Association) plus MIC (Malaysian Indian Congress), together the Barisan National (National Front), and sought national development building upon existing primary-product activities. They secured modest progress until in 1969 a series of race riots broke out. The elite response was to institute the NEP, a programme designed to address the multiple overlapping divisions in Malayan society, in brief, positive discrimination in favour of those tagged indigenous, that is, Malays. Later reforms, undertaken by Mahathir Mohammed, reinforced the drive for national development through a look East policy, drawing on the lessons of the developmental state.

Along the way, the island territory of Singapore became an independent state in 1965, largely an accident of local politics. Lee Kuan Yew's ambitions for a Malaysian Malaysia met the concerns of the Malay elite head on and they resisted, so Lee was obliged to turn his attention to the territory of Singapore island. State-led national development was pursued: a state machine was created, a nation invented and material advance assiduously pursued. It was another variant of the developmental state and the process involved building on the legacy of a colonial port city which was a nexus in global trading networks by inviting in the multinationals and providing them with a disciplined population and a sympathetic and effective legal and regulative framework. The upshot was the creation of a distinctive form of life: conservative, orderly and rich.

Its only regional comparator was the somewhat more rumbustious territory of Hong Kong. Similarly atypical was Brunei – oil rich, protected from the vagaries of democracy by the British – which continues as an absolute monarchy.

2 Dutch sphere: violent dynamics of withdrawal

In the sometime Dutch sphere of Indonesia, the incoming elite faced more intractable problems with a widely scattered territory, multiple language divisions and an economy based mainly on primary products. The Dutch colonial authorities had been displaced during the Japanese occupation and the wartime rulers had encouraged a local nationalism. Figures associated with this period were ready in late 1945 to seize their opportunity. At first somewhat reluctantly, then more clearly, an Indonesian Republic was declared, only to be challenged by the returning Dutch before finally succeeding in late 1949. A species of national development was pursued, first under Sukarno and Hatta during an initial phase of development – guided democracy – which was not successful. In 1965 a violent coup mounted by the army removed the government, destroyed the local powerful communist party and ushered in a development-minded dictatorship lead by Suharto, which was broadly successful over the following decades.

3 French and American spheres: violence

In the sometime American sphere of the Philippines, the economy rested upon primary-product exports. The Americans had large military bases. The territory was home to ethnic divisions along with local violent conflicts. A species of national development was followed. Emergency rule was introduced by Ferdinand Marcos. The rural poor, communist groups and Muslim groups in the south were cut out of political life. The USA supported the elite.

Around the same time, the Americans became involved in mainland Southeast Asia. Following the return of the French colonial authorities, mainland Southeast Asia had become consumed by open warfare as various groups attempted to make projects within a relentlessly violent environment. Vietnam, Laos and Cambodia were riven by warfare until the late 1980s. The problems were exemplified by the case of Vietnam: local aspirant replacement elites, nationalist and communist, sought power; local expatriate plantation owners looked to protect their holdings; metropolitan French authorities had concerns for diplomatic status; plus there were local French administrators taking local initiatives. A profoundly destructive civil war was supplemented by foreign intervention. A division of Indo-China was made in 1953 but there was continuing violence. American involvement deepened with advisors and then troops. The American armed forces in Vietnam reached a peak number of around 500,000 but all to no avail. American withdrawal took place in 1973 with the reunification of Vietnam secured in 1975. But there were further rounds of violence in the guise of war with Cambodia along with an incursion by the PLA into northern Vietnam. After the collapse of the Soviet Union there were reforms in Vietnam, later similarly in Cambodia and Laos, in all variants of Chinese pattern of the party-state plus market-oriented economic reforms.

China: Mao, Deng and the new China Dream

The route to the modern world taken by China was difficult as the Qing Dynasty governments were slowly overborne during the nineteenth century. From 1842 through to 1911 Qing governments gave ground to foreign demands; hence International Settlements, war indemnities and trade deals. Attempts were made to respond with Self Strengthening or the One Hundred Days Reform or the Late Qing Reforms, but all were to no avail. The 1911 Republican Revolution removed the empire and set these territories on a new path shaped by ideas taken from Europe and America, a species of modernity was embraced. The founding father of a modern China is thus Sun Yat Sen, but his early death left the multiple factions in constant conflict. From the late 1920s through to the late 1940s the country was beset by warfare of one sort or another: warlord conflicts in the 1920s, civil war in the 1930s, inter-state war in the 1940s and renewed civil war in the late 1940s. It was not until the victory of the PLA in campaigns against the Nationalists in northern areas of the country and the subsequent October 1949 proclamation of the People's Republic that China attained anything like unification and an absence of warfare. In China the elite pursued national development: initially, in the guise of Mao Zedong's utopian socialism; later, with Deng Xiaoping's pragmatic state-directed reforms oriented towards material prosperity – themes recently cast in terms of the notion of the China Dream pursued by the current core leader Xi Jinping.

Mao was politically active from the early 1920s, a period when the environment was suffused with violence from the failing 1911 republic, through warlords, the Kuomintang and Communist antipathy and to the later civil war. Mao came to lead the CCP and established that the party leads and follows a mass line centred on peasantry. The upshot, via contingency of anti-Japanese warfare and resumed civil war, was the establishment of the PRC in 1949 and thereafter the construction of a party-state system and then the pursuit of national development informed by the nostrums of state socialism, a mixture of Maoist celebration of the potential of the peasantry plus ideas imported from the USSR. The record shows a mix of success and failure until the political upheaval of Cultural Revolution discredited Mao.

Mao died in 1976 and something of an interregnum followed, until elite political positions were settled. Thus in 1978 Deng became a key figure and inaugurated reforms, slowly at first, thereafter accelerating. The reforms focused on economic activity as Deng imported a variant form of developmental state; there were village-level enterprises, export processing zones, plus SOEs (state-owned enterprises) gain local control/responsibility. The reforms were continued by Jiang Zemin and there was rapid growth in economy, rapid growth in corruption, pollution and inequality plus talk of a socialist market economy.

The latest phase was associated with Xi Jinping. The problems of corruption and pollution were being addressed. The party-state machinery was being reformed but kept intact. The leadership has sought to ensure the legitimacy of the party-state machinery by the deployment of a national past celebrating the long history of the Chinese race and noting the recent century-long episode of foreign domination, together offering the moral impetus informing the elite-level discussions around the advocacy of the China Dream. These elite-level discussions have been given more concrete expression in policies for the development project One Belt One Road, a new silk road, comprising a northern land route and a southern sea route, both – in the published schematic maps – connecting China to Europe.

Over the long period of post-war growth, the states of East Asia were celebrated as the Asian Tiger economies but later their success brought them into conflict with their major ally, the USA, in particular over trade issues, and trade links with Japan were the crucial issue. The 1985 Plaza Hotel Accords addressed these problems by revaluing the yen, which, it was thought, would rebalance US/Japan trade. However, the reaction of the business community prompted the creation of regional production networks and thus the germ of an idea of an East Asian region. Later still, in 1997, as financial market speculators attacked the Thai baht and thereafter a spread of regional currencies – in sum, the 1997 Asian Financial Crisis – those traits of local economies that had been celebrated as keys to success were now read in terms of the notion of crony capitalism. Regional states learned the lesson and began building up surplus balances and swop arrangements so as to be able to resist any further speculative attacks. In recent years the regional pattern has changed once again; headlong Japanese growth has slowed, whilst the rise of China has become unequivocally clear, matters celebrated in the 2008 Olympics.

East Asia is now a powerful region within the global economy, however there are significant tensions, in particular:

- the business of the rise of China (changing patterns regional influence);
- on-going issue of status of Taiwan;
- on-going issue of North Korea's nuclear programme;
- on-going integration problems for ASEAN.

It may be that earlier expectations of regional integration in East Asia were either overly optimistic or premature (or both) for there are significant intra-regional tensions and there are significant extra-regional problems (in particular n regard China's relations with the USA and its regional allies). It might also be noted that the other part of the world signalled out for praise – the European Union – is in difficulties.

The record debated: developmental state, expanding system and regional networks

The record of the countries of East Asia has been much debated and contrasts are drawn with other regions which emerged from the colonial era around the same time, thus the Middle East or sub-Saharan Africa or Latin America, and cast in these macro terms the record is good. East Asia has grown from the poor conditions created by the exigencies of multiple wars until by the end of the first quarter of the twenty-first century commentators are confident that it will be one of the more prosperous regions within the global system.

The record in sequence

At the end of the Pacific War the peoples of East Asia were in a parlous state as economies, societies and polities had been turned upside down by years of warfare: millions were dead; millions were injured; and millions were displaced. The task of reconstruction was daunting yet this is the point from which replacement elites began; commentators were pessimistic but in the event the doubters were proved wrong. The region recovered and the political and institutional records of a group of states in Northeast Asia came to exemplify the wider growing success of the region: with the developmental state, thereafter working within the wider context of the post-war boom economy and creating over time the outlines of an East Asian regional system.

A number of key dates could be cited to track this process of recovery:

- 1950 reverse course in Japan;
- 1971 Sino-American rapprochement;
- 1985 Plaza Hotel Accord;
- 1993 World Bank Report;
- 1997 Asian Financial Crisis;
- 2008 Beijing Olympics.

Each of these contingent dates signals either a policy change on the part of key actors or a shift in public perceptions of events, but the overall drift has been towards an integration of regional space – economic, social, political and cultural; however, whilst much has been achieved there are still significant tensions within the region and an institutionally integrated region remains a distant prospect.

Thus, first, the reverse course in Japan saw the American occupation authorities move to disable the local political left, that is, groups that had emerged in the wake of the dismissal of war-tainted elites, and swing behind the machinery of the state and its links to the business world. Scheduled reforms to the big conglomerates were not pursued and a marriage between two key market-friendly parties was organized, thereby creating a business-oriented political elite, what came to be called the LDP system, a political order that ruled Japan for most of the rest of the century and on into the twenty-first.

Then, second, the 1971 rapprochement altered the international politics of great power relations – the triangle of Russia, China and the USA – and it also opened the way for the Americans to pull out of the war in Vietnam. America's established Taiwanese ally was diplomatically abandoned as formal recognition of China was switched to the regime in Beijing, drawing that country, thereby, more into the main stream of global diplomacy.

Third, turning to the economics of the region, the Plaza Hotel Accord attempted to address the problem of Japan's large and growing trade surplus with the USA. The agreed revaluation of the yen was supposed to solve the problem, with Japanese goods becoming more expensive and American cheaper, but the response of Japanese business was to move production off-shore, so the trade imbalance was thus reworked but not changed as had been intended. A related unintended consequence was the creation of regional production networks, that is, linkages, such linkages being supplemented by intra-regional investments from other countries.

All went well until, fourth, the Asian financial crisis was triggered by poorly regulated speculative lending to Thai business, coupled with the withdrawal of lines of credit from regional firms and governments; the region was plunged into a sharp recession. The region did recover quickly but the lesson had been learned and concerted moves were made within the regions to reduce exposures to international money markets with foreign currency reserves, swop agreements. The political lesson was also clear: the region had to look after itself. An issue, finally, celebrated, in a fashion, in 2008, with the Beijing Olympics; described as China's coming out party, it announced that the country was now a significant power within the global system and the key country within the East Asian region.

All in all, this sequence of dates signals a fifty-year record of regional deepening success.

The developmental state

The new nation-states in East Asia, whatever their previous historical trajectories, faced daunting tasks in respect of what has come to be termed development.

The term embraces a vast agenda of state-sponsored action:

- action in regard to the economy;
- action in regard to society;
- action in regard to the polity;
- action in regard to culture;
- action in regard to the new state's structural location – how it fitted into the global system.

At the end of the Pacific War, specialists were under-impressed by the prospects for development in the region. It was noted that the region was largely agricultural, it lacked capital resources, its natural science base was slight and its people were predominantly rural. The region and its people were poor. Plus, along with Europe, it was one of two parts of the world that had suffered extensive losses of people and materials during the war years. However, contingent circumstances worked in favour of the replacement elites. First, the post-war global economy experienced a long period of economic growth and so new states in East Asia could grow within a growing global economy. And second, as the Cold War came to East Asia, the USA sought allies in the region via soft loans, development aid, FDI (foreign direct investment), technology transfer. In short, American actions provided a flood of money for the region. The initial example of a developmental state came to be offered by Japan.

In Japan post-war growth plus American expenditures put the Japanese economy back onto the track of building a strong economy, albeit this time around without a radical nationalist political elite coupled with heavy industry and an overbearing military – in time the state-centred development strategy came to be tagged the developmental state. The heart of the machinery – as discussed by Johnson – was MITI, an organization staffed by technical specialists. In the era of post-war scarcity, the common situation of war-ravaged countries in the late 1940s and early 1950s, they controlled access to credit and to raw materials and they prioritized the distribution of credit and materials so as to grow the national economy. This is a distinctive political and policy stance: the former aspect was in line with Japanese elite thinking since the days of the Meiji Restoration in the pursuit of a strong economy as the basis for national progress; whilst the latter also had local antecedents in the Meiji era preference for the economics of Friedrich List as opposed to British talk about liberal markets. List argued that economic development in the context of a global system containing already developed and powerful economies required a policy of state intervention to protect the local economy until it could compete with established economies – the business of late development. The post-Pacific War role of MITI's expert technicians met these requirements as they planned for national development within a world dominated by already established economic powers. In this they had the direct help of the Americans (aid, technology transfer and access to their domestic market, plus the domestic impacts of the reforms to society enforced by the occupation authorities) coupled with the assistance offered by the general condition of the America-oriented regions of the global system, that is, the post-war long boom, the overall rise in economic activity.

In brief the developmental state had these core characteristics:

- a clean powerful bureaucracy;
- coherent planning machinery;
- national economy focus;
- mobilized population (performance legitimacy plus popular formal legitimacy).

The strategy of elite-led export-oriented development was repeated amongst America's allies in Northeast Asia: thus, in time, South Korea and Taiwan. A variant form was established in Singapore. Hong Kong also prospered (albeit for rather different reasons – domestic and contextual – and with rather different practical results). In all, a series of success stories – economic growth, social advance – led by energetic technically efficient states.

Thereafter, the model was further rehearsed in Southeast Asia, in particular, Malaysia and Singapore, and, following Deng Xiaoping's reforms, in China, a further variant of the model has proved successful.

An expanding global marketplace

The countries of East Asia secured success over a lengthy period of the post-war era for success was not immediate and nor was it readily apparent (early exports to Europe of goods from Japan and Hong Kong were regarded as low-quality copies). Nor was it attained smoothly across the region. The first mover was Japan, thereafter other sub-regions followed at various times and within differing contexts (local and global). When debate about the developmental state began it typically turned to the domestic circumstances of the countries of the region whilst at a general level the region was cast in stereotypical terms: thus Confucian capitalism, a counterpart (it was said) to the role of Calvinism identified (it was said) by Max Weber. However, whilst it was correct to look at the individual situations faced by replacement elites (all politics is local), it was also appropriate to look to the wider situation within which success was over time and in an ad hoc manner attained. Local success was framed by a wider post-war economic boom marshalled by the USA.

Success in East Asia took place within an expanding global market, however, problems of trade began to emerge in the 1970s. The USA was financially weakened by warfare and in 1971 was obliged in part by contingent European financial game-playing to break the link between the dollar and gold. A fixed exchange rate system was replaced by floating rates and the global system became financially much less robust. There were crises in the 1980s as America's trade deficit with Japan became a political problem, although it was in principle addressed by the Plaza Accord: the revaluation of the yen was designed to remedy problems of imbalances of trade and consequent financial problems, but in the event it led to the diversification of Japanese investments as production moved off-shore. Other Tiger economies diversified investments and from 1978 some of the investments were made in China. Overall a Japan-centred regional production network emerged, thereafter multiple cross investments deepened regional integration.

Overall, in the earlier phases, by the 1970s and early 1980s:

- Japan and four tigers are successful – rapid growth over many years;
- Southeast Asia – begins to join in;
- Mainland Southeast Asia – still suffering from war – last to join in.

Thereafter the Asian Financial Crisis – readjustment – rise of China – European and American popular rebellions against elite-led neo-liberalism.

The creation of a species of regionalism

The late 1980s and 1990s saw the development of networks of production within East Asia as Japanese, Taiwanese and Hong Kong businesses moved production off-shore. Complex patterns of investment were the result and new developments were pursued in China and in Southeast Asia. These activities created linkages and early commentators saw the outline of a coherent somehow integrated region – but such optimism has been lately reined in. East Asia continues to offer significant areas of tension and this plus the recent crises in the European Union (the other sometime exemplar of regional integration) has led to a downgrading of expectations in respect of further integration in East Asia – nonetheless, the area remains economically powerful.

1 Linkages

There are trade networks within the region; they foster a mixture of linkages:

- social – during the long colonial period there were population movements around the region – Chinese migration around the region – South Asian inward migration to the region – minority communities developed – hybrid communities (Eurasians, Straits Chinese and so on);

- economic – traditional networks of trade – artisanal – colonial era networks (thus port cities) – recently developed economic links, post-1985 as regional production networks;
- political – attempts at managing regional linkages – some early local efforts, thus non-aligned movement – some foreign sponsored efforts, thus SEATO or Five Power Agreement – some later local efforts, ASEAN – recently talk of an East Asian region (ASEAN plus three or East Asian Summit). One key issue today is the rise of China. Commentators ask how will this large powerful country act within the region, hegemonic in aspiration?

2 Tensions

Notwithstanding the creation of regional linkages and their self-conscious recognition in political interactions and related commentary and scholarly analysis, it is the case that there are significant tensions between countries, elite-level and popular:

- between Japan and its neighbours in South Korea and China – economic links continue but diplomatic relations are poor – elements of aggressive nationalism in all three countries aggravate matters of historical memory – this exchange is also cut-across by security links, thus both South Korea and Japan are allies of USA;
- between China and Taiwan – historical antagonisms (civil war), current issues of sovereignty (PRC claims Taiwan) and links of Taiwan to the USA via security treaties;
- between China and some of its ASEAN neighbours over South China Sea – as China asserts its control/sovereignty over large area of South China Sea it is provoking a sub-regional arms race;
- within ASEAN as China courts allies (divide and rule) – countries adjacent China (Laos, Cambodia) have acted as spoilers within ASEAN when it comes to the bloc's relationships with China.

The issue of regions and regionalism has been much discussed in recent years and it is a debate worth considering – matters for the next section of the text.

Successor elites – retrospect and prospect

The mixture of metropolitan doubts and post-war weakness coupled to peripheral political calls for change undermined the state-empire system. In 1945 they were unsustainable and these large multi-ethnic hierarchically ordered territorial holdings dissolved into a multiplicity of smaller, nominally more homogenous, holdings. Multiple local elites competed for control: they lodged claims for statehood (arguments with departing core authorities and other international agents – some succeeded, others did not), invented nations (a laborious business of propaganda and persuasion) and pursued national development (cast in various terms).

As with other political groups, these new elites had to read and react to enfolding circumstances, discipline their populations and pursue national development. Elites drove this work. The new elites in East Asia faced daunting problems in the legacies of the upheavals of the shift to the modern world, the legacies of colonial rule (institutions, linkages to former cores plus the spread of cultural legacies created by virtue of the colonial era practices) along with the legacies of war. Expert commentary was sceptical but in the event they were wrong as East Asia prospered.

8
ELITES AND MASSES
Domestic power, authority and dissent

The dissolution of state-empires was followed by the construction of a set of replacement political institutions and the available model was that of the state. Successor elites created the machineries of new states, invented nations and thereafter pursued in one fashion or another national development. Here was the basic deal: the elites sought support from the local population and in exchange promised to work to create better lives for these people. The relationship was not one of equals and new states and nations were not assembled by consensus, rather they were fashioned by elites; and opposition or dissent or advocacy of a plan for an alternative future were all disallowed. Elites deployed what power they had to create order and they sought legitimacy, that is, they looked to turn power into authority and they managed dissent. In all this three issues were crucial to domestic politics: power, authority and dissent.

Europeans created the modern idea of states with the 1648 Treaty of Westphalia. The idea informed novel practice. In place of pre-modern kingdoms with fluid borders, each state exists within defined borders within an international system of states. The international system is now grounded on mutual recognition (as each state is formally acknowledged by all the others) and buttressed by state armed forces and networks of alliances (the balance of power). The overall international political system is thus stabilized. At the same time states are sovereign within the territories they control. Internally they are hierarchical. An elite rules the masses. However, over time, absolute elite power slowly gives way to variations on the theme of democracy. Now elite membership is broadened, populations are accorded political status as citizens and representative governments take shape. States create nations to legitimize these arrangements. The domestic political system is thus stabilized.

The system of states should now be stable both internationally (between states) and domestically (within states). External order must be secured against potential enemies and internal order must be secured against dissenting voices and here issues of power, authority and dissent are raised.

The European and American colonial empires ensure that these ideas are then variously exported to East Asia as colonial powers superimpose their familiar practices on extant East Asian polities, that is, they read extant political forms in terms of their own ideas and act accordingly. But all these local polities have their own forms, for example, bureaucratic feudal systems or mandala or galactic states, and so the results of colonial actions are hybrid political forms. Later these ideas are available in turn to incoming local successor elites as East Asia removes the colonialists and secures its distinctive place within the modern world. However, over time three novelties have appeared: first, an appreciation of the context-bound nature of the European and American experience has grown; second, an appreciation of the intrinsic value of other historical experiences has also grown; and, third, the practice of new polities has unfolded novel patterns. So, in general, against any simple affirmation of the historical experience or model of America or Europe it is best to grant that patterns of power, authority and dissent can assume various forms.

In European and American liberal democracies power and authority are taken to revolve around popularly elected parliaments. In its 1950s' guise modernization theory presented this as a universal model or aspiration and a literature on democracy and democratization and transitions was developed. In the 1990s and 2000s these same ideas were re-presented in more corporate friendly terms as globalization theory, with the role of the state and consequently competitive elections reduced. However, in recent years as the pre-eminence of the West has faded more sceptical theorists have looked at the basis of political power and authority in human social relations and have found multiple patterns. So, now, if we note that humankind must deal with certain common tasks (the basic needs of physical and social reproduction such as food, shelter, livelihood, child-rearing, old age and death), then we can analyse domestic patterns of political life in a similar way and suggest that political communities have basic needs, that is, all societies have to order themselves: thus issues of power, authority and dissent.

Formal considerations: power, authority and dissent

These ideas are widely used: power and authority are linked; dissent is another matter, standing somewhat to one side of the core pairing. Power and authority are familiar ideas and they have taken cultural and institutional root in Europe and America; however, these organizational forms are contingent, they could have been otherwise, so the ideas can be revisited in order that they can be seen more clearly and it can then be seen how the ideas unpack in other political cultures, in particular those in East Asia.

The question of power: considered schematically

Turning directly to discussions of power it is clear that there are many competing approaches: Karl Marx used the ideas of structural power (class position), agenda setting (hegemonic ideas) and persuasion (ideology); Max Weber countered with comparative discussions of the modern state (hierarchical, bureaucratic and in possession of the legitimate means of violence); later theorists identified the pervasive role of taken-for-granted ideas (Antonio Gramsci on hegemony or the Frankfurt School on the emancipatory role of critique); others wrote about the inevitability of the formation and power of elites (New Machiavellians); and more recently still, Michel Foucault has uncovered the ways in which power relations can be expressed in subtle and pervasive ways (discourse/episteme).

So whilst the notion of power seems quite straightforward, the most cursory examination reveals it to be thoroughly elusive. In order to clarify the idea of power schematically there are three arenas of debate: philosophy, institution and practice.

1 Power-as-philosophical issue

In European and American work a key distinction is made between democratic traditions of reflection and liberal traditions of reflection. The one looks to human social life pursued within ordered communities, the other to the fundamentally contractual nature of life, where the social world is merely the sum total of individually secured contracts.

A number of political philosophers have worked this distinction.

C.B. Macpherson distinguishes democratic 'power to do', that is, power to secure purposive objectives within a definite social environment, from liberal 'power over', that is, power to secure utilitarian objectives in face of competition from others. Macpherson adds that familiar ideas of liberal democracy are an uneasy compromise between the two lines of argument, with the democratic line preferable.

In a similar fashion Isaiah Berlin distinguishes the ideas of 'positive liberty' and 'negative liberty'. It is roughly the same distinction, but with evaluation inverted, as Berlin prefers the negative liberty of liberal theory. Now positive liberty is to be rejected in favour of negative liberty. More generally, liberal philosophy centres on the putatively autonomous person and regrets socially made rules, these are not enabling but restrictive, hence the idea of negative liberty, that is, freedom from external constraint.

Work lodged within this liberal tradition of thought has been very influential over the last thirty or so years within the Anglo-Saxon world, hence ideas of globalization and the end of history. The material is in essence liberal, looking to the putative superiority of free market individualism. Unfortunately, there are no free markets (economic activity is always and everywhere lodged within systems of social rules and understood with reference to discrete cultural traditions), nor are there any asocial individuals (individuals are always and everywhere elements within wider encompassing social groupings), so its celebrants run the risk of an intellectual and ethical collapse into the vapid foolishness of consumerism or the more absurd adolescent idiocies of libertarian individualism.

From yet another direction Alasdair MacIntyre tackles liberalism head on, arguing that it is a post-Enlightenment nonsense, a mish-mash of claims and injunctions, which fail to substitute for the pre-liberal religious communitarian notions of life lived within community. MacIntyre rejects ideas of negative liberty: aspirations to freedom from social constraint are absurd, for human life only makes sense within the context of communities; it is here that the ends of life should be sought, and it is here that sense can be made of the notion of a life well-lived.

2 Power-in-institutional guise

Again there are sharp disagreements.

In the 1930s a group of Italian theorists presented arguments that rejected the egalitarian impulses of ideas of democracy in favour of an acknowledgment that all societies were liable to resolve themselves into hierarchies – other things being equal, elites would form in all societies. The New Machiavellians argue that natural elites, possessed of intellectual or psychological or other natural attributes, will come to hold power in society. The social world will be hierarchical, so too the political world and a small network of players will make up the elite and they will confront and order a much larger grouping of disorganized persons, the social mass. This natural hierarchy will be reflected – inevitably – in patterns of institutionalized power and authority and an elite will wield power/authority over the much larger mass. In its textbook form, the approach is tagged elite theory.

A contrary view is taken by those labelled liberal pluralists, who argue that society includes multiple social groups, and consequently multiple elites, and so in turn institutions will be multiple and horizontally ordered. This view of the institutional set-up of modern societies opens up the space for enquiries into social diversity and the ways in which such diversity plays into the familiar formal political realm: both institutional structures (machineries of power within society, thus the state, corporate and civil society) and the social bases of competitive political life (which groups vote for which parties). One subsidiary issue has turned out to be inequality: access to positions of power is contested and within diverse communities some groups prosper whilst others do not.

In contrast to both lines, Marxists resist starting analysis with either abstract ideas of communities or equally abstract ideas of individuals, preferring instead to deploy a critical political economy in order to elucidate more directly to the logic of the world as it is: thus they affirm that the social world is best characterized as capitalist; they affirm that capitalist society is class divided; they affirm that elites hold power; they note that this power is contested; and they expect the institutional and civil bases of elite power to be sites of contestation (contest both for state power and public opinion).

3 Power as historical practice

The shift to the modern world is an on-going process. The core ethos of modernity celebrates reason, natural science and materialism. It shapes a distinctive form of life. Social life is lived on an upward curve as social progress is taken to be inevitable over the long run. Modernity looks to the future with optimism.

This form of life has its roots in seventeenth-century Europe – it proved to be very dynamic – intensification and expansion – the form of life has been exported around the globe – most dramatically in the form of the system of state-empires – a multiplicity of extant forms of life were more or less thoroughly remade in line with the demands of the still unfolding modern world – and, as might be expected, this produced a multiplicity of forms of modern life – the process of reconstruction was repeated during the period of the disintegration of state-empire systems – as these geographically large-scale multi-ethnic units dissolved away they were succeeded by smaller, typically more ethnically homogeneous units, all cast in terms of states – but these new states were ordered in a variety of ways – all variants on the modern state.

The historical trajectory whereby contemporary states attained their present configurations can be reconstructed (political histories can be written) – and the distribution of power within such forms of life can be mapped.

The question of power: location and practice

A schematic enquiry offers one way of unpacking the issue of power – another way is to ask more directly: who has power and what do they do with it? – that is, to ask about its social locations and associated practices.

Cast in terms of scale, a range of answers could be available: individuals (operating within domestic and local networks), groups (with operations centred on particular locales), organizations (working within defined territories), states and supra-state organizations, such as the UN or IMF (International Monetary Fund) or European Union (working within the international system).

The shift here is from a recognizable individual agent through increasingly collective agents through to thoroughly abstract ideas of agents. Cast in terms of location and practice, the formulation leans towards the relationships of agents and points to the constraints and opportunities of relationships. Agents are always located within established patterns of social relationships (and the sum of other agents produces the sociological idea of structure); thus, for any agent, the resources/ possibilities of structures can be grasped and deployed in pursuit of the agent's goals.

This strategy of unpacking the idea of power calls attention to the specifics of its exercise: which agent has power, in what institutional location, justified how and turned to what particular objectives in respect of which particular community?

Responses to claims to power

There are two broad ways in which claims to authority can be received by those to whom they are addressed: acceptance (in various forms) and resistance (again in various forms).

1 Claims to authority

These are well-trodden paths and a number of lines of reflection are available. First, inspired by Max Weber – notions of power and authority are clearly linked as both ideas designate ways of self-consciously making social order and many theorists argue that authority is more effective than power; authority is power seen as legitimate so if an agent has authority then obedience follows automatically. Weber's liberal quartet (below) indicates types of authority. Second, Marxist style ideas of ideology or hegemony – if structural power relations have been read into common sense then they become quietly effective (and for those so controlled the mechanisms are in effect invisible, they work, so to say, behind people's backs). Third, post-modernist theorists look to consumer seduction – theorists have noted that the global industrial-capitalist system is so rich that it controls people by virtue of making many consumer choices available to them and so power gives way to seduction (and the poor of the First World are labelled failed consumers and disciplined via welfare payments system). Fourth, recent work on collective memory points to the exchange of elite ideas and the various recollections of subordinate groups; it is out of this exchange that a national past will be constructed, that is, a set or ideas serving as a source of legitimate authority. And, finally, fifth, in respect of post-colonial elites one part of the exchange of elite and mass could be the effectiveness of the elite in delivering material well-being to the population at large, that is, performance legitimacy.

a) Agent-centred analysis

Max Weber is one source for the liberal tradition in political analysis with his agent-centred analysis. Weber investigated various types of elites, their social location and nature of claims to legitimate authority. Weber identifies four ideal-types of power/authority: (1) traditional elite power/authority – those who hold power do so because they have done so for many years – that they have held power for many years is the source of its legitimacy amongst the wider population who acquiesce in their power/authority; (2) charismatic elite power/authority – those who hold power do so on the basis of their unique personal style – this unique style is the source of their authority in the eyes of their followers; (3) affective power/authority – flows from emotional commitments to the power holder; and (4) rational legal elite power/authority – those who hold power do so because they have been appropriately appointed to a position in a system which itself is regarded by the population as legitimate, so the population view the system as legitimate and view power holders as legitimate. And in regard to East Asia it is the case that polities take the form of constitutional monarchies: Michael Vatikiotis points out in Southeast Asia that Malaysia, Thailand, Cambodia and Brunei have monarchs, whilst Indonesia sustains a Javanese royal caste; all are remnants of the pre-contact era, but all are influential; so too, the monarchy in Japan. In all these cases, Great Tradition ideas of kingship – benign, paternalistic authority, secured, somehow, by suprahuman authority – have run down into the present day, intermixing with the local variants of rational bureaucratic states.

b) Structure-centred analysis

Karl Marx is one source for the structural tradition in political analysis with his structure-centred analysis; hence the claim 'men make their own histories but not as they choose', as received structures bear down on actors. In the political world elite groups run projects to advance their interests and they discipline their populations. In this general vein Bob Jessop has considered elites in terms of the broad political-economic projects they pursue: (1) their social base – whom do they represent within ordered society? (2) their accumulation strategy – what economic policy do they favour? – whom does it serve? (3) their state strategy – how do they use the state to organize economy to serve social base? (4) their hegemonic project – how do they explain/legitimate the above to population? Thereafter, using these ideas, a range of modes of production and associated modes of regulation can be identified: (a) the welfare national state – the familiar post-Second World War European system of state-regulated capitalism plus extensive social welfare; (b) the liberal competition state – the familiar Anglo-American model of minimally regulated competitive capitalism with small welfare programmes; to which (c) might be added the East Asian developmental state – the elite-sponsored pursuit of national development stressing industrial advance, providing extensive social infrastructure and avoiding entitlement style welfare payments. Each of this trio identifies a particular substantive mix of power and authority: ideas developed by elites, running through local culture and hegemonic in respect of their respective populations.

In East Asia the elite has made many demands of the masses. As in other political systems such demands can elicit a number of acquiescent responses: (i) the deferential response – the agent accepts status hierarchy and position in it; (ii) aspirational response – the agent accepts status hierarchy and works to move up it; and (iii) passive – the agent withdraws into private realm consumption, family or minority life style and ignores status hierarchy. Another response gives voice to dissent.

2 Patterns of dissent

As with acquiescence, dissenting responses to elite power and authority can come in very many varieties: passive acquiescence; disagreement; resistance and rebellion.

Passive acquiescence is a familiar response to power and authority and it requires only passive acquiescence in the claims of the relevant elite; their ideas are neither accepted nor contested nor rejected, they are merely ignored so far as is possible as subordinate groups prefer get on with their everyday lives. In wartime, this can take the form of collaboration (France/China). In political environments with heavy-handed elites, it can take the form of familial and vocational privatism as people turn away from the public sphere (H.C. Kuan suggests, for example, colonial Hong Kong). And in countries with moribund core governance systems, it can take the form of popular disengagement (thus, for example, European elections, in general, over recent decades, have seen falling participation rates).

Disagreement is also familiar, but there has to be some practical occasion for disagreement and there has to be a way of putting the disagreement into a persuasive form, that is, a way of appealing to a set of ideas that will legitimate action directed at changing the status quo. There also has to be some sort of venue for expressing disagreement, a mechanism (in the liberal and democratic traditions in Europe this is tagged 'the public sphere'). In respect of giving form and voice to disagreement, two ideas from anthropology can help: Great and Little Traditions.

The idea of Great Tradition points to arts and religion and these are the broadest commitments that are made within a form of life; thus the ideas are enshrined in arts, literature, religion, official ideologies and so on. These ideas are carried by particular institutions and there may be particular sites, which exemplify the Great Tradition ideas. The Great Tradition will usually be conservative; it will serve the status quo. However, the Great Tradition also offers resources that may be used by aspiring elite groups in criticizing the status quo, for example: local nationalist groups in a decolonization period; factions within a Communist Party appealing to 'sacred texts'; or growing political parties claiming to best capture 'core traditions of community'; or ordinary people staging demonstrations that invoke the ideas of the elite, thus in China, actions tagged as rightful resistance.

The idea of Little Tradition points to the intellectual and moral resources of patterns of ordinary life; that is, the sets of assumptions about correct behaviour that are simply taken for granted. The Little Tradition offers resources that may be used by subaltern groups, rural or urban, in resisting the elites; the moral resources of the local community inform resistance to the demands of the powerful and these can range from unspoken disobedience through to protest through to outright resistance and rebellion; again, in China, with only poor mechanisms for subaltern groups to express disapproval of local officials, one familiar strategy is the local demonstration where crowds of people gather to harangue the local officials (sometimes successfully, other times not), behaviour recorded by the state as mass incidents.

Popular disagreement can develop into explicit resistance and perhaps rebellion. James C. Scott talks about the weapons of the weak, which as noted are found in the intellectual and moral resources of the local community. Scott notes that these patterns of principled resistance can include evasion, passive-resistance, uncooperative actions and sabotage, and thereafter maybe organized protest such as leaflets, marches, petitioning and the like.

Finally, where dissent finds no other mode of expression, there can be overt violent rebellion; this takes various forms from sporadic and spontaneous violence at the extreme to organized and sustained attacks on the state and its local supporters. There are multiple examples in Europe, over many years, and multiple examples in East Asia, again over many years. The use of violence to advance political aims is not new, indeed the reverse is the case, it is quite familiar – but as such activities are aimed at the state – with all its resources – such attacks are usually of no very great consequence for the state but can carry heavy costs for those engaging in such styles of protest.

Power, authority and dissent are characteristics of all ordered polities. The ideas can be unpacked and put to work in regard to the situation in East Asia. Here there are many instances of the successful deployment of elite power and contrariwise there have also been many examples of dissent ranging from non-compliance, through protests to outright rebellion.

Substantive issues: power, authority and dissent in East Asia

Power and authority enable elites to shape the social world; the masses accommodate to these demands; and the social world functions. It is a subtle dynamic of structures and agents. First, elites are crucial and their concerns drive the polity forwards but they always operate within given circumstances: historical (that is, the resources of the trajectory that the polity has taken); internal (the domestic balance of groups within the polity); and external (the international environment within which they must act). Second, an elite will seek to direct the polity and the underpinning of such actions is their position with wider structures of power (that is, power is always relational (elite/mass or domestic elite/foreign powers)), and their task will be easier if their rule is accepted, that is, if they are seen as legitimate, then they have not merely power but authority. All of which implies that there has to be a mechanism to acknowledge dissenting voices, as a permanent harmonious consensus is unlikely and stifling or suppressing dissenting voices can only weaken claims to authority.

The exchange between elite and mass is a mix of force and persuasion (and persuasion is more effective in securing assent):

- power and authority are embedded in the everyday practical social relations of groups/classes;
- power and authority are embedded in institutional arrangements;
- power and authority are asserted in the realm of ideas – elites create elite ideas – masses create grass-roots ideas – these run together, compromise ideas suffuse the social world.

Everyday life carries multiple strands of cultural resources – ways of reading and reacting to those patterns of social superiority and inferiority – two ideas can help order discussion of these streams of received ideas – as noted earlier, these are Great Tradition and Little Tradition – the former points to fundamental ideas, expressed in arts, religion and the like and buttressed by formal institutional practices – the latter points to the sets of ideas about ordering the social world that are carried in the routines of ordinary life amongst the masses – the two sets of ideas are in tension (thus, in China, the formal claims of the CCP in respect of communism and the role of the party and the local level pursuit of livelihood; or in Thailand, elite claims about the monarchy, the army and the country and the grass-roots preoccupation with the local demands of securing their livelihoods; or, to offer a European example, the formal claims of the British elite in respect of their polity to the effect that it is a long-established democracy and the reality of falling popular participation).

Institutional arrangements carry their own meanings – the party/the people – the stated bureaucracy/the population – the church/the faithful – elite agents can utilize these institutional machineries to transmit – overtly/covertly – particular sets of ideas – explicit as ideology, more indirect via the careful maintenance of hegemonic sets of ideas. In East Asia after the dissolution of state-empires and the process of decolonization, successor elites had to create states, invent new nations and pursue development. It required ideological mobilization – evident throughout the newly created states.

In the realm of ideas, understandings of the past are important: two analytical notions are available: collective memory and the national past. Following decolonization the elites of the new states must legitimate their claims to statehood and leadership and this is done prospectively, that is, promises about the future, and it is done retrospectively with claims about the past. Collective memory designates the way ordinary people forget and remember (what is recalled is selective), whilst the national past designates the exchange between elite and mass in respect of official remembering (again a mix of active remembering and active forgetting); the national past serves to shape official opinions, telling a tale about the nation, its roots, present and ideal future.

Relations between elites and masses are not fixed: they can change; they can evolve; they can change abruptly; and they can also experience long periods of relative consensus where neither side wants to or can change the balance. The resources of these cultural forms provide ideas and ethics which can inform practical action, so when problems arise in society groups turn to the resources of these traditions in order to organize their responses.

1 Chinese elites and masses and the modern world

Imperial China was organized as an agrarian bureaucratic feudal system. It was centred on an emperor and thereafter an elaborate hierarchy of officials. The system was buttressed by Great Tradition ideas in religion/ethic: Confucianism, Taoism (a folk religion mixing vitalism/divination), Buddhism and in places Islam. The Little Tradition worked at local-level village life where rural communities were organized around farming; inevitably, given the scale of the territory, there were multiple variants of tradition, but in general the key was family, so a person fitted into the social world via family, thereafter networks of kin, clan and language group.

The intersection of state and village worked via local gentry and their links to local-level administrators.

The 1911 revolution ushered in a period of great change. Novel Great Tradition ideas were drawn from the example of the modern world; thus nation, democracy and development. Elites debated the relationship between China and modernity: Sun Yat Sen celebrated nation, democracy and development, whilst Chiang Kai Shek imported elements of European/Japanese fascism (celebrations of will and moral example). A little later, Mao blended resources of classical Confucian culture with Marxism-Leninism.

These elites intermixed novel and inherited ideas with the concerns of masses in diverse ways throughout the 1911–78 period and they came to shape contemporary official thought, nominally a body of scientific ideas (Marxism theory), in reality, an evolving mixture of ideas pragmatically shaped in ever shifting circumstances. Mao – for example – remains a key element in the elite-sponsored legitimation of the People's Republic via the notion of Mao Zedong Thought, the mausoleum, the picture on the wall of the Forbidden City, his image on banknotes and, in recent years, an interest in museums of the Long March.

Mao figures as part of the national past. This understanding of the historical trajectory of the country is built around the notion of a century of humiliation, beginning with the Opium War and ending only with the 1949 revolution, the ejection of foreign influence and the creation of a New China. These ideas are unpacked in official culture (formal remembrance) and popular culture (the realms of media – newspapers, television, the arts and film).

And then, cast in another way, there are many examples of ideas emerging from the ordinary people: the May 4th Movement 1919; the 28/2/47 Incident; the death of Zhou Enlai 1976; the Tiananmen Square Incident 1989; the routine occasions of 'rightful resistance'. Such episodes are acknowledged: thus in 2005 Beijing reported 86,000 incidents of low-level violent resistance to officials or developers throughout the country.

2 Southeast Asia – elites and masses and the modern world

Southeast Asia was a realm of small shifting kingdoms and maritime empires; historically, it received cultural inputs from China, South Asia and West Asia, plus there are later inputs from Europe and America. The result is a fusion of cultures with Great Tradition materials informed by Islam, Hinduism, Buddhism and Chinese folk religion, plus Christianity. As with China, there was a multiplicity of Little Traditions threaded through local-level forms of life, fusing with Islam in particular.

After decolonization, successor elites mixed Great Tradition ideas and borrowings from the modern world in the process of making new states, inventing nations and pursuing development. The access of the masses to power was restricted, plus there were additional Cold War problems as anti-communist ideas and actions rolled through the region. And, as above, there were episodes of resistance to the claims of the elites.

In the region there have been many examples of resistance:

- dissenting passive with use of weapons of the weak – small-scale peasant rebellions, worker riots, middle class and/or student protests, gossip, cheating, working slowly and so on – examples from any urban/rural area in East Asia;
- dissenting active with ameliorative resistance – joining NGOs and charities – examples from any urban/rural area in East Asia – thus, the Great Marxist Conspiracy (Singapore 1980s);
- dissenting active in civil society – organizing party or pressure group – offering an alternative status hierarchy and offering alternative models of society – drive for wider participation is strong but often meets varieties of elite resistance – examples: student/unionists in South Korea, civil society groups in Thailand, the Assembly of the Poor (Thailand 1990s), Philippines people power, Malaysia, with minority party alliances – disadvantaged groups can also have recourse to violence: peasant groups in Philippines, various groups in China, religious groups in southern Philippines and parts of Indonesia, occasional terrorist actions;
- dissenting active in rebellion – invoking ideology or ethnicity or religion: the Huk Rebellion in northern Philippines (Philippines 1950s), Moros in southern Philippines, rebels in southern Thailand, minorities in Myanmar, East Timorese, Achinese and West Papuans in Indonesia.

In a comparative fashion William Case uses democratic elite theory to discuss contemporary Southeast Asia and offers three theories of political change: structural (macro forces of class change), modernization (rise of middle class liberal democracy) and cultural (local culture is local). Case argues that all offer insights but so too does elite theory, which focuses on the interests and actions of key political groups. Elite theory starts in 1930s Italy, where it was anti-democratic, and was revived in post-war USA as democratic elite theory. It characterized elites and the political regimes they ran. Cast in these terms, Case distinguishes a series of elite/polity types in Southeast Asia: (1) semi-democratic – Singapore and Malaysia; (2) pseudo-democratic – Indonesia; (3) unconsolidated democracy – Thailand; and (4) stable low quality democracy – Philippines. The benefits of such work are clear as Case uncovers the detail of groups and factions fighting for influence within the polities; but the disbenefits are also clear as Case rests content with a distinctly Western-centric notion of politics.

All that said, in recent years, commentators such as Amitav Acharya report signs of a return – after the divisive impacts of colonial era – to a coherent region ordered via ASEAN.

Unfolding trajectories: elites and masses going forwards

The starting point for analysing power and authority is the historical experience of Europe and America as the modern world is organized into states and nations;

thereafter, the inherited resources of local practices/cultures can be acknowledged – Great Traditions and Little Traditions (probably much altered by the experience of colonialism and the difficult on-going shift to the modern world); then we can take note of the practice of post-colonial local elites over the last fifty plus years.

In recent years East Asia has undergone rapid development. The exchanges between elite and mass have taken place in context of rapidly developing countries. The key agent has been the developmental state. Yet the East Asian developmental state has offered restricted opportunities for active subordinate access to power but a developmental state rests on a sense of community; leaders must be able to fashion consensus and mobilize/legitimize lines of action, so authoritarian top-down control is not enough. One aspect of securing legitimacy is by generating success, that is, material success redeems the promises elites make, but subordinates will still seek to access political power (indeed, material advance might make the subordinate classes more concerned with political power). If there are no effective avenues for political engagement, then politics does not go away, it goes somewhere else and it reappears in novel forms.

All this mixture will uncover the nature of power and authority in contemporary East Asia; what is visible is a multiplicity of locally determined forms of political life. These patterns of events are familiar in post-colonial East Asia.

In sum:

- the replacement elite will typically pursue security, order and development;
- to secure order they must deal with existing groups;
- these can react by supporting elite, acquiescing in elite project or resisting.

Other issues related are:

- groups can engage in conflict in a number of ways (for example, riots, pogroms, discrimination and boycotts);
- groups can stereotype (Malays as lazy, Chinese as ruthlessly materialistic, foreigners as exploitative sojourners);
- groups can have minimal exchanges (plural societies, or ghetto-ization or separatism);
- hostility can develop when one ethnic group comes to be associated with either an economically powerful position or a politically powerful position (or both);
- and such group identifications/tensions are available for calculated political exploitation.

In summary, thus far, the text has tracked unfolding historical trajectories of change and argued that the countries of East Asia:

- have it in common that they have shifted to the modern world (that is, they have accommodated to the demands of the global industrial capitalist system)

via the *episode of colonialism* (either direct or indirect), which generates a dual legacy, including the remnants of ancient civilizations along with the memories/ remnants of colonial episode;
- have it in common that they have *sought to locate themselves autonomously* within this modern industrial capitalist world, which generates typical preoccupations around the goal of national development (identity and development); here the first basic preoccupation is with making post-colonial states for the state is the key and all this generates a typical government form of *the developmental state oriented towards elite engineered change*;
- have it in common that these *unfolding trajectories can be grasped* in part in terms of the activities of elites in asserting their power/authority in order to make states and nations;
- have it in common that these *projects of identity/development are uncompleted* and there are multiple domestic and international tensions in the on-going pursuit of development.

Power, authority and dissent

All polities can be unpacked in terms of elaborate relationships of power and all polities will have equally elaborate common understandings of these patterns, but neither patterns of power nor patterns of understanding are fixed for both are contingent; relationships shift and change and ways of understanding also shift and change.

Cast in terms of elites and masses, the former must seek to shift the basis of their power away from force (explicit or implicit) and towards authority. If the elite can persuade the masses that extant political arrangements are reasonable, that is, legitimate, then their authority is secured (for the moment) and potential dissent will be held in check. But claims to authority will need continual attention, for the political world is inherently turbulent and elite claims to authority will need to be reaffirmed as events unfold.

9
DEVELOPMENT ISSUES FACED

Successor elites had to pursue development. In this regard pressures came from two directions, external and internal. The former drew together departing colonial authorities, corporate interests and the specialists of the United Nations and they imputed to successor elites the goal of becoming an 'effective nation-state' (essentially a variant form of liberal market-based liberal democracy). The latter, internal, pressures were so to say self-chosen, thus elites had promised supporters better lives and now they had to deliver and elites embraced programmes of national development (a somewhat different goal, set locally). As they assumed power, East Asian successor elites faced daunting problems: in rural to urban migration, in poverty and welfare and finally in external relations involving aid and trade. Yet over a thirty-year period, constructing and deploying the machinery of the developmental state, they achieved great success.

The literature of development is vast, so here, first, a note on the theories available to successor elites (many voices, much advice), followed more directly by a quartet of issues that elites had to address. All were awkward in the early days of development and some remain awkward today as domestic demands crowd in on elites, as do those within the international sphere.

Available theories of development

A number of broad approaches to the issue of development can be identified; these are large comprehensive theories and they offer a characterization of the condition of being underdeveloped and policy advice about how to organize change so as to achieve development. They rest on complex judgements about how societies work, how change can occur and how desired change can be secured. They are usually made in the rich countries and recommended to the poorer weaker countries. They are prescriptive. A large number of theories have been offered in the post-Second World War period but only a few have commanded widespread attention:

major theoretical approaches have been produced in America, Latin America, Europe and East Asia.

The promise of modernization theory

The earliest theory was presented in the 1950s. It was a time of high optimism within the USA and amongst its subordinate allies. The theory combined a Keynesian inflected preference for liberal markets (that is, it granted a key role to the state in managing the economy) with a description of the difference between traditional and modern societies taken from classical sociology along with a resolute hostility towards socialism and communism. From this mix it offered the new elites of the new countries of the Third World a way of thinking about development, which would let them quickly join in the life style of the rich countries, that is, modernization.

The distinction between traditional and modern used late nineteenth-century work: traditional societies were said to be religious, stable, static, rural, non-scientific and hierarchical, whereas, in contrast, modern societies were said to be secular, mobile, dynamic, urban, scientific and democratic. The business of modernization entailed replacing one set of characteristics with the other. Then a series of stages for the process was identified by the American theorist Walt Rostow, which all countries in the past had followed and which new countries could also follow under the direction of the modernizing elite. The five stages were: (1) traditional society – static, superstitious and so on; (2) preconditions for take-off – the country accumulates some wealth, introduces some scientific education, builds basic infrastructure and the first elements of the machinery of a modern state; (3) take-off – a period of around twenty years during which time investment is poured into industry, infrastructure and social upgrading; (4) the drive for maturity – after the hectic phase a quieter period of supplemental growth follows; and then finally (5) high mass consumption – the country is modern.

The theory was very influential in the West. It was influential in international organizations. It was also heavily criticized. It was said to be ahistorical, that is, it gave the modern countries the histories of their emergence, but denied any history to those it called traditional; they were just static. Yet this neglected the entire episode of colonial empire – the history that they did have, that is, the externally determined reconstruction of their hitherto existing civilizations. The distinction between traditional and modern was said to be biased, as modern was defined according to the model of rich Western countries, whereas the traditional were not considered directly, but merely compared unfavourably with the rich, so traditional seemed to be merely a residual category, an ad hoc list of ways that non-Western societies differed from those of the West. And, finally, the programme was said to be impractical: how could the key phase be specified so clearly as twenty or so years?

In the event the theory was overtaken by events as the optimism informing the approach ran into a series of problems. These included: an intractable war overseas,

Vietnam; the financial costs of that war plus pressures on dollar as key reserve currency; and the stirrings of the Civil Rights Movement. By the mid-1960s the fundamental optimism of modernization theory (and its domestic counterparts in claims about the inherent functional logic of industrialism), seemed simply implausible and confidence in the model of the USA faded away.

The approach was reprised in the 1980s and 1990s when renewed optimism about the American model of industrial capitalism coupled to the collapse of the Soviet Union, plus the construction of trans-national supply chains along with the creation of a very influential corporate financial realm, ushered in the notion of globalization. Highly ambitious claims were made for the idea and the world it described; thus globalization was simultaneously idea, project and practice; but as before these claims ran into the sand as events turned against its proponents. The American elite embarked on futile overseas wars (this time in the Middle East), became detached from large sections of its population (race plus inequality and the rise of the one per cent) and facilitated the creation of a financial bubble. The bubble collapsed in 2008 and with it, over the next few years, the neo-liberal project that had propounded the idea of globalization.

Doubts voiced: structural and dependency theory

A second major strand of thinking comes from Latin America. It is a structural theory, that is, it tracks the historical development experience of countries and identifies the internal class groupings and their external linkages. It is the mix of established historical trajectory, the existence of discrete groups and the resultant pattern of external linkages, which is used to explain the current situation of poor countries and to sketch out what has to be done to improve matters. The work was produced in the 1950s and then extended during the next couple of decades.

The earliest statements were structuralist economics. The approach grew from reflection upon the episode of the Second World War when Latin American economies were cut off by warfare from their traditional links with Europe, with whom they had shared a relationship of primary-product exporters and manufactured goods importers. When they could not import, they made the goods at home thereby inventing the strategy now known as 'import substituting industrialization' (ISI). The practical experience was supported by theoretical work and, in particular, the rejection of a long-established theory of trade dealing with international specialization and exchange. The Latin American structural economists said the theory was false and in practice – as policy – it allocated to Latin America a subordinate role in the trading relationship; whilst this might suit primary-product exporters, it did not do the economy as a whole much good.

The key figure is Raul Prebisch. The structuralist economists proposed a programme of ISI oriented to the development of the whole society; the approach was successful for a while but then began to run into domestic problems: small markets; protected local producers; governments spending too much money; difficulties of importing advanced technologies; and so further proposals were made for poor country cooperation such as organizing primary-product exports so as to raise prices (for example, OPEC), or forming trading blocks to encourage local industry and increase size of market, or arguing for changes in the global trading system to give better chances to the poor. Some further success was recorded and the basic insights about different social sectors with different interests plus their linkages overseas has proved useful, but in the 1960s Latin America drifted into debt and military coups and a new version of the theory emerged.

The later version expands these insights to stress the political relationships within Latin American countries and their linkages with the wider global system, in the past Europe but now America. The new theory was called dependency theory; it insisted that the poor countries were poor because of the ways in which their historical trajectories of development had lodged them in a weak position within the global system and had locked them in place by drawing the local elites into alliances with overseas powers. A key figure was A.G. Frank who proposed the idea of the development of underdevelopment, which asserted that being poor was not an original condition; rather it was generated by social relationships over time. The solution was pretty much the same: a national government was needed committed to general national development and it would probably have to be fought for as such a policy would upset powerful domestic and international groups.

Dependency theory was very influential. It uncovered the historical dynamics of poor countries, lodged them within the global system and sketched out the linkages that kept them in a subordinate position; it called attention to patterns of structural power. However, the theory was also criticized: (1) it was seen to be impractical as its diagnosis implied that a solution could be found in separating the poor countries from the wider global economy, but they were already integrated in a system centred on the rich; (2) it was seen to be overly confident in the mobilizing power of the state in poor countries, but it was the state that had lodged the countries in a subordinate position; and (3) the historical analyses of how the poor came to be poor were sometimes overstated, for the people of the poor countries were not just passive victims. And then, in practical terms, dependency theory was overtaken by events; domestic class and ethnic tensions festered, popularly elected governments were overthrown by local militaries; and the American government offered overt and covert aid to friendly regimes; development advanced, but, broadly, along free market lines.

Cautious optimism pursued: institutional development theory

A third major theoretical approach was produced around the same time – the late 1950s and 1960s – and was influential amongst sometime European colonial powers and within the arena of the United Nations. It has continued to exert influence on the thinking of large numbers of development policy makers: it is characteristically sceptical, identifies multiple factors in development and presents technically specialist planners with a key role.

Institutional development theory has roots in a particular strand of economic thinking, that is, institutional economics, which insists that it is not possible to conceive of economies without lodging them within social systems. It is a sociologized economics: the focus is not on buying and selling stuff in a marketplace, but on the ways in which people make their livelihoods. The enlightened state was the key to controlling the market and securing development. A key theorist was the Swedish scholar Gunnar Myrdal who spoke of circular and cumulative multiple causation, whereby a country once set in a path-dependent direction would continue along that line until something acted to change it, so for the poor countries the state had to try to upgrade across a range of areas – economic, social, cultural and political (all interconnected) – and once a positive trend was established it would be automatically reinforced. One theorist who followed Myrdal was Paul Streeten, who argued that development theorists were often too hasty in their pronouncements and needed to go more slowly and listen to the people of the poor countries whom they wished to help. This is a key move. Instead of treating the poor as needing outside expert treatment, it brings the poor back into the discussion; development projects should start from the existing patterns of life of the poor, rather than just follow a set recipe for development.

Institutional development theory looks at the evolution of poor countries over the long run and identifies complex internal patterns of life and complicated linkages with the wider global system; it is disposed to argue for small-scale incremental change. It has been influential but it has also been criticized: (1) it has been associated with the United Nations – the record of this organization has combined success in technical areas (for example disease reduction) with failures in the political sphere (with a series of 'development decades' and other initiatives which have not in general worked); (2) for playing down the reality of global politics – it was not disposed to acknowledge the effects of the Cold War; (3) for playing down the reality of global economic relations – where rich countries have been careful to look after themselves even where this was damaging the poor; (4) intellectually – the sociologized economics might have allowed a more subtle grasp of detail but it still neglected the histories of the poor and still adopted a Western-centric perspective. All that said, the approach has continued and it finds official expression in the work of the UNDP.

An East Asian approach: the developmental state

In 1945 development experts thought that East Asia had rather poor prospects: it had many peasant farmers; it had few modern industries; it had limited sources of capital; plus it had been extensively damaged by decades of warfare (thus: deaths, injuries, displacements plus material losses, with cities and resources destroyed). Yet against these expert expectations, the actual record has been quite different. The countries of the region have recorded great success. The reasons have been much debated and scholars, policy analysts and political commentators have all tried to discover the secret of success: the central area of debate has been the idea of the developmental state (or East Asian model); a related idea is that of Asian Values; there was some discussion about the Asian financial crisis; and a recent influential area of debate looks to the idea of regions.

The debate about the developmental state or Asian model began in the 1970s amongst development theorists and the issue was how to explain the success of Japan and the East Asian tigers because their success was in sharp contrast to perceived stasis or failure in other parts of the Third World. Society and culture were mentioned but the role of the state was picked out as important. The debate grew in scope in the 1980s as Japan–USA trade problems grew and numerous scholars and policy analysts considered the record. However, by now the debate had become somewhat intemperate as strong positions for or against were adopted.

First, some asserted that there was nothing special about East Asia as the economies were merely undergoing a process of catching up with the developed West; this mainly entailed bringing into use factors of production otherwise neglected, thus the shift from mainly rural to urban living and production. Second, some asserted that there was nothing special about East Asia as they were merely pursuing mercantilist policies to advance their trade at the expense of others and that these policies should be resisted. Third, some granted that there were some novel features in East Asian economies such as the role of state, the nature of systems of financing and the widespread elite-level habit of long-termism, but then added that all these novelties were merely supplementary to fundamental market functioning. Finally, fourth, some asserted that there were significant differences between East Asia and standard Western versions of modern industrial capitalism and that these differences merited study, in particular the role of the state was crucial.

Possible lessons of these debates

These debates amongst theorists are part and parcel of the business of development and they frame discussions of more practical issues. What many scholars would say is needed is: (1) an appreciation of history; (2) an appreciation of domestic social structures; (3) an appreciation of global links; (4) an appreciation of the pragmatics of policy oriented to national development; and (5) most of all an appreciation that many actors are involved who all have their own concerns, and this means that the pursuit of development is highly political and highly contested.

The successor elites in political power in the new states, those created following the dissolution of colonial empires, faced daunting problems. They had to secure better lives for their newly created citizens. That was the basic political deal: popular support in exchange for better lives. The issue of development moved to the foreground and the scale of the problems elites faced can be illustrated. As populations grew,[1] three broad areas of concern were tackled: the domestic business of agriculture, urbanization and social health. And to these were added the external business of aid and trade.

Domestic concerns I: agriculture and the drift to the towns

Until quite recently most of the population of the planet lived in rural areas and many were involved in agriculture. In terms of scale, roughly: 3 billion people live in rural areas; 2.5 billion work in agriculture; two-thirds of the world's poor live in rural areas; and most are engaged in subsistence agriculture. If rural areas are compared with urban, then for output and employment in these rich and poor countries, data shows that in poor countries agriculture has a high share of labour force but produces a much smaller share of total country GDP; and for productivity in the rich and poor countries, data shows that in rich countries agriculture is much more productive per unit of land, whereas, contrariwise, poor rural areas can be more productive per unit of labour.

Early policy expectations

Development experts have followed other social scientists in expecting that the historical pattern of presently rich countries would be repeated in today's poor countries; that is, that agriculture would decline as manufacturing became more important, and in time this too would decline as services became more important. This assumption meant that attention was turned to urban areas, sometimes called urban bias. However, rural areas have not disappeared and nor have they kept pace in terms of levels of living with urban areas; the global pattern is patchy, but over recent decades more attention has been paid to rural areas.

Types of agriculture

In rich First World countries agriculture is now just one more industry: farms depend upon inputs from industry (chemicals, machinery and IT), and they are financially supported by governments (price support, farm income support, export subsidies). Farms are fully integrated into the modern industrial economy (many are large corporate organizations).

In contrast, in the poor Third World the standard pattern is subsistence agriculture or peasant agriculture; it has typical characteristics. First, it is household-centred – production is for the consumption of the household unit and surplus is traded for additional goods, but it is not a commercial operation and the household will be a site of production and consumption. Second, land tenure is typically other than legal title – that is, households hold land by customary rights (used over the generations) and by agreement with village elders (controlling land so long as it is used). Also, as the modern world impinges they may become tenant farmers or sharecroppers or estate workers, so in today's Third World there can be many ways of holding land, unlike the First World where land title is law-based and contractually clear. Third, resources are low-level – labour power is used in household and in farming, simple agricultural tools are used and high-tech chemical industry fertilizers, herbicides and insecticides will be in short supply or not available.

FIGURE 9.1 Village field, Sichuan, November 2016.

FIGURE 9.2 Washing leeks, Sichuan, November 2016.

Folk knowledge about farming will be available but technical knowledge is in short supply or not available. And finance for investment will be in short supply or not available. Fourth, crops are grown for subsistence and there are only restricted possibilities to market surplus products. As the modern world encroaches, plantation agriculture may be adopted. Fifth, environmental problems may affect subsistence farming with competition for land, competition for water and competition for grazing land. All these place stress on the carrying capacity of land and problems of land degradation follow. In some areas these problems are exacerbated by climate/geography; thus marginal lands are more readily stressed by overuse. And such episodes of over-use and environmental degradation impact the poorest and can contribute to social unrest.

In the Third World one particular form of commercial agriculture has developed, that is, plantations. The essence of plantation agriculture is the production of tropical crops using industrial techniques. Small holding production is replaced by large units. Plantation agriculture requires land, the peasants to work plus industrial inputs and global marketing systems: for example, oil palm or rubber or cocoa or flowers or vegetables are all grown in the poor Third World for export to the First World.

The plantations can be large family-run businesses or corporate organizations (for example, Latin American banana companies), with the former running in a patron/client style and the latter more commercially (the shift from one to the other can create problems, for example, in the Philippines the 1950s Huk Rebellion). But the advantages of plantations are that cheap land and labour can produce a large output; the disadvantages are the impacts on existing forms of life or the social costs of established plantation businesses, and finally that the crops are low value and depend on First World markets (any agricultural primary product).

FIGURE 9.3 Farming, Zhenjiang, Spring 2017.

Most poor countries have poor agriculture but the pattern is not the same: (1) in Latin America land distribution is uneven, with a few large holdings and many smaller holdings – overall, not efficient or equitable (routine conflicts over land holdings and peasant representation); (2) in South Asia there are many very small holdings – overall, not efficient and there are problems with landlordism, landless labour, money lending and debt bondage; and (3) in Africa more traditional subsistence farming – successful in stable conditions but population growth and impact of modern world (thus, encouraging crops for export) cause disturbances.

Newer policy ideas about rural development

Integrated rural development – instead of an expectation of a decline in agriculture and its replacement by industrialization and in place of mega-schemes such as plantations or communes (the state socialist experiment), the preference is for small-scale activities to upgrade levels of living: (1) agricultural extension services (technical advice on improving output); (2) reasonable price support (to provide basic incomes); (3) land reform (to redistribute large holdings, to aggregate those too small to support families); (4) health and education services (raises general levels of living); (5) transport networks (link rural areas with core urban areas); (6) electrification (bring power to rural areas); and (7) off-farm employment (look for ways to provide alternative employment in the rural areas).

Rural–urban migration

Where rural life cannot support the population the result is migration to the cities: (1) seasonal working (adults travel to take up seasonally available work); (2) contract working (adults travel to take up short contracts in town); (3) remittance working (adults travel to take up short contracts overseas); (4) family relocation (the basic family unit relocates to the town); and (5) chain migration (the newly established urban family acts as facilitator for further migration). For the future, given that rural populations cannot all move to urban areas – rural development is crucial.

Yet the process of rural–urban migration continues. The process of migration to the cities (domestic or overseas) is often traumatic: one social network is left behind and another must be constructed; in poor Third World countries the receiving area is likely to be marginal housing, squatter camps, slums or, in the worst case, the street.

Domestic concerns II: urbanization – the rapid growth of cities

Human beings invented settled agriculture around 3,000 years ago; for most of the following period most people lived in rural areas close to the land they farmed; there were large cities, but not many. Literate cultures emerged around 2,500 years ago, thus Confucianism in China or the body of work produced in Ancient Greece; these were the earliest steps on the long road to the modern world of today.

FIGURE 9.4 Village, Zhenjiang, Spring 2017.

In Europe the shift to the modern world was driven by trade and science; urban centres prospered; a slow movement from rural to urban areas began; the rise of industrial society approximately 250 years ago accelerated the movement towards the towns; in the nineteenth century in Europe there was rapid urbanization which was concentrated in certain areas and along a few major rivers. That process has been repeated in East Asia and in the wider Global South. Today, the majority of human beings now live in urban settlements.

Urban growth and patterns of city life

The global population is growing and by 2025 it is estimated it will be around 9 billion. In 2025 total global urban population is projected at 5 billion and 4 billion (80 per cent) are projected to be in Third World cities. As a consequence, urban growth is very rapid. In 1950 total global urban population was 724 million and 275 million (38 per cent) were in Third World cities. In 2001 total global urban population was 3.6 billion and 2 billion (66 per cent) were in Third World cities.

Cities are very complex social organizations. First, they are highly productive – very high outputs of material products, knowledge products and cultural products, and so cities have been the drivers of human development over millennia. Second, they are highly expensive to sustain – the basic physical infrastructure of a city is highly expensive (water, sanitation, housing, transport along with manufacturing and commercial sites). Third, they are highly structured economically – cities are typically zoned either formally or informally according to the activities carried out and zones must be policed and zone boundaries must be maintained. Fourth, they are highly structured socially – cities are typically class structured; classes generate formally or informally residential segregation, so mechanisms for securing residential segregation must be in place, as boundaries must be policed. And, sixth, they are highly contested politically – the city organization is very complex and the city cannot function without continual maintenance of these systems, so control of these systems is vital and it is thus a key site of power (resources/rewards), so it is contested.

The natural growth of rich cities is readily absorbed; population growth enhances the productive power of the city. But the natural growth of poor cities is more difficult. Rapid population growth places stresses on the urban system and flows of inward migrants make these problems more difficult: (1) employment and the informal sector – the lack of regular employment encourages the growth of low-level informal working, thus petty traders, small-scale services and the like; (2) accommodation is poor – the rapid increase in numbers of people often with little money means the spread of informal provisions such as shanty towns, squatter camps and slums; (3) social stress rises and the coherence of the city society weakens – crime rises, taxes are not paid, administration is corrupted, business evades marketplace demands via networks with politicians; and (4) state capacity is weakened – the ability of the state to sustain the complex organization of the city declines: ethnic or class divisions are deepened, the rich and middle classes withdraw and the poor slip downward.

FIGURE 9.5 Ramkhamhaeng Road, Bangkok, December 2009.

City planning

Around the turn of the nineteenth century in the context of burgeoning industrial capitalist growth, modern city planning began. Settlements were experiencing rapid urban growth: initially inward migration, later urban population growth. There were many problems – unplanned expansion entailed poor physical provisions

FIGURE 9.6 Café, Ramkhamhaeng Road, March 2014.

(poor infrastructure), poor economic conditions (unregulated activity), poor social provisions (incoming migrants had to fend for themselves) and unsatisfactory political conditions (elites divorced from masses and a ready propensity for violence). At back of this drive was population growth; global population is expected to top out at around 9 billion.

Various groups are involved in the overall task of upgrading life in the cities. First, elites and city governments look to organize infrastructure: (1) land registry (who owns what); (2) building codes (minimum standards for construction, light and air); (3) transport systems (road designs and provision); and (4) hygiene (water supplies, waste systems or housing layout designs). Second, elites and civil society groups (charities/philanthropists/unions) provide social infrastructure: (a) hospitals; (b) schools; and they offer some poor relief for the destitute. And third, city governments and reforming civil society groups looked to organize social welfare infrastructure: (i) affordable housing; and (ii) mass schooling.

Elites had always planned their own estates and palaces, and urban guilds had attended to the needs of small trading towns, but the development of industrial society and the rapid growth of towns required action on a greater scale: at first from elites, later from city governments. The initial impetus is security (health/political) but later the business of designing towns takes on a social engineering or utopian aspect.

The shift to urban areas is likely to continue. Cities must absorb more people and the authorities will have to help them make new better lives, whilst rural areas will likely loose population, but they are vital as sources of basic food stuffs so they too must be dealt with by offering their populations the same chances as those in the cities.

FIGURE 9.7 Public housing, Singapore, December 2008.

Domestic concerns III: poverty, education and health

Development theorists distinguish absolute poverty and relative poverty: (1) absolute poverty means levels of living that put physical survival in question; such low levels of living put great stress on social systems; (2) relative poverty means levels of living so low that a person or group cannot join in the mainstream activities of their society; now the comparisons are often made internationally, that is, groups or societies who cannot do what most/many people on the planet do – so the issue of relative poverty raises the issue of inequality.

Absolute and relative poverty and policy options

Absolute poverty means being unable to satisfy basic needs for physical survival and there is an agreed official definition used by development agencies. There are technical debates about how to do this but the figure is set at US$1 per day and this is called the poverty line (using the idea of purchasing power parity, that is all different currencies are scaled to the basket of goods that US$1 will buy in the USA, so in effect this offers a physical comparator, that is, the basket of goods). It is crude but useful. If your income falls to this level you cannot survive. A related idea is the poverty gap, which is the shortfall in a country's total income needed to bring everyone above the poverty line. A related idea is the human poverty index in which poverty is measured against a set of criteria including life expectancy, education and material resources. In the case of absolute poverty the problem is rather obvious, that is, people cannot survive and either their societies collapse or the individuals die or both.

Relative poverty means the income a person or group has relative to the rest of their community. It is interesting because a person's position within a society will shape their life-chances. There are various ways of expressing these social relationships.

The people of a country can be ranked in order and then the share of total income of each quintile (20 per cent set) or decile (10 per cent set) and the data can then show which set of population gets what. Similarly the Gini coefficient is widely used. A graph of income against population can be drawn; a line at an angle of 45 per cent means each section of population receives same share of income, but if the line falls from 45 per cent then it means that different sections of the population are receiving different shares of total income. The divergence of line from 45 per cent can be expressed as a coefficient: thus 0 equals perfect equality and 1 equals perfect inequality. In practice rather equal countries have a Gini coefficient of 0.2 to 0.32 and rather unequal countries have a Gini coefficient of 0.5 to 0.7.

In the case of relative poverty the problems are more subtle: (1) diminished life chances of the population; (2) diminished social functioning – thus economic problems and social problems; and (3) unfairness – inequality – it seems that a claim to fairness might be familiar in human societies

A range of policy options have been tried at macro scale and micro scale: (a) fix the market – if the market worked properly then it would allocate resources efficiently and the poor would find jobs; (b) fix the pattern of asset ownership, that is, redistribute – thus land reform or upgrading human capital by making better access for poor; (c) progressive taxation; (d) raise public provision via spending on health, welfare, subsidies and the like. All in all, it is a slow business but over last sixty years great advances have been made, especially in Latin America, South Asia and East Asia.

The issue of education

In general, for people in the rich world, education is an issue because it has an intrinsic benefit, that is, it helps realize individual talent, and thereafter contributes to social welfare. For development theorists it is an issue because formal education contributes to pursuit of development in three broad areas: (1) practical skills such as literacy and numeracy; (2) employability (as formal job markets expand); and (3) social skills such as in hygiene and food preparation and social organization.

Specialists have asked questions about enrolment rates and access. First, enrolment rates are now good – years of schooling are improving and the figures are converging on First World models, but access is often biased. Second, gender bias – educating girl children is less popular but very important in pursuit of development and the data shows evidence of differential treatment of boy and girl children.

In general, the former get more years of education than the latter. There is also a distinct geographical pattern to this: thus the Middle East and South Asia have lowest percentages of female participation in education. This bothers development theorists, as there is widespread agreement that the education of women is crucial to development. Third, class bias – the middle classes and rich receive better schooling and so the system may reflect their preferences with over-provision of high schools and universities combined with under-provision of primary schools, and the syllabus might be skewed towards academic rather than practical learning. Fourth, the issue of health, for learning is better if students are healthy, and health status is skewed by class, with differential access to food and health services.

Related debates

The idea of human capital has been used. Thus a healthy and knowledgeable population can contribute to development, therefore invest in health and education systems; usually this means the state or charity or NGO as the marketplace does not work well in this area. The translation into economics terms helps make the point.

A concern with child labour has been voiced. The data suggests that child labour is extensive. Child labour brings in wage or contributes to family earning, but loss of schooling lowers individual/family contribution over the longer term, for poorer education means poorer work means poorer family, so the problem transmits down the generations. ILO data records about 120 million children working full-time and 130 million working part-time, plus those working at home, plus those working with relatives. It is most prevalent in Asia and Africa. Responses vary: (1) some argue it is inevitable, so work to eliminate poverty (World Bank); (2) some argue it is not inevitable, so get more kids into school (NGO line); (3) some argue it is inevitable, so regulate until it fades as poverty reduces (UNICEF); (4) some argue it is not inevitable, so ban it (ILO); (5) some argue it is not inevitable, so the First World should use trade sanctions.

Development policy on education

Education pulls people out of the job market and then they need facilities and teachers and administrators, sourced in private market or via charity or provided by the state. In most places for most people the state is the key provider. It figures in most currently rich countries, for mass education was linked to the rise of industrial nation-states. Education provides benefits for the individual through increased lifetime earnings plus satisfactions of greater skills or knowledge, and also for the community as education provides a smarter workforce/population. Calculating the mix of individual and community benefits is difficult and there are different views, which result in different opinions about how it should all be paid for. In the Third World debate is somewhat irrelevant as most are poor and cannot pay much. The state is key provider: the system must exist and there is plenty of scope for debate planned (what sort of schools? where? and teaching what syllabus?). And, finally, government policy determines the pattern of educational spending and provision. There is data to suggest that spending can be skewed towards the needs of rich/middle classes; thus high schools and tertiary systems (rather than primary/secondary schools). There is data to suggest that expenditure on education can be a burden to poor people. And there is data to suggest that poor countries can find themselves financing education for people who then work in rich countries

Health issues and policy

As with education health is a key preoccupation of development theorists: health is a necessary condition of development, a key basic need. There are simple measures available to judge the health of the people in a given society: life expectancy and infant mortality. First, national governments and UN organizations collect data on life conditions, including life expectancy at birth, as it is a simple measure of the health of a community. The figures show great differences (Sierra Leone 36m/39f or Hong Kong 78m/83f (2003 World Bank), but note that the figures obscure differences in social class and age). Second, national governments and UN organizations collect data on infant/child mortality. The data typically records infant mortality under one-year-old and also child mortality under five-years-old. In addition to the raw data this gives an indication of the general level of living of a country (the poorer levels of living, the more infant/child mortality). The data show great differences (Sierra Leone 166/1000 or Norway 3/1000 (2003 UNDP)), but again also obscure class differences within countries, because the lower one's class, the higher the infant mortality.

There are also more subtle measures. First, there are patterns of disease (which illnesses? caught by whom? treated how? with what impact upon family incomes? with what costs to community?). People in poor countries have different patterns of illness and premature death from those in rich countries. In poor countries people suffer from poor hygiene, poor nourishment and the impact of preventable disease. Treatment can be rudimentary and people in poor countries may have to rely on family members for help; the burden of caring can weigh heavily on community. People in rich countries experience diseases of affluence – treatment is good – those in rich countries usually have access to welfare systems (of variable quality, paid for in various ways) and rich countries can fund health systems (but these are now debated). Second, there are the impacts of malnourishment, which is widespread in poor countries. It has various impacts on individual, family and society. Poor food leads to greater susceptibility to disease and it leads to poorer performance in school and poorer performance in work.

There are issues with preventable diseases in poor countries and also pandemics. Preventable diseases can be managed; two issues are of noted concern: first, malaria, which used to kill and debilitate many millions in tropical areas until brought under control by DDT, has recently made a comeback as insects have shown resistance to standard treatments (spraying, bed mats); second, HIV/AIDS, a recently emerged disease, which is debilitating before allowing secondary infections to kill; it has a high mortality rate. And there are others: round worm, hook worm, schistosomias, leishmaniasis and so on. Then, relatedly, pandemics can sweep through populations causing many casualties and presenting severe difficulties in organizing a response. Disease can spread uncontrollably and historical examples abound (in Europe in the Middle Ages, plague killed between one-third and two-thirds of the population; in the early twentieth century a flu pandemic killed 30 to 60 millions). There are recent examples, thus SARS (severe acute respiratory syndrome) created anxieties and H5N1 ('bird flu') continues to cause worries. Fears of pandemics have been heightened in the last thirty years with the expansion of large-scale migration flows, and in particular mass long-haul air-travel can spread a disease very rapidly.

As with education there are questions about how health care should be delivered to the population, but unlike education health care spending is potentially open-ended with steeply rising costs. So the debates are sharper. There are three mechanisms of provision: state (funded by taxation), charity (funded by gifts) and corporate or marketplace (funded by purchase price). The mix of mechanisms and income streams varies. In poor countries only the rich can buy medical care, charity provision offers only partial coverage and so the state must carry a large part of the burden. The choice of type of provision is awkward. Primary health care can reach the most people, whilst urban dwelling middle classes tend to prefer higher-tech hospitals. The former are cheap whilst the latter are expensive. How to train medical professionals is a further question: training can be enough for local needs or up to best international standards. There are unintended consequences: trained medical professional are valuable as it takes time and money to train them and rich countries poach trained staff; yet medical treatment is needed, so where the poor cannot access the state system and there is no charity provision they must return to folk medicine and untrained personnel.

By way of a summary comment: it may be true that there are many outstanding problems with poverty, health and education, but it is also true in general that the human population today is better fed, better educated and enjoys better health than earlier generations of humans.

External concerns: aid, trade and the environment

Mainstream development theory focuses on both the domestic situation of poor countries and also their external relations: the *domestic issues* include poverty, population, agriculture, migration, urban and industrial growth, health and welfare; the *international issues* include debates about trade, trade policy, financial flows, development finance and debt along with the role of international financial institutions such as IMF and World Bank.

Trade in theory

There has been a long debate amongst political economists and mainstream market economists as to why international trade exists. In the nineteenth century, David

Ricardo argued that trade was a good thing; if countries specialize where they have an advantage, then, if all trade, general prosperity is encouraged. The key idea was that comparative advantage helps individual countries uplift their economies so they and everyone else are better off. In more recent times, mainstream market economics have argued the same where particular factor endowments underpin comparative advantage in trading and so, once again, everyone is better off. The idea has recently been celebrated as part of the project of globalization. However, in contrast Raul Prebisch looked at historical and structural circumstances of different countries and diagnosed an advantage for those who developed early. They dominated the high value parts of economic activity and controlled the terms of trade with poorer countries, leaving the latter in a structurally disadvantaged position. For the poorer countries the solution was national development behind protective tariff barriers. The idea was picked up by others and expanded into dependency theory which was influential amongst various groups who doubted the claims of the mainstream. More recently, institutional theory, looking at the detail of multiple exchanges within social life, has argued for the state to play a key role in fostering development; thus, there is no reason to privilege trade *a priori*, the better approach is to ask how it helps (or doesn't).

Trade policy

International trade makes a significant contribution to economic progress and – cast in macro descriptive terms – since 1945 trading economies have typically prospered, whilst more autarchic systems have not. However, quite how the benefits of trade can be captured by a particular state has long been in question. A number of lines of argument can be noted. First, import-substituting industrialization (ISI) – the policy strategy is to protect the domestic economy until it has caught up with the powerful and then negotiate reductions in barriers so that local economic activity benefits from liberalization. The intellectual roots of this position go back to Friedrich List and it has been advocated recently by Raul Prebisch. Second, export-oriented industrialization (EOI) – the policy strategy is to promote local industry with the immediate target of competing in the markets of advanced economies in the expectation of rapid learning and rapid advance in order to negotiate market access agreements as quickly as possible. The approach was taken post-war by East Asian client states of the USA, with spectacular results. Third, it might be noted that these matters are debated: optimists say trade drags poor countries upwards and that bi-lateral and multi-lateral strategies available; whilst pessimists say that the poor cannot compete directly with the rich, so instead protection, cartels and regional trade zones are favoured. Fourth, institutions have been constructed to facilitate trade and resolve difficulties. The World Trade Organization (WTO) was designed to regulate international trade and resolve disputes: again, enthusiasts affirm ideal model of free market trade, whereas critics see the rich using it to exploit further the poor. It might be that a middle route is to say that the WTO machinery is an institution embodying a ritual truth, which is

Financial flows

International trade has long been measured. It must also be financed. The two ideas are often run together. The idea of national accounts presents the situation of a county on the analogy of domestic household account, they measure income and expenditure of a country. The idea is relatively new (associated with Keynes in the 1940s) and it is now very elaborate. The accounts are disaggregated. Thus, the current account records goods imported and exported and monies paid out and remittances received. All these involve financial flows to pay immediate bills. On a longer term, the capital account records flows of finance not immediately attached to goods: foreign direct investment, portfolio investment, inter-bank lending, aid transfers and the like. One particular issue identifies disturbances to regular money flows, which make problems for the wider economy, thus 'capital flight' and 'hot money'. Finally, the state has a cash account or foreign reserves, the funds readily available to state.

In respect of finance, it is the case that the global financial system is centred – and thus regulated – in a few key centres: Wall Street/US Treasury; IMF/World Bank (both headquartered in Washington); the City of London; the European Union (European Central Bank (ECB)/Bundesbank); plus there are powerful centres in East Asia (Beijing (Central Bank of China), Japan and the financial centres of the other Asian Tigers). Together, these centres control and regulate global flows of finance – they are thus politically powerful.

Development projects have to be financed and there are a number of possible sources: (1) domestic taxes, where state income is used to fund expenditures; (2) foreign direct investment, where outside money sets up business ventures (benefits and disbenefits); (3) aid money, which can be bi-lateral, multi-lateral, government or charitable, and it can come with or without conditions (benefits and disbenefits); and (4) bank finance, that is, commercial loans – here there are questions of terms and conditions. Where foreign state money is made available to fund projects (aid and business are often linked, thus aid, trade and foreign direct investment are intermingled (benefits/disbenefits). Where foreign corporate money is made available, there can be problems – powerful banks, relatively weaker borrowers. Granted that the finance can be arranged, lenders have gone on to pay attention to the ability of local elites to service debts or collect taxes or manage foreign investment, and there have been many failures in these regards.

Debt problem of 1980s onwards

The emergence of many new countries following decolonization created demand for development and it created demand for development funding. The 1973 Middle

East War saw OPEC sharply raise the price of oil and this created a large stock of petro-dollars, which were recycled into development projects in the Third World. When development projects faltered, many states found that they had unsustainable sovereign debts. They were supported by international lending, but poor countries were unable to service these debts and found that they were locked into debts they could never repay. At the same time the flood of petro-dollars into the global money markets created inflation in the richer countries, further destabilizing the system.

The World Bank and IMF became involved. Structural adjustment programmes were designed and linked to structural adjustment lending; the overall plan was to shift poor economies into the marketplace in the expectation that this would solve their problems, but it resulted in failure. The issue has been reprised in recent years with a further debate around liberalization, globalization and debt relief.

The global system of finance is inherently unstable but most of the time it functions. Nonetheless, when it goes wrong it can cause great distress; hence recently the 1997 Asian Financial Crisis and, more recently, the Anglo-American 2008–10 financial crisis and relatedly the seemingly interminable crisis of the euro currency from 2015 onwards.

The environment: industrialization – costs incurred, problems created

Contemporary concerns for the condition of the natural environment began to be voiced in America in the late 1950s when the use of agricultural chemicals was discovered to have negative effects on wildlife. Rachel Carson's 1962 book *Silent Spring* announced the problem; in the 1960s two writers were particularly influential as Paul and Ann Ehrlich introduced to a wide audience the core idea of ecology, that all living things are connected and interdependent, and went on to argue that the human population was impacting upon the natural environment and in the long-term this would damage human society. In 1972 the Club of Rome published *The Limits to Growth*. All this was phase one of the debates about the environment; it was noted that industrial society was placing unsustainable stresses upon the natural environment. A debate began with two sides forming, those who argued in favour of industrial society, claiming that it produced richer, healthier people, and those who argued that its excesses, that is, pollution of one sort or another, had to be curbed; unfortunately, this debate came to be cast in terms of economic growth versus environmental protection.

Phase two of the debate moved debates to a larger scale as evidence began to be accumulated about the long-term impact of industrial manufacturing on the atmosphere. Industrial activity has produced an effect in the planet's atmosphere. In the relatively short period of a couple of hundred years humans have added thousands of tons of greenhouse gas to the atmosphere and this produces the effect called global warming. Projections suggest that if the warming continues it will have serious negative effects on the environment and its human population. Those who say that climate change is happening say that it is caused by humans and that it is unsustainable (that is, if left unchecked it will cause great damage to human beings). On the other hand, climate sceptics say the science is not well established and so we need not worry too much. But there are now international agreements about the atmosphere and individual states have declared that they will act to reduce the output of harmful gases (mostly from burning fossil fuels); however, agreement is difficult and action is even more difficult, and greenhouse gases are only one element of the waste produced by industrial societies.

Summary: aid, trade and the environment

The elites of poor countries usually control economies skewed in the direction of a few primary products; maybe minerals, maybe plantation crops, plus in recent years some industry relying on cheap labour will have been added. Heavy indebtedness means they are subject to external pressure and so their situation is very difficult. The countries of East Asia have kept debt under control and many are now creditor nations, but the countries of sub-Saharan Africa are indebted, whilst other areas show various patterns. Overall, debt remains a fraught issue; environmental issues are acknowledged, but tend to take a back seat to economic or financial concerns.

The tasks of development – retrospect and criticism

Development theory has a quite distinctive starting point. It emerges from the collapse of empire and the needs of successor elites for economic development. The whole business was further shaped by Cold War competition amongst great powers for allies amongst the new nation-states. And over forty years much work has revolved, one way or another, around the pursuit of the goal of becoming developed. It has been thought that deliberate action could secure that goal either by effective planning (by international organizations, states and private sector actors) or efficient market mechanisms (regulated by the state, ordered internationally and pursued by private sector actors). There has been a great deal of debate about policy strategies, but the end goal has remained in place. However, in recent years a groundswell of criticism has been heard; some of it is towards current policy and some of it is towards the entire approach to development.

First, the general orientation of development theory has been criticized. It has been characterized as biased: (1) it is biased because it draws uncritically upon the historical experience of the West; (2) it is biased because it affirms unquestioned the current pattern of economic and social arrangements in these rich countries; (3) it is biased because it ignores alternative approaches to development generated by the experience of people who live in the poor countries.

Second, the practice of development work has been criticized. It has been argued that the rich are less concerned with development than securing continued access to poor countries' resources and markets (neo-colonialism). It has been argued that the mechanisms of development, that is, the apparatus of planning and aid, are intellectually implausible (the knowledge/expertise is lacking), hopelessly corrupt (aid is now a business and those involved have their own agendas) and in practice act to misdirect the efforts of those involved (aid as upmarket welfare payments which debilitate the recipient). And it has been argued that the development game routinely ignores the voices of the poor; that is, their knowledge is ignored, their concerns are ignored and their desires for the future are ignored.

Third, the First World public view of development has been criticized: (a) there is a pervasive habit of viewing the poor as incompetent (rather than being those at the bottom of the global heap); (b) there is a pervasive habit of fixing on the deserving poor (children, those suffering from natural disasters and so on) and neglecting the people as a whole; (c) there is a familiar habit of thinking that charity events or contributions are enough (they make little difference); (d) there is a pervasive habit of disregarding the responsibilities of the rich for the situation of the poor (debt is presented as the responsibility of the feckless poor rather than feckless lenders); and (e) there is a familiar and maybe fading habit of seeing the situation of poor countries as separate from the rich, but migration, crime and disease do not respect rich countries' boundaries.

Recently the mainstream view has been analysed as a discourse. The mainstream position in respect of development can be associated with the United Nations style institutionalist analysis discussed in the company of Todaro: the goal is to replicate the levels of living of American and European countries; their role as the presently most powerful countries is noted and made the basis of claims to their responsibility to help; the diversity of the poor countries is also noted; giving help is a responsibility which can only be discharged through negotiations with poor countries.

The position generates a distinctive discourse: (i) First World governments offer aid cast in terms of discharging a duty to common humanity; (ii) poor country recipients acknowledge aid, ask for more and accept conditions; (iii) First World NGOs criticize their own governments for not doing enough; (iv) poor country NGOs criticize both donor and recipient governments for providing too little wrongly directed.

The discourse is sustained by national governments, international agencies and the various NGO participants: it functions as a taken-for-granted framework for policy debate; it is routinized; it involves many people; it is lavishly funded.

It has been argued that this routinized sphere of policy debate is now part of the problem: it directs debate and money into long-established channels; it offers few new ideas; it has demonstrably failed (after forty years there are still very many poor); and some critics condemn the entire discourse – from those who deny any continuing rich world responsibility through those who see only poor world corruption to those who say it really would be better if all these matters were left to the marketplace.

Over the years a number of responses to these criticisms have been made. First, the rich countries are the only plausible models and poor countries must adapt to the demands of the global system built around them because there simply is no alternative (realist modernization/globalization). Second, the rich countries are dominant but do represent the future of the poor and further open-minded debate can reveal how all countries can participate in the current global system (optimistic modernization/globalization). Third, the rich countries have run down their own trajectories and the poor have run down different trajectories and these should be studied directly, because if theorists embrace the historical particularity of development experiences then they will be better able to advise poor countries (optimistic multi-trajectory development). Fourth, the model of the developed West is not the only model for there are many local resources whereby development can be understood and ordered and the resources of local cultures are available (embrace ethno-development). And fifth, the rich have run down their own trajectory and wrongly advised the poor, so the model of the rich cannot be replicated in poor countries because the model is unsustainable, therefore poor countries should find their own distinctive trajectory based on their own resources (embrace sustainable development).

Development work (theory/practice) involves many agents and early optimism that massive social change could be easily engineered has given way to a much more sceptical stance: it is no longer clear that there are simple development gaols. What seems to be left is a widespread continuing concern for drawing the poor into the mainstreams of modern life but expectations are low whilst proposals for action are various. It is a highly contested sphere. And it remains a central concern for most of the countries of East Asia.

Note

1 The population of the planet was around 500,000 million in 1750 (roughly the 'start of the modern world'); by 1900 it had slowly increased to around 1,000,000,000 (one billion); over the twentieth century it rapidly increased to around 6,000,000,000 (6 billion); and current early twenty-first century projections suggest it will finally settle at around 9 billion sometime this century.

PART IV
EAST ASIA IN THE CHANGING GLOBAL SYSTEM

By the middle of the 1980s the global system was reconfiguring. The USA and its North American neighbours remained the single most powerful grouping in the global system. The key international economic institutions, the IMF and the World Bank, were headquartered in Washington, so too the US Treasury, plus links to Wall Street. The United Nations itself was headquartered in New York. The European Union was in the process of institutionally embracing a neo-liberalism fashioned in the main in the USA albeit reinforced by German intellectual and institutional ordo-liberal proclivities; thus the programme of the Single Market, enshrined in treaties amending the constitutional machinery of the European Union in 1985. The European grouping now resembled the USA in terms of its economic profile, with sophisticated natural science-based industrial production serving an affluent consumer society. The links across the Atlantic Ocean were strong and in political and security terms the USA was clearly the senior partner. In the 1990s American pre-eminence was celebrated as globalization and the ethico-political end of history was confidently announced. However, the balances were shifting. European governments acting collectively were better able to secure their local interests. And, more importantly, in East Asia regional production networks were generating a species of integration. East Asia was in process of emerging as the third major economic area within the global system: sophisticated natural science, equally sophisticated manufacturing and a powerful export sector. Foreign scholars pointed to the effectiveness of the developmental state but they also noted some downsides, such as rising inequality and environmental problems, but, overall, they were impressed by the region's successes. Local scholars and political actors were sometimes more bullish; thus Lee Kuan Yew and Mahathir Mohamad spoke of the 'Asian Model', the World Bank announced an 'Asian Miracle', whilst more enthusiastic nationalists of all stripes spoke, somewhat contradictorily, of East Asia's rise to power – the twenty-first century, they claimed, would be the Asian Century.

10
THREE SPHERES OF CONCERN
Domestic, regional and international

As successor elites secured their power and authority they faced numerous problems. There were domestic issues to deal with, the heartland of their political support; there were regional issues to deal with, the immediate context of elite goals for development; and there were international issues to deal with, new states were states within an international system of states, and dealing with these had, perforce, to be something of a priority. In this respect matters were peculiarly difficult for new elites, as the dissolution of state-empires had left the politics of the entire area in flux. The most significant power was the USA and in the years following the end of the Pacific War it was this country that set the agenda, shaping, thereby, the context within which new elites had to operate.

After 1945, the new elites of the new countries of East Asia faced a host of problems; expressed schematically, there were three areas of problems: (1) immediate domestic problems (that is, order, stability and growth, where this trio were the minimum demands placed upon successor elites); (2) local regional problems (that is, maintaining stability as the new local political system settled into place); and thereafter (3) the arena of broad international problems, that is, managing the diverse demands of the changing international system, the system of which the new states were now integral parts.

In all this domestic problems were the first concern of new elites, as they had to secure their borders, establish internal stability and pursue growth and welfare. These were the minimum conditions of elite survival; fail here and the whole enterprise could go wrong. Thereafter, the second area of concern was the local region, as they had to work to minimize conflict and create stability. But drawing borders and settling issues of citizenship (and minorities) is not straightforward, and all this was made more difficult by the activities of external powers, both departing colonial groups and the participants in the nascent Cold War. And finally, the third area of concern was the ways in which the countries of the region and the region itself fitted into the wider global system. The behaviour of outside powers could impact domestic and regional concerns: local states had outward-oriented alliance linkages with USA and USSR (trade links, aid links and military links); local states could become involved in Cold War proxy wars (notably Korea and Vietnam); or local states could combine as with the Non-Aligned Movement (which pleased neither Cold War power) or more recently as ASEAN (which has been found to be useful); and local states could also find they were subject to demands of larger powers (in regard to terrorism or trade in weapons or drugs or other goods)). And there wider issues here relating to the increasing importance of countries within the wider global system (thus Japan and more recently China are large economic powers). These large powers can set rules (thus over product standards or trade regulations or intellectual property or contract law – and so on – that impact weaker states). Overall, the demands of the international system provide one further set of problems and opportunities for the governments of countries within the East Asian region.

Domestic and regional concerns

The first concern of successor elites was with ensuring their power and authority, that is, creating a local functioning state machine along with ensuring that the population took the regime to be legitimate: in brief, a mobilized polity-in-the-making. Much of this could be taken to be domestic, in the sense that the tasks of state making and so on were the immediate local concern of the elites, but this would not be correct, for players in the region had multiple overlapping agendas and so the activities of regional neighbours were important; states were not isolated units.

Domestic agendas

At the end of the Pacific War the East Asian region was in a difficult situation: war damage, population displacement, interruption of economic, social and political order. Various groups contended for influence. The militarily victorious allies sought to organize the area in line with their interests: the Americans sought security in regard to Japan and trade within the wider region, including China, whilst the Europeans sought the return if possible of their colonial empires. And local nationalist elites including communists sought independence from foreign rule. This was their first concern. If they could organize support amongst the population and secure a territory, then they could pursue state building, nation building and economic development.

So, as colonial empires dissolved away the first order of business was to secure a clear territory, the basis of a modern state, the key to all further developments. It meant that leaders in Asia were concerned with drawing borders and separating themselves out into distinct states; they were concerned with differentiation and the populations that they controlled became their citizens. However, as with Europe after the Great War, creating boundaries for citizens of putative nations also

TABLE 10.1 East Asia – states[1]

People's Republic of China (China)
Republic of China (Taiwan)
Democratic Republic of Korea (North Korea)
Republic of Korea (South Korea)
Japan
Socialist Republic of Vietnam (Vietnam)
Lao People's Democratic Republic (Laos)
Kingdom of Cambodia (Cambodia)
Kingdom of Thailand (Thailand)
Malaysia
Republic of Singapore (Singapore)
Republic of Union of Myanmar (Myanmar)
Republic of Indonesia (Indonesia)
Nation of Brunei, Abode of Peace (Brunei)
Democratic Republic of Timor-Leste (East Timor)

Note
1 In this text these countries will be taken to constitute the broad region of 'East Asia'. The official name in English is given followed by the more familiar name in parentheses. The idea of 'regions' offers one way of thinking about the histories of these peoples but it is not an unproblematic term; for discussion of the nature of 'regions' and the nature of 'East Asia' see – as a first move – M. Beeson and R. Stubbs, eds., 2011, *Routledge Handbook of Asian Regionalism*, London, Routledge.

had the effect of creating minorities and some future problems become bound in during the initial phase of state making. That said, it was only when they had secure states could they think about domestic advance and regional relations and maybe cooperation.

Regional institutions

As with any other state elite, the elites of the countries in East Asia had to read and react to changing circumstances, and domestic agendas were their main concern, another their relations with neighbouring states. In the early years of post-colonial Southeast Asia there were disputes about the borders between Indonesia and Malaysia, related questions about borders drawn in the island of Borneo – here the Philippines government has intermittently laid claim to parts of Sabah, those adjacent local island chains, on the basis of the existence of the pre-modern Sulu Sultanate, which had embraced this territory. And the border between the northern states of Malaysia and the southern states of Thailand was also an issue. Historically, it has been changed a number of times, most recently when the British moved their colonial border northwards. It remains an issue down to the present day, with the four Southern Thai ethnically distinct regions troubled by intermittent violence, with a suspicion that some of the actors have links across the border.

In other parts of the region there have been similar problems of demarcating borders. China ran campaigns shortly after 1949 to re-establish borders in Tibet and in the north to demarcate borders in Xinjiang and with the USSR. Japan and South Korea have a disputed maritime border. Japan has claims on the four Northern Islands presently held by Russia. Japan and China have a dispute over sovereignty of the Senkaku-Diaoyu Islands and further south, and more recently, China has laid claim to a huge swathe of the South China Sea, unequivocally encroaching at one point on the exclusive economic zone of the Philippines.

One aspect of this issue has been the construction of regional organizations. Some early organizations were sponsored by the USA and were concerned with security and military questions, for example, SEATO; or in similar vein the Five Powers Agreement; or there were networks of bi-lateral agreements such as USA/Japan Security Agreement or USA/South Korea Security Agreement or USA/Taiwan Security Agreement. There were other alliances between the USSR and PRC, and the PRC and North Korea. Such arrangements proliferated in the Cold War period because governments were preoccupied with geo-strategy.

After the end of the Cold War, both in Europe (where the ending was quite clear, 1989–91) and in East Asia (where the ending was more of a phase-out with outstanding issues put on one side, thus Korea, thus Taiwan and so on), countries began to focus more on geo-economics, that is, patterns of trade and investment, rather than the distribution of weapons systems. In East Asia, as the countries of the region became prosperous, elite concerns shifted towards economics, that is, trade and investment. A newer set of regional institutions became important – most are officially focused on economic issues but some commentators think that they have proved most successful in the political sphere.

Regional bodies: ASEAN Plus Three – ASEAN Regional Forum (ARF)

There are numerous regional bodies, they have different specified tasks, mostly focused on trade, and they have different records of success or failure.

ASEAN is the longest established regional body in East/Southeast Asia and in addition to its internal consultations it now seeks to engage with other countries. While it has often been criticized for its ineffectiveness it has nevertheless survived for over thirty years and has helped the countries of the region solidify their identities and positions within their region and wider global system. It has produced several offspring. More positively Amitav Acharya argues that with the end of colonial divisions a newly reintegrated Southeast Asia is in process of formation around the organization ASEAN.

TABLE 10.2 ASEAN membership, 1967–99

1967	Malaysia, Indonesia, Thailand, Philippines, Singapore
1984	Brunei
1995	Vietnam
1997	Laos and Myanmar
1999	Cambodia

APEC (Asia-Pacific Economic Cooperation) began in 1989 and links the countries of the Pacific Rim. APEC adds Australia to the core East Asian countries. It seeks to foster trade and dialogue and has a secretariat to coordinate activity, but has no legally binding agreements. It has been criticized for not achieving very much.

There have been other proposals at one time or another. Thus Dr Mahathir of Malaysia proposed a regional body EAEC (East Asia Economic Caucus), which would have excluded Australia, New Zealand and the USA, but the idea was watered down and the proposed grouping was subsumed in APEC. Then ASEM (Asia–Europe Meeting) began in 1996 linking the East Asian countries with the European Union. It too seeks to foster trade and dialogue but it has been criticized as merely a talking shop.

There have been more recent proposals. President Obama pressed for the creation of a trans-Pacific trading area (TPP, Trans-Pacific Partnership), arguing that it would allow the USA to set the rules of trade. It did not include China. Unsurprisingly an alternative proposal came from China for a Free Trade Area of the Asia Pacific (FTAAP) and then, most dramatically, in 2017, President Xi Jinping held a conference to launch the idea of a new Silk Road, tagged 'One belt, one road' (OBOR). Later President Trump pulled the USA out of the TPP, seemingly leaving the next moves in region-making diplomacy to Beijing.

The point of all this politico-economic manoeuvring revolves around the business of setting global or regional rules for trading, because, commentators assert, setting the rules will favour some but not others, and so within the context of a broad regional trade arrangement being the rule-setter is preferable to being the rule-taker.

International relations in a changing regional setting

The changing relationship between parts of the global system can be illustrated with a simple map: a global map drawn with three circles, representing East Asia, the USA and Europe. In 1945 the USA is the largest circle with approximately 50 per cent global output; in 2000 all three circles have grown much bigger but now the three circles are more or less the same relative size; and moving forwards to 2010, East Asia has grown larger, whilst the USA and Europe have become slightly smaller.

By the late 1980s East Asia had emerged as an economically powerful region; its record was considered, its character debated and numerous lines of analysis were proposed.

Amongst the more familiar were these:

- East Asia had got the market prices right (the liberal market line);
- East Asia had adopted mercantilist policies (sceptical liberal line);
- East Asia had used wisely the developmental state (the statist line);
- East Asian culture was the key (culturalist line celebrations of Confucianism);
- the US role was crucial (the US hegemonic power line);
- the impact of the Second World War was crucial (historical shocks line);

- then, after the 1997 crisis, reasons for success were inverted, failure was a result of corrupt elite networks (the crony capitalism line).

There were also debates about Asian Values, the Asian Financial Crisis and the East Asian Region. All these debates had in common that they addressed an important preoccupation: it was clear that something special was happening in East Asia and political actors, policy makers and scholars wished to understand, the better to inform their decisions, policy and scholarship.

In all these debates many lines of argument presented the East Asian experience as a variation of the historical experience of the West (thus East Asia was joining in and catching up); in this vein one line suggested that nothing special was happening (East Asia was simply experiencing rural to urban migration and this showed in the data but didn't amount to anything special); but other lines of argument stressed that something novel had happened in East Asia (thus East Asia was joining in but it was not catching up because it was following its own trajectory). In this text it has been argued that East Asia has been making its own trajectory as it joins the unfolding shift to the modern world in a process of continual adjustment and readjustment to enfolding structural circumstances. The whole business is contingent. Thus success and progress are not guaranteed. The optimistic claims of modernization/globalization theory are false; trajectories can falter and fail as with, say, the USSR in the last decade of the last century, or Thailand post-coup, no longer a rising tiger, or the European Union in the recent post-financial crisis years of the early twenty-first century.

Today, towards the end of the second decade of the twenty-first century in East Asia, there are three key players: USA, Japan and the China. The European Union, as noted, is a significant global economic power but its presence in East Asia is low key, notwithstanding historical links and the rather more superficial connections afforded by ASEM. There are also significant secondary players in the Tiger economy countries and ASEAN countries. There are distinctive contemporary issues: legacies of decolonization, legacies of Cold War, the effects of decades of economic success upon patterns of relationships within the region and between the region and the wider global system, and most recently there have been changes in country interactions following the end of the Cold War.

1 The USA – key power, perhaps in relative decline

Bruce Cummings has argued that the USA was involved from the nineteenth century with the slow shift to the modern world in East Asia – traders, missionaries and adventurers travelled to Japan, China and the Philippines. Americans were also active throughout the wider region. Thus, for example, the American promulgation of the doctrine of the 'Open Door' affirming that all foreign powers could trade equally with China. Or, in more detail, one reason for the success of modern Singapore was the development of the tin and rubber trades – serving US canning and automobile industries. However, America's position in East Asia was – like that of the Europeans – overturned by the events of the Pacific War: at first, total exclusion, as Imperial Japanese forces overran the area; then, during the war years significant changes, with rights in China formally relinquished, the UN established, with its institutional commitments to human rights (and thus opposition to notions of colonial authority); and then, with the end of the war, the rapid shift into Cold War thinking. The Pacific War and related Cold War saw East Asia divided, with one bloc focused on the USA and the other on China.

At the end of the war the USA was the strongest military, economic and diplomatic power in the region. The USA sought to resist what it took to be an expansionist communism and lent support – material and political – to a range of allies throughout the region: Japan (reworked from enemy to ally in a few years), South Korea (with its imposed right-wing nationalist leader), Taiwan (protected from the CCP by US military), Philippines (reoccupied and made safe for US interests), Thailand (drawn into the US sphere), Indonesia (after the 1965 coup) and then, at a distance, parts of a hitherto UK-focused network, Malaysia, Singapore, Australia and New Zealand.

At this time, China and North Korea withdrew into variant forms of autarchic state socialism ordered around party-state systems. Communist parties were active in parts of Southeast Asia, along with local peasant movements and similar popular nationalist groupings. All were read negatively by the USA. The Cold War saw two major wars and both pitted forces marshalled by the USA against local forces backed by China and the USSR: Korea and Vietnam. These two wars were catastrophically destructive for the people of the countries – Korea was laid waste, so too large areas of Vietnam and the adjacent countries of Laos and Cambodia. The Cold War also saw a number of other conflicts, which were read, by the Americans, and their allies, in Cold War terms: in the Philippines (Huk Rebellion 1945–54), in Malaya (Malayan Emergency 1948–60), in Singapore (Operation Cold Store 1963), in Indonesia (1965 Coup), in Thailand (multiple military coups), in South Korea (Gwangju Massacre 1980); plus in these decades the more routine repression of opponents in many of these countries. Matters were not any easier for ordinary people in China or North Korea where state-party systems in pursuit of state making, national building and development were not averse to either utopian experiments or harsh repression of domestic critics.

However, all that said, the late twentieth and early twenty-first century has seen significant changes in the overall posture of the USA – economic, political, cultural and military changes have swept through the region – changes occasioned by developmental success in East Asia – in significant measure these follow from benign economic policies adopted by the USA (allowing allies access to markets and technology) – they also flow from the post-1978 policy changes adopted in China, which have made that country the key player in East Asia.

For US policy makers the key issues include:

- strategic – how to update policy and reconfigure alliances and forces in order to meet the challenge of the rising power of China – this was pursued in regional trade terms by President Obama whilst his successor President Trump has been rather more aggressive and direct in his public statements;

- strategic/military – how to manage problems in North Asia – the Korean peninsular continues to be a site of tension – America is the military guarantor of allies in the region – there are a number of players – North Korea's disruptive quasi-military posturing – China's anxieties in regard to the actions of a socialist ally and unreliable neighbour – South Korea's anxieties about its northern neighbour and the role of the USA – Japan's anxieties about its neighbours and the role of the USA – Russia's unease about the demographics of its easterly territories in an apparently unstable area;
- diplomatic – how to manage the on-going Taiwan issue in context of relations with China;
- security – how to contain radical Islamist networks in Southeast Asia;
- generally – how to accommodate the evident rise of East Asia in general and China in particular.

2 The case of Japan – an economic power

In the years following the Pacific War, Japan was drawn into the American sphere. The 1951 peace and security treaties bound Japan to America.

Within this framework, Japanese policy makers set out to reconstruct the nation's economy – this they did. By the early 1980s America was voicing worries about trade imbalances, whilst scholars were following Chalmers Johnson and theorizing the developmental state. The economic recovery was spectacular and – as a consequence of the 1985 Plaza Accords, which addressed the issue of the US trade deficit by revaluing the yen – Japanese firms had the funds and motivation to disperse investments throughout the region – aid, trade and foreign direct investment reinforced each other – these activities constituted one starting point of a process that has in time given rise to discussion of an East Asian region, one distinct from North America or Europe.

The military alliance had a Cold War rationale – taking shape during the Korean War – and being sustained down the subsequent decades. In the later years of the twentieth century the USA was concerned to encourage the Japanese to raise their military profile within the region, a contentious strategy both within Japan and the wider region. In the early twenty-first century matters have become more complex: the rise of China, economically, militarily and diplomatically, have made the calculations of Japanese policy makers that much more complicated.

Domestically, Japanese pubic opinion is divided: there is strong peace movement, centred on memories of the atomic bombing of Hiroshima and Nagasaki; there is a conservative nationalist movement that rejects the Peace Constitution and looks to a more assertive international stance, with Yaskukuni Shrine playing a totemic role; there are internal division informed by ethnicity – thus the bulk of American bases are in the southern islands but in Okinawa locals distinguish themselves from main-island Japanese and resent the presence of the bases – and in Japan there is a resident population of Korean heritage, some supportive of North Korea, thereby sustaining both colonial and Cold War tensions within the domestic population.

Such domestic problems find wider Northeast Asian resonances – governments in the region formally resent the Japanese nationalists' activities, suggesting, repeatedly, that the Japanese government should either apologize sincerely and/or pay reparations, whilst finding an external enemy convenient for domestic political purposes.

The key issues for policy makers include:

- security/diplomacy – whether/how to revise the peace constitution;
- military/technical – how to respond to China's military build up;
- strategic – whether or not to go nuclear (urgent given the actions of DPRK);
- diplomatic/economic – how to manage changing relationships with PRC;
- diplomatic/economic – how to develop relationships with USA;
- social/economic – how to deal with a declining domestic population;
- thereafter, how to sustain present links with the wider East Asia region.

3 The People's Republic of China

The People's Republic of China was formed in the context of civil war. The USA had supported the KMT and factions within Washington spoke of the loss of China. In 1950 China supported the North Korean government and their troops fought against the USA. The situation stabilized after 1953 into a Cold War pattern. The Chinese government's pursuit of an autarchic state socialism meant a low international profile with an alliance with the Soviet Union 1950–58. The link was broken and rapprochement with USA organized. President Nixon's visit in 1972 gave rise to a period of triangular diplomacy. In 1978 Deng began the process of reform in China and the country slowly became more engaged with the international community, that is stability and growth domestically meant that country became more of a player in global politics. The 1989 Tiananmen Square incident damaged this process; thereafter there was slow recovery and further economic advance, in time resumption of diplomatic linkages. The late 1990s and early twenty-first century have seen further economic and political integration within global system. The Beijing 2008 Olympics was read by many commentators as the announcement of the arrival of China as a great power in the making.

Having ended the period of sustained violence in the country with the establishment of the People's Republic of China, the government turned towards an essential autarchic development strategy, albeit assisted for a period by the USSR. A decision for reforms was taken in the late 1970s and change has run through the country. This included opening up to the global system. Today, in the early twenty-first century, the country continues to integrate into the international community. Matters are not straightforward; the situation it faces includes a number of elements. First, relations with USA are uneasy: there is much trade and much mistrust – trade volumes are not in balance – financial flows are problematical – US arms budget is huge – PRC arms budget is much smaller but growing. Second, relations with Japan are awkward – competition for role in East Asian political networks – direct competition over seabed oil resources – the issue of war/memory routinely emerges (Japanese nationalists plus convenience to PRC government playing nationalist card domestically). Third, relations with EU are good – trade – no diplomatic/military anxieties or tensions. Fourth, regional problems – managing relations with Taiwan – much trade plus measured nationalist bluster – a distinctive ritual diplomatic status competition. And fifth, China has growing links with ASEAN and problems of accessing oil in South China Sea now seen as resolvable – issue of Chinese settled in region is sometimes awkward.

The key issues for Beijing policy makers include:

- economic – domestic reforms – shift from investment led to consumption led growth – supplemented by deeper international links (OBOR);
- economic/social – reign in the corruption consequent upon earlier phase of reform and opening;
- economic/social – bring pollution problems under control;
- security – continue the process of upgrading and reorienting the military (from a focus on domestic security and development to a more conventional international war fighting stance);
- security/diplomacy – manage relations with Taiwan;
- security/diplomacy – manage relations with Japan;
- security/diplomacy – manage relations with USA;
- security – manage North Korea;
- economic/diplomatic – continue to deepen links with global south;
- general – continue to raise the profile of the country on the global stage.

4 Tiger economies: Taiwan, South Korea and Southeast Asia

Taiwan's route to the modern world has been via the experience of colonial rule by Japan – the territory was removed from Qing control as a result of the 1894/95 Sino-Japanese War – the Japanese developed Taiwan as a subordinate economic element of a Japan-centred empire – but as with other Japanese holdings outside the home islands, Taiwan was removed from Tokyo's control – instead power was inherited by the ROC – at the end of the Chinese Civil War the defeated KMT forces retreated to the island and in alliance with the USA established their own – dictatorial – regime. The island prospered economically and with the death of Chaing Kai Shek began a process of political reform, creating in time, variant forms of liberal democratic institutions, along with an underpinning provided by a growing sense of Taiwanese identity (as distinct from simply Chinese).

For Taiwanese policy makers there are several issues to be faced:

- economic – sustain economic growth;
- economic/security – manage deepening economic links with the mainland;
- security/military – manage Chinese military expansion;
- security/military – sustain security links with USA.

South Korea is in a somewhat similar situation – the territory was drawn into the modern world via the experience of Japanese colonial rule, sustained from 1911 to 1945, and thus having considerable impacts on economic and social developments. The end of the Pacific War saw the Japanese withdraw and a locally led government was disregarded by the outside powers, which went on to divide the country along the 38th parallel. A civil war fixed the division in place. South Korea, in time, prospered with a series of dictatorships backed by the USA. Political reforms were undertaken in the late twentieth century and the country now has a variant form of liberal democratic government along with Korean tradition-inflected social and cultural modernity.

Policy issues faced by South Korean government are:

- economic/domestic – sustain record of success;
- economic/international – sustain record of success;
- security/domestic – manage relations with North Korea;
- security/military – sustain links with USA;
- generally/socially – deepen the countries economic, social and political development.

Finally, turning to Southeast Asia, where the region is ordered via the organization ASEAN – the organization has been sustained for some forty-odd years – often criticized as a talking shop it has provided a framework for regional countries to order their exchanges – it has also allowed wider discussions involving countries in East Asia. The association now has ten members – as noted – but they are not all of a piece – the earlier members have relatively sophisticated economies and have developed a wide network of economic, social and diplomatic networks within the global system. In the case of the trio of later Indo-China members, this is not the case: they are poor, not well integrated in the global system and have China as a northern neighbour; Laos and Cambodia are economically and diplomatically closely linked to China. The other late joiner, Myanmar, faces analogous problems – it is poor and ethnically divided.

ASEAN members face internal policy issues:

- economic/developmental – discussions over economic development plans;
- social/developmental – minorities within countries – differing situations and problems;
- social/security – minorities in border areas – refugees;
- security – local radical Islamist groups;
- security/economic – illegal migrant workers;
- economic/environmental – haze;
- governance – reforming the machinery of ASEAN;
- diplomatic – ASEAN has sought to assist regional diplomacy.
- generally – the organization continues to be active, to make links with other countries and to serve its members.

The East Asia region is broadly prosperous. The elites of the various countries – the ASEAN ten plus China, Taiwan, North Korea, South Korea, Russia and Japan – have variously pursued national development. There are many differences in the circumstances of the countries of the region and within the region there is much work for diplomats and this is true of external linkages. What is perhaps most noticeable about the region is its lack of any formal overarching institutional apparatus. The end of foreign state-empires prompted a successor elite concern for differentiation and this preference seems to remain in place. It might be that in the future problems will only be solved piecemeal, but the elites of East Asia are mostly in the happy position of being able to address problems from within generally prosperous and stable countries located within a generally prosperous and stable region.

The shift to the modern world in East Asia: success debated

Before the slow rise of the modern world of industrial capitalism East Asia was the centre of the global economy; it was rich and powerful with Europe and America peripheral and unimportant. But European and American agents slowly joined in existing East Asian systems of social production and these systems were slowly remade. East Asia became a subordinate periphery in the modern industrial capitalist system. Then the general crisis 1911–75 saw extensive dislocation. The system of empires ended bit by bit with the establishment of regimes dedicated to national development. A crucial element of this process was the Pacific War; it destroyed the European and American empires. The industrial capitalist system in East Asia was reconfigured as local elites took political power and sought a better position or niche within the global industrial capitalist system. They sought this via projects of national development and the institutional mechanism for the political and economic project was the developmental state.

Looking at the post-1945 record it is clear that each elite-ordered trajectory reveals a specific mix of global, regional and local political and economic factors. Local actors have used the developmental state to pursue their own distinctive projects. For the region as a whole success runs through a sequence: Japan, Tigers, Southeast Asia and China. It is true that success is the major part of the story but there are two other elements: continuing underdevelopment in much of Southeast Asia and inland China; and throughout the region a growing environmental catastrophe.

The success has been debated: scholars sought to understand the reasons for the success; policy analysts wondered what procedures might be replicable elsewhere; and political actors sought to grasp the implications of shifting patterns of political and economic power. All agreed that the record in East Asia was remarkable and much debate revolved around the nature of the developmental state. The debate was opened up again with the related issue of East Asian region. And debates shifted again with the Beijing 2008 Olympics; China announced its arrival as a potential great power in the making.

The East Asian region

Early talk about the East Asian region was inspired by the post-war record of Japan, its invention of the developmental state and the copying of the model around East Asia. The debate opened up in the 1980s as the issue of trade deficits became acute and the debate stalled somewhat in the late 1990s following the 1997 Asian financial crisis. Today, in the second decade of the twenty-first century, talk of the region has shifted its central focus. China is rapidly becoming an important regional player but the process is not without severe difficulties: relations with Japan are poor, links with Taiwan problematical, relations with ASEAN countries coloured by aggressive expansion in the disputed South China Sea, and the country has one key foreign power to consider, the USA.

There is a clear distinction to be drawn between regionalization in East Asia and the same processes in North America and Europe, and these contrasts are a product of different historical trajectories.

In Europe, the long crisis of the dissolution of state-empires that assumed its most acute form in the wars of the period 1914–45 issued in an elite-level commitment to unification – in part pragmatic (the economic costs of the damage), in part moral (revulsion at the loss of life and related trauma) and in part partly obligatory (the opinions of the USA weighed heavily as Europe reconstructed) – institutional machineries embracing the continent were constructed (their history is complex, coloured by national concerns and overarching Cold War) – but they begin with heavy industry and have developed since then in an ever more complex series of layers of essentially economic cooperation.

In North America, an analogous process had led to the nineteenth-century unification of the USA through local and domestic wars, assorted land purchases and overseas colonial expansion. Americans created a federal system embracing weaker member states. In the twentieth century, during the neo-liberal era, further machineries had drawn in neighbours to the north and south via the organization of NAFTA.

However, in East Asia, the collapse of European and American state-empire systems during the wars of the early part of the twentieth century had left a legacy of a multiplicity of new states concerned to create nations and pursue development. One aspect of this historical process was the elite concern for differentiation, for drawing up clear borders and creating within them coherent nations thereafter ordered by sovereign states. This entails separating themselves from neighbours, thus there were no overarching institutional machineries and the key organization of the region has been ASEAN, famously proceeding by consensus amongst sovereign states.

All that said, as the East Asian region has prospered and regional networks centred on trade have been developed; these important linkages have been acknowledged in a number of institutional structures – ASEAN – ASEAN Plus Three – EAEC – EAS. However, East Asia has not developed any of the supra-national machineries that typify the European Union and nor, evidently, does it have the integration found in the federal system of the United States. It might also be noted that the region is burdened by both inherited and novel tensions, including the legacies of the wars of the early part of the twentieth century, the confusions of the era of decolonization and, recently, the impacts on neighbours of the revisionism of a rising China, in particular, the grab for territory in the South China Sea – issues underscored by ambiguities in the OBOR plan.

And there may be further problems on the more distant horizon. The second decade of the twenty-first century has seen a number of popular rebellions in rich countries and they seem to have a common theme, that is, a rejection by large sections of the population in rich countries of neo-liberal globalization. There are signs of similar doubts amongst East Asian middle classes in respect the costs of growth, in particular pollution and corruption (thus China, thus, recently, South Korea).

The 2008 Beijing Olympics and the rise of China

The historical development trajectory of China was different from its regional neighbours. The revolution of 1911 was in part an early exercise in progressive resistance to the demands of foreign state-empires. The revolutionaries looked to create a modern China but the experiment failed and in place of the hoped for republic the country dissolved into warlordism. Two progressive parties formed – KMT and CCP – and for a period they cooperated until late in the 1920s a civil war began. This was to run on until 1949. It was not until the civil war was resolved that the country was free of foreigners and united under one government, but re-establishing a single state was not simple and was accompanied with significant domestic violence and, thereafter, the new CCP government began its programme of building a socialist society.

Mao Zedong and the CCP mobilized the country. They began from a very low material base: few resources, cities ruined by war, society divided by the recent civil war, and from this low base they sought to build an egalitarian society. The record in the early years was good with reconstruction and growth; however, there were elite-level disagreements about policy, roughly, socialist reform versus pragmatic economic growth. The balance between these contending factions was not stable. The Cultural Revolution was one expression of these debates, but in this case the debate ran out of control and a destructive decade of political struggle ensued, which was only brought to a halt when the proponents of Cultural Revolution turned their attention to the PLA. The military was the backbone of the state and so at this point the CCP called a halt; shortly thereafter in 1976 Mao died. His nominated successor led the party and state for a short period before being side-lined and removed by Deng Xiao Ping. A pragmatic policy of economic reform was begun, tentative at first but more enthusiastically embraced later which led to the transformation of the economy and society. The state socialist economy and society was remodelled and a new variant form of the developmental state was embraced; the state was central but commercial markets played an ever-larger role.

Deng's reforms included establishing a number of export processing zones. Here available stocks of labour could be mixed with foreign capital and expertise to create export-oriented manufacturing, plus associated technology transfer, plus associated capital accumulation. A virtuous circle was established, as foreign funds and expertise were married with local labour and the economies of those regions designated as Special Economic Zones (SEZs) grew rapidly. An early success was Shenzhen in Southern China as funds and expertise from Hong Kong moved over the border and helped turn a village into the southern city of a metropolis reaching along the banks of the Pearl River.

The reforms inaugurated by Deng generated rapid economic growth plus a host of problems, including corruption, pollution and inequality; that said, China became a major exporter of industrial goods. The profile of these goods slowly changed as they became more technically sophisticated and moved up the value-added chain. By the turn of the twenty-first century, China was clearly what international relations scholars in America dubbed a rising power. The 2008 Olympics were something of a diplomatic coming-out party as they announced the arrival of China on the regional and global stage.

Moving forwards: the second decade of the twenty-first century

In Europe and the USA the costs of free trade and migration have been topics of debate along with evidence of a more vocal nationalism. Any rejection of neo-liberal globalization would have implications for the countries of East Asia via a new set of problems. It might be that these debates would impact policy, that is, popular pressure might force elite action. Any pressure on trade deficits, that is, moves to curb East Asian exports, in particular those from China, would have an impact on local economies – however, any pressure on migration might have a slight local impact as neither Europe nor the USA have major inflows from East Asia – though there may be some local impacts, thus possible curbs on Chinese in the American and Canadian West Coast, or curbs on overseas working of expatriates from the Philippines.

Any restrictions on trade might have further impacts. It could impact defence spending. There is something of a regional arms race underway as countries upgrade their military forces in response to the upgrades and reconfigurations of the PLA (from domestic control to high-tech war fighting). Should trade restrictions impact local economies it is possible that local nationalisms could be encouraged and here, of course, there are both available flash points and long-nurtured historical grievances. East Asia does have the sort of problems that can, if elites are unlucky or stupid, lead to violence; once recourse has been made to force it is easy to make further turns of the screw, but, against that, it is clear that the region as a whole has prospered over the last thirty years and why would any rational leader want to risk that?

11

GLOBALIZATION, THE END OF HISTORY AND THE DEBATE ABOUT REGIONS

The 1990s and early part of the twenty-first century saw extensive debates about the idea of globalization. Proponents celebrated what they took to be an inevitable economic and social process. Opponents decried what they took to be hubristic American nationalism. These debates also turned to the case of East Asia and the ideas were deployed to read the present circumstances and likely future directions of the area. Politics, policy and scholarly commentary were interlinked as formal organizations were established to foster globalization. Other organizations were established in opposition, to foster regionalization. All these debates took one thing for granted, that is, the pre-eminence of the USA – an assumption that has come to look ever more unsustainable; not merely as a result of domestic problems in the USA (and amongst its close allies), but also because of the continuing success of East Asia along with the seemingly inevitable rise of China.

Argument in social theory is centrally interpretive and critical, and this implies that it is concerned with contingent circumstances, tracking and elucidating shifting patterns of change. It is also concerned with its own location within those processes, which it claims to elucidate. It is reflexive and in practice it is often dialogic so that enquiry becomes part of a conversation with those whose forms of life have become for whatever reason a focus of scholarly reflection.

However, not all social theorizing evidences these traits for positivistic work, that is, exercises in argument making that borrow from the received model of the natural sciences, takes the social location of the theorist to be either unimportant (the business is about the accurate description of the given facts and this is in principle straightforward) or where the possibility of interpretive pollution of reliable description is suspected, as amenable to procedural controls (purging biases and remaining objective). So far as those working within and with reference to the classical European tradition are concerned, positivistic work is unsatisfactory. It can fail for a variety of reasons. The most obvious is that substantive ideas and opinions running within the society in which the theorist is located can be introduced without scrutiny into work that otherwise claims to be accurate description of how things are in fact. Thus it can be asserted that a necessary condition of scholarship is reflexive self-embedding, that is, the theorist has a double task both of grasping the substantive problem at issue and reflexively checking the argument machineries that carry the analysis, for if the latter is skimped or omitted altogether, then the result is misanalysis, or, more familiarly, the production of ideologically skewed material.

It is often very difficult for a theorist to spot the assumptions underlying his or her work, as ideological ideas work best when they work behind the backs of the subjects, hence the notion of hegemony. Where work is un-self-critical, bias may be suspected and the arguments investigated. One way of uncovering such unconscious bias is to contextualize the work in question so as to see how it fits into a given society, asking whether it investigates or merely reflects currently taken for granted ideas. An analogous strategy involves constructing a timeline to show how theoretical machineries can be adjusted to shifting common opinions, or recycled in newish contexts: once again a source of unsatisfactory argument.

Modernization theory in the 1950s ('first time as tragedy')

In the 1950s American pre-eminence was celebrated with a collection of interrelated social scientific ideas: for the First and Second World, industrialism, convergence and the end of ideology; and for the Third World, modernization. The future was to be a species of America-centred liberal market systems. The ideas came as a package but they came in various forms; they were not a simple block of ideas. They were also recognizably a reworked expression of the nineteenth-century concerns of the classical European tradition, so change was at the core. Change was seen to have multiple aspects but, crucially, it was understood in evolutionist and teleological forms; that is, there was an evolutionary progression and the end point was known. In the jargon of one theorist, Walt Rostow, it was the age of high mass consumption; informally, it was the model of the USA in the late 1950s, the high tide of the post-war celebration of the American dream. The optimism was warranted, as the 1950s, in the West, were a period of rapid post-war growth and reconstruction. The early statements of modernization theory were optimistic and hence its failure, when it came, was regrettable.

The core driver of change in the modern world was taken to be the logic of industrialism. The role of natural science in underpinning production and innovation was celebrated. Natural science was placed at the core of the logic of industrialism, which, reasonably enough, was taken to be neutral as between competing ideologies of capitalism and socialism, for the same logic worked in both Cold War camps. Science informed technology, which in turn informed production, which in turn drove the social world forwards. This being so, a slow process of convergence could be expected between the two Cold War camps. The logic of industrial life would erase ideologically created differences in forms of life and the future would be industrial, innovative and planned, so, thereafter, there was confidence that it would indeed by very productive. The logic of industrialism pointed to growing material wealth and both Cold War territories would become materially wealthy; that being the case, finally, there would be little to argue about, and debates, such as they were, would revolve around the best technically informed policies oriented to sustaining productive outputs; ideology would wither away, hence the expectation of the end of ideology.

The core trio of ideas worked as a package: industrialism, convergence and the end of ideology; in brief, the idea of the industrial society. The theory was evolutionist and teleological, thus the end point was the model of the USA around the late 1950s and early 1960s. In this period America was not merely the richest and most powerful country in the global system, but it was also an object of admiration, a model to which many people (elites and masses) looked, in particular in Europe, where post-war financing had helped the continent recover (at least the western half). The core set of ideas produced a spin-off that could be put to use amongst the new nation-states created from the territories of dissolving state-empire systems. The derived idea, which was saleable to the successor elites, was the idea of modernization. This notion took the evolutionary and teleological package (of industrialism, convergence and end of ideology) and put it to work in the context of the poor sometime peripheral countries in the global system. Modernization theory – as it was known – drew a simple distinction between traditional and modern societies and proposed that the traits of the latter could be acquired in fairly quick time. At its most optimistic, it was claimed that poor countries could catch up and join in within twenty or so years; this was the process of modernization. It was an optimistic theory, produced by an optimistic elite that was generous to its allies in Western Europe, and in East Asia – thus Japan, Korea and Taiwan – along with a host of other countries scattered around the Third World.

In the event, circumstances intervened in the guise of war and finance, coupled to social distress at home. The American war in Southeast Asia went badly. It was a disaster for the people in the affected countries and it underscored problems within American society both in the form of an anti-war movement and with the Civil Rights Movement. And the costs of the war also became a problem. The finances of the American government became overstressed and the dollar, which had been the core currency of the post-1945 Bretton Woods system of fixed exchange rates, was allowed to float. Now the currency market would determine day by day the value of the dollar and the internal coherence of the hitherto coherently managed Western system began to weaken.

In the early 1970s familiar confidence in the American nature of the future collapsed. But, arguably, only for a little while as a series of changes were made. The Americans withdrew from Vietnam in 1973; the authorities discovered they could easily live with a floating dollar; reforms were made to domestic politics with the claims of the Civil Rights movement granted in principle; and internationally the administration of Jimmy Carter (1977–81) made attempts to recover lost ground by advancing the cause of human rights. Overall, it was a period of creative retrenchment.

A more aggressive reaffirmation of the model of the USA had to wait for a Republican president. President Ronald Reagan (1981–89) rekindled enthusiasm for the model of the USA with one slogan announcing that it was 'morning in America'; however, such public vacuities covered an aggressive policy agenda, which included successful interventions in Latin America, successful interventions in Central Asia, reforms encouraged in Central Europe and then the end of the Cold War bloc system and the subsequent collapse of the USSR. All these changes worked to usher in a period of unrestrained enthusiasm for liberal market systems – American-ness was now emphatically re-presented as a model for all states and societies.

Globalization and the end of history in the 1990s ('second time as farce')

Intellectually, amongst social scientists and other commentators, the enthusiasm of the period took two forms, the notion of globalization and the idea of the ethico-political end of history. Celebrants worked with ideas of liberal markets and liberal democracy, whilst sceptics doubted that either celebration made much sense, but their doubts were swept aside.

1 Globalization

In regard to globalization, where commentators pointed to deepening economic integration via trade as the basis for deeper social links and cultural convergence, theorists and commentators offered elaborate characterizations of the underlying process, its direction and the benefits that would ensue for all peoples. Globalization was also linked to ideas of the end of history and post-modernism. This intellectual fashion was not given to modesty. It emerged in the last decade of the twentieth century. At that time, following the end of the Cold War in Europe and the self-abolition of the USSR, some commentators spoke of a uni-polar system whilst others upgraded the USA from super-power to hyper-power. American commentators tended to be rather more direct; thus America won the Cold War.

The proponents of globalization included political theorists (Francis Fukuyama), business theorists (Kenichi Omae) and journalists (Thomas Friedman), and politicians (America's President Clinton, Britain's Tony Blair). Modest opponents of the idea spoke of internationalization and preferred to track detail of interlinkages (Paul Hirst and Grahame Thompson). More radical opponents suggested that globalization was mostly rhetoric designed to serve the political project of expanding the reach of a neo-liberal economic system centred on the USA and European Union (Wolfgang Streeck). And similarly, development theorists diagnosed recycled modernization theory designed to serve interests of the mostly Western global corporate sector (thus, anti-globalization activists).

The core of the globalization programme was radical market liberalization, which proposed that trade in finance should be unrestricted, trade in goods should be unrestricted, trade in services should be unrestricted and movement of people should be accepted, welcomed and facilitated, for in this way collective benefits would be maximized. If the arguments are taken at face value, then the core of the model of humankind affirmed is that of a rational maximizer (or 'rational economic man') and the focus of this agent is taken to be on the maximization of material benefits – more stuff is better than less stuff. Proponents of this stance were happy to dismiss a series of long-standing debates; a number of issues are set aside: (1) the nature of the rationality thus affirmed is set aside (instrumental means/end affirmed with all other forms of reasoning subordinated to it or disregarded, thus, arts, humanities, social, pragmatic and so on); (2) the ethic affirmed that 'greed is good' set aside all familiar Western ethics; and (3) the nature/costs of the stuff to be accumulated (advertising/pollution) were disregarded (matters of individual choice and anti-capitalist over-reaction or outright scientific fraud).

Many agents took these claims at face value (or claimed to) but they can be read as the claims of special interest groups, in particular, the denizens of the world of finance. A global market liberal system offers maximum opportunities for moving money around the planet – profit seeking, disregarding all other considerations – the justification, as before, is that the magic of the marketplace will ensure that all peoples benefit to the maximum.

Globalization theory and the neo-liberal view of the world that underpinned it was enthusiastically promulgated during the 1990s and the early years of the twenty-first century; it offered an easy and non-critical explanation for the pre-eminence of the USA. However, in the USA critics noted the arrival of a new 'gilded age' embracing the one per cent of the population who accrued great wealth, whilst others noted the vast accumulation of debt amongst the population in general. When doubts about its sustainability were voiced, elites disregarded them and mainstream economists invoked the 'rational market theory', which explained the market was both resilient and efficient and so there were no problems.

Then in 2008–10 the system collapsed. Problems in the sub-prime mortgage market, where salesmen had given loans to borrowers they knew could not service the debts, erupted and brought down the entire house of cards; thus globalization theory's most enthusiastic proponents, that is, the worlds of finance, proved to be corrupt and incompetent. The financial system centred on Wall Street and the City of London came to the edge of collapse and the banks were then bailed out by the state: Washington inaugurated the TARP (helping the banks unwind the mass of bad debts that they had on their books) and in London the state simply nationalized key banks (and their bad debts became the tax-payers' bad debts). At the time European commentators looked on with feigned sympathy; it was the Anglo-Saxon model of financial capitalism that had proved fragile, but a little later it became clear that key banks in Germany, France and elsewhere in the European Union were just as overexposed to bad debts. In Europe the manner of their rescue was somewhat different, involving a mix of state action, ECB intervention and the inauguration of a policy of austerity. European critics point out that as in the Anglo-Saxon debacle, the public is being asked to foot the bill for the errors of the banks.

Globalization theory was a rehash of modernization theory. The parallels are clear:

- the 1990s were like the 1950s in that domestic confidence in America was at a peak, because in the 1950s the USA had no economic or political equals (the USSR was recovering from 26 million dead during the Second World War, Europe was ruined and so too East Asia) and then in the 1990s the surprising 1989–91 end of the Cold War in Europe coupled to the economic impacts of financialization powered optimism in regard to the American model;
- in the 1990s as in the 1950s a theory was assembled, which offered an abstract-general characterization of the USA at that time as a model of the functioning of the system and a goal to which all could aspire;
- in the 1990s as in the 1950s the theory ignored the domestic problems of that country (in particular inequality, race divisions and poverty); and
- like modernization theory, globalization theory made claims not merely in regard to the sphere of the social production of livelihood (or, 'the economy') but also in respect of the wider social world.

The fatal parallels are also clear:

- the country became involved in an overseas war that was unwinnable, costly in terms of lives and materiel and evidently hugely costly to the denizens of the countries attacked;
- the state found itself overburdened by costs and, this time around, partly the enormous costs of the machinery of war but also those associated with rescuing a failed financial system.

However, all that said, globalization theory was only one of two influential theories, and where globalization offered the planet a model of economic and social life, exemplified by America, the second theory offered that same country as not merely a political model but in practice the only plausible model available.

2 The end of history

Francis Fukuyama published an influential text in the 1990s, which celebrated liberal democracy as the ethico-political end of history; that is to say, the system represented a peak of human achievement, which, by implication, could not be surpassed. This was the model of the USA represented as a historical achievement of unparalleled scope.

Fukuyama argued that the system of liberal markets and the related politics of liberal democracy constituted a system that effectively met the needs of liberal mankind and – by implication – was without significant flaws so that all systems of social ethics were likely to converge upon this one model. There could be no better way of grasping the fundamental nature of humankind and so politico-moral progress had therefore reached an apogee in neo-liberal America.

The argument garnered much attention: some of it simply misunderstood, taking the author to have argued that history itself had stopped, and some of the attention was positive, proponents of globalization theory were content to be reassured that their politics and ethics were of a historically superior kind. However, on the other hand, critics suggested the proponents of the thesis were simply deluded and the model was merely an abstract-general version of the contemporary USA, an unreflexive nationalism. There was no reason to offer this as universal model, for American nationalism with its mix of John Locke, Protestantism and unreflexive hubris (the city on a hill) was a quite particular historical construction. It was no more general or generalizable than any other nationalism. And, more prosaically, it was perfectly clear that the USA had many domestic problems; and nor was the country likely to stay unchanged, as natural science and global system together were innovative and restless, modernity unfolding.

3 Post-modernism and neo-conservatism

It might be noted that two other ideas made their appearance around this time, spin-offs of the core ideas of globalization and the end of history. The first, post-modernism, popular amongst some scholars and cultural analysts, posited the end of system-occasioned social repression and its replacement by system-facilitated seduction, the putative overweening power of consumption. One critic dismissively called it the disappointed consciousness of left-wing American intellectuals. The second, popular amongst sections of elite-linked commentators, was neo-conservatism. This was an aggressive, nationalistic, militaristic, expansionist doctrine advocating an inchoate mix of hierarchy and autonomy for people at home coupled with the use overseas of American power for American ends.

Both sets of ideas faded in the early twenty-first century. The domestic scene in America revealed growing inequality, race conflict and political reaction, whilst events overseas in Afghanistan, Iraq, Ukraine and Libya undermined whatever plausibility arguments in favour of the use of the military might once have had: neither the celebration of consumption nor the invoking of conservatism long survived the financial crash of 2008.

The arguments in favour of globalization and the end of history were influential for around two decades, that is, the 1990s and the first decade of the twenty-first century, and they foundered in the confusions of financial collapse and warfare. First, the financial crisis of 2008–10, with its double centre in Wall Street and the City of London, revealed the systemic corruption of the financial world, with the scale of the crisis requiring international state-led rescue interventions. And second, the wars of the Middle East, which saw American ideas about externally imposed marketization and democratization end in military failure, great loss of life amongst targeted populations and the concomitant emergence of a militant Islamism (hostile to the West and, most commentators argued, bankrolled by the US ally, Saudi

Arabia). By the second decade of the twenty-first century, the arguments of the enthusiasts for globalization made little sense.

It might be noted that the wider context of the failure of globalization theory recalled the earlier problem career of modernization theory, that is, hubristic claims centred on the model of the USA followed by failure as that country encountered domestic and international difficulties. And in contrast to all this work, sceptics suggested that an examination of the available data pointed less to a global system than a tri-regional arrangement – three powerful blocs, in North America, Europe and East Asia.

Regions considered critically – vocabularies and audiences

As simplistic ideas of globalization were rejected, critics called attention to the facts of the matter, that is, they measured standard claims against standard data sets, and what they found was that whilst the claims of proponents of globalization did have merit in the realms of finance, in respect of the rest of economic activity, the pattern, if there was one, was one of regional linkages taking shape and being variously acknowledged in the creation of institutions and associated discourses. When these matters were examined, scholars found evidence of trans-national linkages almost everywhere. People move and they trade and borders are a recent invention; but that said, there were areas where economic interlinkages were both highly developed and regulated, that is, they were organized trading areas and these economic links were deepening in a process of regionalization, plus there were signs of self-conscious activity, thus the notion of regionalism.

In all this talk of regionalization, regionalism and regions there are a series of complexes of questions: (1) first, the diverse ways in which the notion of region can be construed (as concept and as substantive instances); and (2) second, the multiplicity of ways in which the idea (or idea set) can be used by various agents to make particular sorts of arguments (implying thereafter certain schedules of actions). Regions are not simply given by geography; rather they are elaborate social constructions, practical and ideational.

Regions – families of concepts and multiple substantive instances

The idea of region has been around in the social sciences for many years. Thus, in the context of economic policy making, the European Union has a regional policy, which channels funds to those regions whose standard data reveal certain specified divergences from the common data profile: there are poor or disadvantaged regions. But these designations of a region are driven by administrative convenience. In order to hand out cash a recipient must be specified; pointing to a geographical territory, one where data is already available, is a solution to the question. The problem with this approach for scholarship is that it makes regions look obvious and natural and bounded, whereas it makes much better sense to see regions as historically constructed territories. Not fixed and not particularly sharply bounded either, as historically regions are subject to definition and redefinition. All of which presents the task of clarifying how regions come to be defined and how the region so defined enters administrative, political and popular consciousness.

Peter Winch – invoking the philosopher of language Ludwig Wittgenstein – has argued that new ways of thinking imply a new way of construing the world and new ways of acting within it. So, first, we can think about the diversity of the notion of region, where in ordinary language we use the idea in a multiplicity of ways. In an analogous fashion, we can note the diversity of the substantive territories that are tagged as regions in contemporary political, policy and scholarly debate. The notion of region is used in a multiplicity of ways – noting this multiplicity might help us clarify matters in regard to substantive analyses. Wittgenstein argues that forms of life and language games are intertwined (social life is a subtle process, so too are ways of conceptualizing these patterns) – we can open up a little space in respect of the notion of region – we can sketch out a series of meanings.

1   *As geography*
    Delineate some area or other on some criteria or other:

    - location (that is, position in space, relations with other delineated areas);
    - climate (the demands and opportunities of climatic conditions);
    - geology (the demands and opportunities of geographical character);
    - topography (the demands and opportunities of topographical character).

2   *As human geography*
    Delineate some area or other on some criteria or other:

    - livelihood (agricultural, pastoral, urban, etc.);
    - as racial type (Caucasian, Mongoloid, Negroid, Melanesian, etc.);
    - as language family (Indo-European, Chinese, etc.).

3   *As social organization*
    Delineate some area or other on some criteria or other:

    - an economic region (networks of investment, production and trade, etc.);
    - a social region (networks of social interaction, family, work, leisure, etc.);
    - a cultural region (ideas/practices);
    - a political region (agents and projects).

Having sketched the readily available diversity of the concept the diversity of real world circumstances that are swept up in the term region can be noted. For example, Amitav Acharaya offers a long list of acronyms all designating regional organizations. analyses ASEAN as a self-conscious attempt to create a regional identity. In sum, in brief, in respect of regions, both concepts and substantive claims are complex.

Rhetoric – arguments and audiences (official/popular)

A political region is not a natural given; it is a construct, the out-turn of the interacting projects of diverse national agents. One aspect of all this will be the ways in which these agents tell the story of the region. Turning to the rhetoric of region, there are a multiplicity of available arguments addressed to a multiplicity of audiences. There are discourses of region; claims to the existence of regions and proposals for action.

There are different arguments for different audiences, for example:

1 *Planning talk (projects/rhetoric)*
   As maps and plans:

   - maps (lines on maps – sketching out areas);
   - plans (schemes for what can be done in sketched areas, for example, 'growth triangles'.

2 *Political talk (projects/rhetoric)*
   As political schemes:

   - constructing the idea of a region (Acharya on ASEAN);
   - institutional vehicles (the organizations that embody and carry the project);
   - popular dissemination (for example, the ASEAN gift shop at Changi, or the ASEAN filler on ChanelNewsAsia – plus the ASEAN reports on news broadcasts (the photo ops)).

3 *Popular talk (rhetorics/prejudices)*
   As popular talk:

   - picking out large areas – on some criteria or other – adding in simplified judgements – for example, the Muslim or Christian world (one might recall S.P. Huntington for an upmarket version of this style of stereotyping).

4 *Corporate talk (instrumental/project)*
   As corporate talk:

   - picking out an area, for example, the European or American market.

In general, in regard to the rhetoric of regions, a series of issues could be pursued:

- the role of official truths (official discourses);
- the nature of these truths (the metaphors etc.);
- the manner of the construction of these truths (by whom, how deployed);
- how the truths are sustained (institutions etc.);
- the reach of these truths (audiences);
- the nature of alternatively located truths (whose, and how promulgated);
- the extent of the possibility of rationally debating various truths.

In conclusion, the familiar claim that regions are social constructs is both true and rather innocent as the whole business looks much more complicated.

East Asia: regionalization, regionalism and regions

East Asia there has been the focus of much recent scholarly and policy analytic attention; matters of novelty in livelihood along with rising political power. Scholars look at East Asia and they see something that is new. In the years since the Pacific War the area has become rich. It has done so in a distinctive fashion. One aspect of this has been role of developmental state, another has been the outward directed nature of trade and another has been the development of regional networks. Scholars ask: so how does it all work? Political actors look at East Asia and see a rising regional power and ask: so who is setting the rules?

In sum, conversations amongst scholars and policy analysts, which focused on the experience of East Asia, became familiar during the late 1980s and 1990s. These conversations involved a number of ideas:

- the shift from geo-strategy to geo-economics;
- the distinction between open and closed regionalism;
- the notion of the developmental state (and its pejorative counterpart 'crony-capitalism');
- the appropriate response of European and American elites to burgeoning trade deficits with East Asia (wait for the inevitable logic of the marketplace to provide a remedy or deploy the power of the state to curb damaging imbalances).

There were various intellectual responses to the increased salience within the global system of East Asia, some anxious, some celebratory. One area of work turned out to be influential. It was a rehearsal of earlier strategies of analysis; thus political economy was represented as international political economy as the community of international relations scholars in America, Europe and elsewhere began to write about geo-economics, read as a replacement to concerns for geo-strategy. What mattered now, it was argued, was not a country's possession of armies, but its natural science-based industrial and export power.

There have been a series of debates; they have had different intellectual centres of gravity; but their concerns overlap and the same themes tend to reappear. It is an on-going debate.

Three ideas have been presented:

- regionalization – the practical business of building low-level links;
- regionalism – the self-conscious elite recognition of patterns of linkages;
- regions – the resultant more or less coherent units.

Regionalization is also seen as a discernible trend as recent years have seen areas of the global system develop dense economic linkages and thereafter deepening social linkages and cultural/political linkages. Proponents suggest that whereas globalization was (probably) hype, regionalization seems to be happening. These proponents point to the European Union, to East Asia, and thereafter to smaller groupings such as Mercosur or ASEAN, and thereafter to sub-regional enthusiasm for coordinated activity (Pearl River Delta, Greater Mekong Sub-Regional System, SIJORI and others). In all this, anxious commentators draw a distinction between open regionalism and closed regionalism, where the former integrates economies, does not discriminate against outsiders and leads towards globalization, whilst the latter distinguishes members and non-members and does not lead towards globalization.

The idea of regionalism unpacked – regions can be seen as 'social constructions', thus a further line of commentary suggests starting with regions not as simple givens or accretions of activities but as more or less self-consciously constructed: the results of projects. Proponents of this view point to the ways in which economic activities can be gently coordinated (for example Japanese aid, trade and foreign direct investment in East Asia) building networks of activity that slowly encompass not merely the economic spheres but also social, cultural and finally political as formal institutional mechanisms are established (thus, for example, EAEC or ASEAN Plus Three or East Asian Summit). Doubters respond in several ways: some reject the constructivism as an implausible approach whose results are not worth the effort; others affirm the key role of states in any regional organization, suggesting that what is agreed today can be revised tomorrow; and some affirm the overriding power of liberal market relations anticipating that regions are merely way points in the move towards a global system.

The idea of regions unpacked – a number of such regions have been identified and they vary in the nature of the economic interlinkages and their related institutional expression; thus, illustratively: MERCOSUR – ECOWAS – ASEAN – SIJORI – EAEC – EU – NAFTA. But three regions came to be picked out: Europe (EU), North America (USA) and East Asia (Japan, the Tigers, Southeast Asia and China).

These debates are on-going. The nature and future of ASEAN has long been debated; more recently scholars and political actors in America and Europe have turned their attention to the rise of China. For the USA, China's remarkable record over the last few decades presents a host of questions: how to deal with burgeoning trade deficits; how to deal with the associated flows of money (Chinese earnings deposited in Wall Street) and how to respond to the rising effectiveness of the PLA and the associated robustness of Chinese foreign policy (thus, the South China Sea issues)?

Retrospect: the idea of regions

These arguments belong to the period of neo-liberalism, roughly, the last decade of the twentieth century and the first decade of the present century; a twenty-year period beginning with the dissolution of the Soviet Union and ending with the collapse of these claims in the debacle of the 2008–10 financial crisis. During this period theorists took the view that America had won the Cold War and that the type of money-centred society they had created represented a model for the rest of the world: not merely an optional model, but the outline of the inevitable future, the end of history.

But it was all nonsense. Globalization theory rehearsed the claims made earlier for modernization theory. Both intellectual exercises were produced during periods of heightened domestic optimism within American elite circles. Both theories were lines of commentary upon elite-led political projects. Both theories were concerned to inform and advance the overall position within the global system of the USA and its subordinate allies.

Problems in the early twenty-first century

In early twenty-first century the USA ran into a number of intractable problems. There were failures in the financial system. There were failures in the wars of choice in the Middle East. The political project of globalization came to an end. More recently there has been a widespread electoral rebellion amongst 'those left behind' in the populations of America and the European Union. Dismissed by elites on both sides of the Atlantic Ocean as populism, these rebellions can be read – quite easily – as resistance to the costs imposed on the weaker members of society by privileged elites. The political direction of travel for these polities would seem to involve a shift towards policy making that is more directly focused on national agendas (not the general reassurances that a 'rule based free trade system' will benefit all). It points to a spread of issues that will have to be addressed:

- persistent trade deficits and associated monetary imbalances;
- the freedom granted over recent years to the financial sector;
- the transfer of technologies out of America and Europe;
- the transfer of employment for some sectors out of America and Europe;
- the detachment of American and European political elites from the mass of their populations;
- the issue and implications of the emergence of 'the one per cent'.

It seems clear that some of these policy changes will impact East Asia. It may be that the post-1945 model of the developmental state with policy oriented towards the national economy, a stance which was permitted by the USA during the Cold War days, and which, much questioned (not least by citizens in East Asia – too much elite, not enough democracy), has continued to the present day, might now be challenged. It is not clear what a replacement could look like; perhaps less export-oriented growth and more concern for domestic sphere along with more interest paid to notions of sustainable development.

At present it is not clear how events will unfold. But the recent turn to populism in both America and Europe suggests that these two polities – key trading partners for East Asian countries – are rethinking the historical development logic of their state policies.

Prospect – unfolding lines of change

East Asia had grown during the post-war period as the USA granted allies privileged access to its markets and technologies. China, too, benefited in the later 1990s from the celebration by American and European elites of neo-liberalism in the guise of globalization, as this allowed it to run huge trade deficits. However, as the tri-regional global system settled into place, and was acknowledged by scholars, policy makers and politicians, a reaction set in. Electorates in Europe and the USA moved to reject globalization as the costs in terms of economic and social dislocation became too much to bear for large sections of the populations: the rise of nationalist parties in Europe, the 2016 Brexit vote in the United Kingdom, the election of Donald Trump in the USA and murmurs of dissent in China, as the costs of rapid and growth became evident in rising inequality and appalling environmental damage. In the second decade of the twenty-first century there were signs that the system might be undergoing a further process of change but quite how a fading commitment to neo-liberal globalization might interact with a continuing elite commitment to a burgeoning if flawed developmental state was not at all clear.

PART V
East Asia
Success and its costs

The countries of East Asia now offer a mixed picture where great success is joined with problems inherited from the past and with newer problems created by their recent development record. Many urban areas in the region are well off, some are wealthy, but many cities in East Asia are also home to poor people and there are large rural areas where levels of living remain low. However, that said, the countries of the region are in the main settled and the more direct legacies of the violent upheavals of the twentieth century have been at least in material terms overcome, with infrastructure rebuilt and new cities developed. Yet political tensions remain. Cold War divisions linger. Collective memory and national pasts provide ample occasion for diplomatic and popular ill temper. And the region is paying the costs of rapid economic development with inequality, pollution and corruption. Nonetheless, cast in historical terms, the countries of the region have embedded themselves in the modern world. They have joined in and they have caught up. But they have not simply copied available models (USA, Europe); rather they have created their own variants forms of modernity. The region is now home to a number of successful and distinct forms of life. These forms can track their distinctive routes into the modern world and these tracks have shaped current institutional forms and in many cases bequeathed complex problems of historical memory.

12
ELITE PROJECTS AND POST-COLONIAL GOALS

The countries of East Asia have it in common that they have shifted into the modern world (that is, they have accommodated to the demands of the global industrial capitalist system) via the episode of colonialism (either direct or indirect). This has generated a dual legacy comprising the remnants of ancient civilizations and the memories and remnants of colonial episode. The countries of the region also have it in common that they have sought to locate themselves autonomously within this modern industrial capitalist world and this generates the typical preoccupations of national development (identity and development): the first basic preoccupation is with making post-colonial states; the second is with identity, creating a nation; and the third is with development. For all these issues the state is the key and it generates a typical government form, the developmental state. Unfolding trajectories can be grasped in part in terms of the activities of elites in asserting their power/authority in order to make states and nations. But thereafter it is clear that the new countries of the region have it in common that these projects of identity and development are uncompleted. They confront multiple domestic and international tensions.

East Asian elites read and reacted to enfolding circumstances and the upshot over time was to embed the communities that they led in the modern world. The forms of life typical of colonial peripheries were remade – one way or another – on the model of sovereign states as the context of the dissolution of state-empires pressed upon the newly independent states a particular goal. Former colonial authorities sought continued economic trading access, new international organizations were open to the membership of states and intellectually ideas of modernization were available: all pointed new elites towards the goal of effective nation-statehood. It was a generalized goal, which was imputed to replacement elites, but they had their own agendas. These were shaped by local circumstances and local ideals, and sometimes they ran with the general goal but at other times they ran along other tracks. Their local agendas were shaped by given contexts and agendas were shaped by three concerns: security, order and development. The key players were local elites and they determined the projects to which the new states were oriented, that is, national development.

In sum, new elites in new countries sought security, order and development. The first two issues were addressed via their assertion of power and relatedly the creation of legitimacy, the latter, as noted, via development, and this entailed the pursuit of a complex set of interlinked objectives – economic, social and cultural advance – starting, in UN terms, with basic needs. So in considering elites, two issues are central: power and authority. And in East Asia, new elites were typically successful; power was asserted, authority established and development energetically pursued.

The historical trajectory in overview

Power and authority in contemporary East Asia mix resources from the pre-colonial period (the resources of long established civilizations), the colonial interlude (ideas taken from this particular experience of the modern world), the episode of state-empire dissolution (typically, violent, contributing to the thinking of later leaders) and the lessons of the period of independent nation-state development. The familiar interpretive resources of political analysis can be used to grasp the contemporary scene, critically and dialogically.

Pre-colonial East Asia was a key part of a wider trading economy, which included Southeast, South and West Asia: trade moved goods along established networks; trade moved flows of people along these networks; and trade moved cultural resources so contemporary East Asia reveals influences from this wide area, Buddhism, Islam and Hinduism, in particular.

It is useful to note the historically available ideas about power/authority.

Power and authority in pre-modern East Asia

Pre-modern East Asia was home to long-established successful civilizations. The historical core of the region, China, had a written history that reached back some 2,500 years and its influence had been exported around Northeast Asia and parts of Southeast Asia. Other ideas had flowed into the region: from India, Buddhism, and from Arabia, Islam. The region was also home to a number of different modes of government: none were states in the modern sense; none were nations in the modern sense; and none pursued development in the modern sense; but all at a minimum functioned, many flourished.

China – hierarchy and order

In the long years before contact with the modern world in the guise of traders from Europe, East Asia centred on China. The country was the economic, social, cultural and political key to the entire area. The form of life can be characterized in brief as a centralized agrarian feudal system and the key to wealth was land and peasants. The governmental structure was hierarchical. The state machine provided law, regional and local officials were appointed and the local landowners dealt with them. A local-level class system took shape: officials, gentry and, broadly, the peasantry, with the last noted grouping embracing all those working within an agricultural economy.

The system of administration could be accessed via the examinations, which centred on received classical texts that constituted the religion/ethic of Confucianism. The examination system meant that these classic texts were central to the life of educated people and linked to the associated cultural status hierarchy of scholar, farmer, artisan and merchant. Other religions served other functions: Taoism, Buddhism and Islam. At the local level of village life the key was family. A person fitted into the social world via family (including ancestors) and the circle of relationships would be family, kin, village, gentry, local officials, followed by regional or central officials and then finally the emperor.

Kenneth Lieberthal characterizes pre-contact Imperial China as bureaucratic, agrarian and feudal; power flows from the centre and loyalty and obligation bind subordinates into the system, obedience is required from the masses. Lieberthal identifies a number of factors: first, hierarchy, the system is ordered from the centre and the emperor heads the system, exemplifying Confucian virtues; second, the Confucian philosophical system, which is centred on order, obligation and correct behaviour; third, the bureaucracy: the emperor rules through an elaborate bureaucracy, which reached from the centre through a series of defined levels – appointment to the bureaucracy is via examination in Confucian classics so that bureaucrat/scholars run the system; then fourth, the lower levels of bureaucracy intersect with local farming communities such that rich farmers gain access and the bureaucrat/scholars gain influence at lowest levels of society; then overall, fifth, the system depends on both hierarchy and dense networks of obligation.

The Chinese bureaucratic agrarian feudal system was reproduced throughout much of the region. The Chinese exported their culture (ideas and practices), their law, their institutional models, their language/script, their science and their medicine. Local leaders and cultures received and adapted these influences as the Chinese exported their form of life from the Han Chinese heartlands of Northern China, to areas south of the Yangtze River, further south into Indo-China and into Southeast Asia, settling in numbers throughout the area. The Chinese also exported their form of life to Korea and Japan. The Chinese elite ordered its relations with these territories via tributary relationships such that local leaders would acknowledge the key role of the emperor and in return receive trading preferences.

The Chinese elite turned inwards in the sixteenth century as the dynasty faced problems in the north. Overseas trading links were neglected, and the result was to leave the trading sphere open to foreigners. Their timing coincided with the rise of European seaborne trade. The Europeans arrived on the back of a powerful dynamic system, that is, natural science underpinned an industrial-capitalist system whose logic entailed internal intensification and external expansion. From the early sixteenth century onwards, European traders, soldiers, missionaries and assorted adventurers arrived in ever greater numbers in the region. They came for trade and, where negotiations failed, violence was available; by the nineteenth century the Europeans had built a system of state-empires. The incoming powers advanced along trading routes, moving from the Indian sub-continent, into the archipelago of Southeast Asia and thence northwards to the regional heartland, China. They accumulated large peripheral colonial holdings in South Asia and Southeast Asia but they were increasingly concerned to trade in Eastern Asia, in particular with China. The Chinese authorities refused, the Europeans insisted and violence was deployed: gunboat diplomacy plus opium. The long established Sino-centric system was undermined and the authority of the core territory of China slowly overborne.

Europeans and later Americans established multiple trading concessions in China, which became a quasi-colony. At the height of the Treaty Ports system there were around 150 concession sites scattered throughout China. The shift to the modern world was very chaotic. There were attempts at reform made during Qing years, including Self Strengthening, One Hundred Days Reform and Late Qing Reforms, but all to no very great effect. The first sustained attempt to redirect China's historical development trajectory towards the modern world was the Republican Revolution of 1911. Sun Yat Sen presented three ideas: democracy, nationalism and people's livelihood, but the revolution collapsed. The warlord period followed with a half-dozen large warlord units, dozens of smaller ones along with extensive inter-warlord violence. Two progressive political groupings were founded around this time: the Kuomintang was direct successor to Sun; the Communist Party of China also acknowledged Sun but looked to a somewhat different political ideal. There was continuing foreign involvement during these years and from 1928 civil war raged. Then from 1931 onwards the country suffered Imperial Japanese advances in northern areas and in time these exchanges turned into the 1937–45 war. The Imperial Japanese armies were able to defeat Chinese forces but given the size of the country they could not effectively garrison the territory they seized; that said, by mid-1944 they could lay claim to occupy most of lowland China. But it was not to last as the Japanese were militarily defeated by the USA. The Chinese Civil War resumed. The decisive battles took place in the north of the country and in 1949 Mao Zedong and the CCP declared the foundation of the People's Republic of China; followed by the period dominated by Mao, and then the cautious but deep reforms inaugurated by Deng from 1978 onwards; this last, the most obvious line to contemporary China.

Political culture in China has four elements (roughly): (1) received tradition – that is, what continues from pre-contact Great and Little Traditions; (2) the memory of the quasi-colonial period (thus the century of humiliation); (3) the memory of 1911–49 (civil war and inter-state warfare); and (4) the era of the People's Republic of China with Mao Zedong of 1949–76 (utopian socialism), Deng Xiaoping (pragmatic reform and opening era 1978 onwards) and the present day leadership of Xi Jinping (the China Dream).

Contemporary Chinese politics are tackled by Flemming Christiansen and Shirin Rai who identify five theoretical approaches. First, totalitarianism: the approach posits a top-down system which disciplines/polices the population and which neither needs nor allows popular participation. Second, factionalism and elite conflict: this perspective notes that within the state/party bureaucracy networks and alliances form and these constitute factions which manoeuvre around policy and position. Third, clientelism: this approach extends the elite/faction view to include a wider group of lower-level supporters. Fourth, complex bureaucracies: now the focus is on how decisions are made in the machinery of governance. Fifth, the culturalist approach: this perspective argues that the key to Chinese politics is precisely that people are Chinese and thus inherit centuries of Confucianism. Sixth, to these can be added a recent characterization, which is offered by Zhang Yongnian, who argues that the CCP is key to local politics. The Chinese political system has a double hierarchy of party and state: the former deals with political debate and organization, whilst the latter executes decisions. Zhang argues that the system is an 'organizational emperor': it is centralized, hierarchical and wedded to continuity, and in principle it requires obedience whilst in practice operating pragmatically, embracing piecemeal reform.

The exchange with the modern world is complex: (1) there are political-cultural borrowings as the Chinese elites have tried to borrow/adapt ideas from the modern world (Sun Yat Sen, Mao Zedong and Deng Xiaoping); (2) there are memories of chaos (imperialism, warlords and civil war); and (3) there is an elite preoccupation with maintaining order. The current situation gathers numerous characterizations: rational authoritarianism – how the elite's concern with order can be read; socialism/nationalism – how the CCP presents itself to its population (legitimization); the East Asian model – China's variant.

The Chinese system slowly collapsed over the course of the nineteenth century. Japan was drawn into the modern world and late development was followed by late empire building in Northeast Asia. The Japanese seized Korea in conflict with China and Russia, acquired Taiwan, territories in the north and island chains to the south.

Japan – feudalism overturned

Pre-contact Japan was ordered in a quasi-feudal fashion with an emperor, nominally the supreme power, in practice, exercising authority in a shifting exchange with regional lords, these lords ruling a number of more local landed territories. In Medieval Japan the system came to have three sources of power: the landed families, who were spread throughout the territory, the religious foundations and the Shogunate, a military ruling house nominally representing the emperor.

The Tokugawa Shogunate ruled the islands from 1603 until 1867. Eighty per cent of the population were peasants, however, the economy advanced, population grew, commerce grew, the economy was monetized, credit facilities increased and a sophisticated urban life developed. Society was hierarchical, influenced by Confucian caste ideas (lord, samurai, farmer, artisan, merchant), and allegiance and obedience were owed to superiors in the hierarchy. The key social organization for the mass of peasantry was the continuing family; people were located in the social world via family membership. The ethos of the system was informed by long cultural exchanges with China and thus Confucian ideals of enlightened rule and social harmony.

The system was undergoing slow change when the modern world in the guise of Commodore Perry arrived. The appearance of this fleet of American warships in Tokyo Bay caused consternation. Perry's demand for trading privileges provoked a domestic crisis as factions debated how to respond to these entirely unwanted demands. A brief civil war ensued as an alliance of regional lords overthrew the Tokugawa Shogunate. The emperor was restored and a process of top-down reform was begun – the Meiji Restoration. The new leadership despatched study missions to Europe and America and inaugurated a rapid programme of modern state building, nation building and development. The reforms were sweeping: a bureaucratic rational administration ordered around the figure of the emperor was created; a notion of the Japanese as a national family led by the emperor was established; and contemporary ideas in respect of science and industry were imported and embraced. The new elite sought to create a strong economy as the basis for a strong military, the key to an independent membership of the modern world.

The Japanese elite were dazzlingly successful. Within twenty-five or so years they were able to challenge both Qing China and Czarist Russia for influence in the Korean peninsular – two short and highly destructive wars saw them decisively defeat both these much larger powers. The Japanese elite went on to deepen their nascent empire territories in Northeast Asia; from Meiji onwards a process of territorial expansion had been undertaken (the modern world of states required clear borders and was cast in terms of state-empires): the Ryukyu Islands, Hokkaido, Sakhalin, Korea and thereafter in the twentieth century claims to parts of Shandong, then Manchuria and parts of Northern China. The process of expansion was buttressed by the elite embrace of notions of 'Pan-Asianism' – ostensibly an ideology arguing that Asia should be ruled by Asians, that is, not Europeans and Americans; however, given the failures of Qing China to resist the depredations of foreign powers, the ideology drifted into a tacit endorsement of a Japanese nationalism.

In the late 1930s a clash with the USA over access to China resulted in war, defeat and reconstruction as a species of liberal democracy within the frame of the American-ordered West.

Chalmers Johnson has discussed contemporary Japan and argued that there is a distinctive state form, with a similar pattern found in Korea. The notion of a developmental state is used to capture the elite-level cooperation of highly trained powerful bureaucrats, business leaders and popularly elected politicians. These elites have been committed to projects of national development where economic growth has been a central preoccupation, the citizens of these polities have been effectively disciplined and the rewards have been recovery from disaster and rapid continual economic growth. However, following decades of successful economic growth, younger educated generations are much more sceptical of familiar elite preferences, particularly in South Korea.

Southeast Asia and the ASEAN countries

Scholars have discussed pre-contact elite forms in Southeast Asia, characterizing them in general as dispersed, fluid and personalist systems. Elites gather support around themselves and more distant sub-rulers surround them; personal loyalty binds in subordinates, whilst deference binds in the masses. Acharya identifies three patterns of political power/authority. First, the Mandala State, which comprises concentric circles of authority: the core embraced the king, the capital and the immediate surrounding areas, then a second ring comprised princes along with their followers and finally there was an outer ring of more or less independent kings acknowledging the core figure. The system is centred on relationships to the king, not on holding a defined territory. It is fluid. In Southeast Asia, the state system was a patchwork of overlapping mandalas. Second, the Galactic State: here there is central king, authoritative within the central core and acknowledged throughout the wider territory. Clustering around this figure are other kings and they reproduce within their territories the same characteristics. The image points to circles of authority, greater and lesser, each both self-sufficient yet subordinate to the next circle of authority. Again the system is not fixed, it is fluid: the circles of power change, growing stronger or weaker. Finally, the Theatre State, where the central king must order relations with other kings (equal and lesser) and this is accomplished via ritual: dress, objects and sites; loyalty and respect are secured through these rituals. Again, these are fluid polities.

These local systems were overwritten during the period of their absorption within foreign-centred state-empires – the Dutch, the British, the French and the Americans all put their own domestic ideas to work in organizing these distant peripheral parts of their systems of empire. Hybrid systems were invented: local elites could be co-opted, local minorities either supported or suppressed, other minorities imported for this or that economic reason and the local masses left – to a greater or lesser extent – to their own devices in what until quite recently were predominantly rural agrarian societies.

As these foreign state-empire systems absorbed and remade those parts of the region, which they controlled, they sought to develop these areas – political, economic, social and cultural links were made with distant metropolitan centres – and the hitherto loosely integrated character of Southeast Asia was weakened. Such broad scale divisions – the Dutch, British, French and American spheres – were supplemented as the empires disintegrated by the interests of their successor elites in drawing clear boundaries as they laid claim to their political inheritances. For a period, division was reinforced. However, Acharya argues, optimistically, that a newly reintegrated Southeast Asia is in process of formation around the organization called ASEAN.

Lessons learned

A number of points can be made in summary. First, the starting point for analysing power and authority is the historical experience or model of Europe and America because the modern world is organized into states and nations. Thereafter, second, the inherited resources of local practices or cultures can be acknowledged, thus Great Traditions and Little Traditions (probably much altered by the experience of colonialism and the shift to the modern world). Then, third, there was the episode of violence as colonial systems were dismantled. Fourth, we can take note of the practice of post-colonial elites over the last 50 plus years. Fifth, this mixture will uncover the nature of power and authority in contemporary East Asia. And sixth, what are visible are a multiplicity of locally determined forms of political life.

Domestic politics: the role of successor elites

As the colonial empires dissolved away replacement elites sought power. The pursuit of domestic order involved asserting their power/authority. The elite had to do this in the context of their relationships with existing local groups.

Social groups constitute themselves in routine social practice. They have a common identity. Such identities can be the basis of exchanges with elites (these can be initiated by elite or by group and these exchanges can be cooperative or conflicting). In practice replacement elites in East Asia usually confronted a multiplicity of groups with whom they had shifting relationships of cooperation and conflict. In the new nation-states domestic stability took time to establish.

In general, there are various ways in which groups can be constituted.

So, first, it can be thought about in terms taken from political economy (these focus on ways of securing livelihood): (1) position in market economy (liberal strategy); (2) position in division of labour (after Durkheim); and (3) position within industrial capitalist class system (Marxist strategy). The criteria for membership of this sort of group is that all members have a similar way of securing their livelihood; typically participants and observers would look at income (employment) and wealth (material resources and cultural resources). In liberal market terms it gives us the elaborate occupational categories supplemented by differences in wealth; in functional terms it gives us position in a complex division of labour, where position and reward are in principle determined by functional contribution to the system as a whole; or in structural terms, it gives us classes (peasant, worker, landlord, financier etc.).

Then, second, it can be thought about it in terms taken from anthropology and sociology (these focus on location within important social categories): (1) geographical area – place of origin or assumed regional identity; (2) physiological type – imputed identity or ethnic identity; (3) language group – imagined community and possibility of linguistic nationalism; (4) religious group – imagined community, claimed superiority over non-members; and (5) age and sex – age group and gender. These categories can be invoked by participants in order to make self-conscious groups. Identity is socially constructed and these distinctions help make local communities, they can help to make diasporic communities and these categories (and others) can be combined in a multiplicity of ways.

Either way, as the empires dissolved, incoming successor elites were faced with a multiplicity of different groups. The first task was for elites to assert their power/authority. It was not simple as groups can engage in conflict in a number of ways, for example, riots, pogroms, discrimination and boycotts. Groups can stereotype: thus Malays as lazy, Chinese as ruthlessly materialistic, foreigners as exploitative sojourners. Groups can have minimal exchanges as in plural societies, or 'ghettoization' or separatism. Hostility can develop when one ethnic group comes to be associated with either an economically powerful position or a politically powerful position (or both). And such group identifications/tensions are available for calculated political exploitation.

Having secured power they had to build states and nations. They faced a trio of problems: security, order and development.

State-empire dissolution: successor elites take their chance

The process of the dissolution of state-empires was accompanied by extensive violence. In East Asia from the Chinese Revolution of 1911 onwards, local nationalist groups began organizing around the goal of independent statehood. Local figures had made their colonial pilgrimages to their respective metropolitan cores and had learned how the modern world worked: its science, its productive industry and its patterns of self understanding, in particular political ideas of reason, progress and democracy. These informed a variety of nationalist rhetoric and allowed nationalists to make promises of better lives to those whom they aspired to lead – the putative citizens of the states they envisaged.

These local groups had relatively little impact before the events of the 1930s and 1940s. The Chinese Civil War, the Sino-Japanese War and the Pacific War formed a sequence of overlapping large-scale conflicts that fatally undermined foreign state-empires. These state-empire territories were now available for aspirant nationalists as they sought control of territories carved from these state-empires. This was not a simple process.

In Northeast Asia, the abrupt end of the Japanese empire was followed by further conflicts involving the withdrawal of Japanese soldiers and civilians from China and colonial territories in Taiwan, Manchuria and Korea, the latter followed by civil war. In China the civil war raged until 1949 and thereafter there were further local conflicts as the Communist Party built the machinery of the PRC. In Southeast Asia sometime European spheres experienced anti-colonial wars in French Indo-China, in the Dutch East Indies and in British Malaya. The Philippines too had local problems, exacerbated by American involvement. In all these cases elites emerged to replace those holding power before the wars: new states were made, new nations were invented or radically reimagined and, thereafter, elites pursued development, again in different ways.

And, as noted, put schematically, replacement elites were concerned with control, order and development.

First, control: taking control of a territory was crucial. It meant creating agreed borders for the new state and agreements made with outgoing colonial elites, neighbouring elites and other aspirant elites within their territory. It was not a smooth process in an area filled with multiple ethnic groups whose forms of life were overlain by wider state-empire systems. Patterns of allegiance were tangled: local in the main, occasionally wider (intellectuals, colonial functionaries (administrators, soldiers and the like)). In China, civil war resolved the issue only slowly; and in Korea, civil war was buttressed by outside involvement. In Indo-China the process entailed long drawn-out wars of liberation and Thailand's borders were redrawn. In Southeast Asia, various mixtures of conflict and collaboration are seen.

Second, order: having secured an external border, having thus laid a claim to a territory that was in some measure agreed by relevant contending parties, the elite were faced with creating order within their territory. This entailed: constructing the machineries of the state, the administrative machinery and the political machinery, the sets of symbols and agreed histories with which the population could be ordered (that is, brought under control or disciplined). And again, in an ethnically diverse region, recently disturbed by war, with consequent displaced persons, this was a difficult process: in China, continuing low-level violence in which millions died; in Korea, the costs of the civil war were severe, thereafter, regimes backed by outsiders took control (with resistance in the south – Kwangju Massacre – and military regimentation in the north); and in Taiwan, the KMT imposed itself violently upon the local population. In Indo-China the wars of liberation ran on for some 30 years and communist party cadres were eventually to form new states, ruling devastated populations. Thailand saw a series of military regimes. In Southeast Asia, British Malaya split on ethnic lines. Malaysia made the split formal, whilst in Singapore ethnic dominance was clear but veiled via policies of meritocracy. And in Indonesia, the new regime had to deal with a population speaking around 200 languages; eventually, the army staged a coup and violently imposed its authority, thereby establishing a long enduring regime.

Third, development: having secured control and created order, promulgating in most cases novel nationalisms, celebrated with flags, parades and anthems, all buttressed by national pasts, elites committed themselves to development. On a general scale it was part of the deal made during the pursuit of independence, in part it was wished upon them by departing colonial powers (a way of sustaining economic interests and links), in part it was wished upon them by extant international organizations and in part wished upon them by the pattern of the global system (membership was as nation-state and the expectation of such states was the pursuit of development). Thereafter, quite what was to count as development and quite how it was to be secured were questions to which local elites gave a variety of answers. It is true that foreign ideologists offered recipes during the Cold War (capitalism or communism) and foreign theorists offered a spread of ideas under the head of development theory, but, in the event, local elites read and reacted to enfolding structural circumstances in terms of their own schedule of ideas. Political projects of development were always local and thus in practice quite varied.

Thus, in the early phases, and in highly schematic terms:

- China – utopian state socialism oriented towards the peasantry;
- South Korea – authoritarian variant of developmental state;
- North Korea – nominally state socialist, garrison state;
- Japan – nominal liberal democracy and developmental state;
- Taiwan – military regime variant of developmental state;
- Indo-China – state socialisms oriented towards development;
- Thailand – elite military regime oriented towards development;
- Philippines – nominal liberal democracy oriented towards status quo;
- Malaysia – nominal liberal democracy oriented towards development;
- Singapore – nominal liberal democracy variant of developmental state;
- Indonesia – authoritarian elite pursuit of development;
- Myanmar – military regime oriented towards status quo.

In later years, as countries not merely took shape (differentiation) but became rooted (that is, firmly established), both within the immediate sub-region, the wider region itself and finally the global system, these national development strategies were subject – as might be expected – to revisions. Dramatically in China, as Deng's slow reforms swung the country onto a variant developmental state style of trajectory. Rather less dramatically in other places: thus Singapore advances along a line set early in its history, accumulating productive multinationals, accommodating inward flows of migrants, overall, becoming affluent. The countries of Indo-China finally escape from warfare and one episode of domestic insanity, then follow their northern neighbour in relaxing the party-state system; Indonesia advances; the Philippines drift; whilst Thailand slides backwards, beset by the posturing of the military, in turn tolerated by a reactionary Bangkok elite, and so on, all now within a broadly successful region.

On-going elite projects

In East Asia the dissolution of state-empires left geographically large multi-ethnic territories somewhat politically adrift. The global system was constructed in terms of states and local aspirant successor elites were constrained to act with this in mind. Local conflicts ensued and local successor elites took shape; they lodged and secured claims to statehood and thereafter they had to build states and nations and legitimate the whole enterprise in the minds of its newly specified citizens.

The most direct way to secure authority was to implement the promise made – more or less clearly – in the context of movements for independence, that is, mass support of elites in exchange for the provision of better lives. The manner in which such promises were redeemed differed, for example: it was delivered in Singapore, it got somewhat lost in the Philippines and it was for many years buried under warfare in the sometime French territories of mainland Southeast Asia. Other promises proved rather more problematical: thus Mao's promise of an egalitarian peasant-centred socialism foundered; Kim Il Sung's Korean style autarchy set his country onto a path leading in the early twenty-first century to a developmental dead end; Malaysian promises of inter-race development have proved awkward; others – Myanmar, Indonesia, South Korea – have only recently reformed otherwise heavily top-down systems. Further reforms can be expected, building on established historical trajectories.

13
ELITES, MASSES AND THE IDEAL OF DEMOCRACY

The base line of the claim to legitimacy made by successor elites was the provisions for the masses of the population of better lives, what might be tagged performance legitimacy, but there was also an idea of formal legitimacy available at the time of the formation of new states; that is, political ideals, typically cast in terms taken from the lexicon of modernity; thus, liberalism or republicanism or socialism or progress or the people and so on. The notion of democracy was one of these ideas. It has continued to be a source of both inspiration for some domestic groups (thus Thailand's 'red shirts', or Hong Kong's 'democracy movement') and has been read as a threat by some domestic elites (thus Singapore's PAP (People's Action Party) and its habit of 'surplus repression', or Beijing's reaction to the student and worker demonstrations associated with the Tiananmen Square incident). The ideal of democracy has also animated the membership of the United Nations, a key post-1945 international organization, most of whom claim to be democratic but, given the spread of actual regime types, this tends to empty the notion of meaning, provoking the thought that an ideal apparently so flexible and all encompassing is in need of critical inspection.

The idea has informed political practice. Idea and practice have simultaneously expanded in scope so as to embrace a multiplicity of regime types. Disentangling these strands of argument and action is necessary in order to grasp the business of democracy in East Asia. In this chapter, two intermingled lines of enquiry are followed: first, a philosophical element, looking at the fundamental elements of the ideal (starting with how the idea gets variously written into formal theories of development); and, second, attention turns to the actual elite practice in respect of their domestic politics, asking how the notion has found practical expression in the years following the collapse of the system of state-empires.

In the domestic sphere newly installed elites had to secure the support of the populations they aspired to lead. The base line is an issue of power: the networks at elite level – politicians, administrators, key agents in the economy and key agents within the wider social and cultural sphere. This elite-level set of deals creates the basis for social order and thereafter the elite and its core supporters could pursue the further tasks of creating the machineries of the state, including administrative machineries, political machineries and cultural machineries. The emerging new system impacts the lives of people in the economy (work) and in society (welfare) and then also in politics and culture (the spheres of argument and action, of ways of understanding). Elites must work to become legitimate in the eyes of their populations; legitimacy secures authority and so the realms of culture must be drawn into the project of the elite.

Aspects of this process are quite visible: the role of the local political and administrative systems (accessible or not, responsive or not and in day-to-day interactions efficient and honest or not); the official ideas promulgated, thus the national past (and its interactions with collective memory); the realms of popular opinion or common sense; the role of the local media and more recently the realms of commercial popular culture. It is within these areas that elite ideas are presented and, thereafter, embraced and made part of common sense (becoming hegemonic) or rejected to a greater or lesser extent (encouraging disengagement or dissent or, in the extreme, rebellion).

It is also in this sphere that the notion of democracy is contested as idea, as institutional form and as practice. Again, in highly schematic terms:

- in China – the notion of New China – free of foreigners, local exploiting classes and concerned with the livelihood of the masses – represented as a heroic achievement – thus the role of the CCP – thus the 'China Dream';
- in Northeast Asia – elite pursuit of developmental state – appeals to technical expertise to guide national reconstruction – in Japan, social relations governed by ideal of 'harmony' – in South Korea, hierarchy; in North Korea, the ethos of a garrison state;
- in Indo-China – Vietnam, Laos and Cambodia – long episodes of warfare issue in elite rule by local communist parties – socialist development – and reforms;
- in Thailand – appeals to Nation, King and Buddhism/Place;
- in Philippines – American-style liberal democracy plus Catholic church – status quo sustained;
- in Malaysia – Malay priority and thereafter development via NEP;
- in Singapore – claims to vulnerability, self-reliance and meritocracy;
- in Indonesia – development – double-function – *pancasila*;
- in Myanmar – Buddhism and Burmese priority – local road to socialism.

After the collapse of empires and the formation of new states replacement elites in East Asia have pursued a variety of political cultural projects. The pursuit of national development has been one such project and it is recognizably modern, for example, the communitarian democracy of Singapore or the corporatist democracy of Malaysia. But there have been others, for example, the alleged kleptocracy of the Marcos regime in the Philippines or the 'autarchic nationalism' of the North Korean regime or the Buddhist socialism of the army-centred regimes in Myanmar.

All these projects have been much discussed. East Asia is seen by many commentators as a success, but some dissent from this view and others point up particular alleged failings. The trajectory of development has favoured economic growth at the expense of the environment and there are severe problems with pollution. The drive for economic development has encouraged rural to urban migration and this has led to problems within burgeoning cities: overcrowding, poor infrastructure and informal settlement or slums. Another alleged failing relates to the situation of minorities in the polities of the region – there are minority groups – it is alleged that they are not well integrated and in some cases this is true, in some not. The situation is made more awkward by the creation by unfolding global economic forces of new social minority groups including migrant workers (legal and illegal), religious radicals and the like. The list could be lengthened and made more detailed but one key failing in the eyes of foreign and some domestic critics is evident in the political dynamics of the countries of the region: a democratic deficit is identified. Rebuttals are made by local elites, for example, in terms of 'Asian values', and other defences can be offered which point to the long-term historical achievement of democracy. But attention turns quite often to the business of democracy (or not) and, as the ideal of democracy is part and parcel of the modernist project, it is worth investigating its expression in East Asia.

Democratic ideal: theories, criticisms and confusions

The shift to the modern world of the countries of East Asia was mediated by the experience of colonial rule, the confusions of decolonization and the conflicts of Cold War. In the latter phases local elites sought and achieved power. They proceeded to build new states and new nations. They made political communities. At that time three macro theories were available – theories of development – each had lodged within it an ideal of democracy as a model to which development was oriented.

1 Modernization/globalization: liberal democracy as minimum rules

In the optimistic late 1950s, American scholars presented modernization theory. It affirmed the logic of industrialism, anticipated convergence between capitalist and state socialist systems, spoke of modernization for poor countries and looked forward to a wealthy world where there would be an end to ideology. It was criticized in the 1960s. In the 1980/90s in a similar period of optimism globalization theory was presented. It spoke of a universal market capitalist logic, convergence on a single market-consumer society, anticipated that the poor countries would be drawn into the system and looked for the ethico-political end of history as liberal-democracy became accepted worldwide. The model of democracy affirmed is a familiar one; tagged liberal-democracy it embraces a political ethic fusing liberal and democratic ideals and all the machineries of republican ideas; in North America and Europe it has served to legitimate relatively successful developmental trajectories (thus, ideal, machinery and practice).

In substance, both theories affirm the economic, social, cultural and political model of American global market-centred liberal-democracy, which was assembled during the latter years of the Second World War. In the wake of that war, other countries were assimilated to this model under the Cold War label of the West (thus Western Europe, Canada, Australia, New Zealand and the nominally market capitalist countries of East Asia, subsequently the tiger economies plus, in some respects, the countries of ASEAN). The shift around the 1980s and 1990s from a discredited modernization to a resurgent globalization also involved a corporate world-sponsored programme to upgrade the market and downgrade the liberal democracy – now only periodic elections were needed to validate the shrinking sphere of the state.

Liberal democratic polities have their own logic (schematically, the triangle of state, public sphere and private sphere which has developed over many years), which can be summarized as an ideal list of governmental and institutional arrangements: political parties to aggregate individual interests, competitive elections, parliaments, a free press and so on. A lengthy checklist can be assembled once the central model has been affirmed, and other non-core system countries can then be ranked against this model.

William Case in his otherwise good detailed discussions does this for Southeast Asia:

- Indonesia – a pseudo-democracy;
- Singapore – a stable semi-democracy;
- Malaysia – a semi-democracy with strain points;
- Thailand – an unconsolidated democracy;
- Philippines – a stable low quality democracy.

And the American organization Freedom House does it for the planet.

However, the procedure can be criticized:

- the model affirmed is the outcome of a particular history and there is no reason to take its universality for granted (if indeed it is universal then this has to be argued for directly – as with, say, Francis Fukuyama's attempt);
- the model is not well established in the West (there are variant forms, thus the USA is Lockean liberal and Europe only became generally liberal democratic in 1945, plus, narrowly, there are problems in many Western countries from falling voter participation, scorn for politicians through to disaffected minorities);
- using the model to judge other polities is foolish (it misdescribes their own logics and consequently is liable to misdiagnose any problems).

2 Dependency: democracy as critique of comprador elites and distant goal

In the post-war period in America and Europe (in particular) the work of the political economist J.M. Keynes was used to theorize mixed economy systems (mixing a role for the state and a role for the private sector), which were linked to large welfare systems. These debates continue. Other debates looked to the situation of countries outside the West. An influential family of theories drew on the experience of Latin America.

Dependency theory affirmed an ethical model of socialism, that is, it prioritized society and state and insisted that the liberal market and its local elite beneficiaries must be subordinated to the needs of society and state, and it affirmed the priority of the national economy over alternative policy stances that favour participation in the open global liberal marketplace.

Dependency theory offers an analysis of the global capitalist system: it is fundamentally expansionary and is organized with powerful core economies and weak peripheral economies. Elites in the core are powerful, elites in the periphery are weak and the core elites co-opt weak elites. Peripheral masses are weak and poor and are likely to stay that way. Dependency theory diagnoses compromised local elites; it does not speak of pseudo-democracy and so on, rather it speaks of neo-colonialism and it argues that local elites are concerned for themselves and do not care about general social progress. Dependency theory calls for the replacement of compromised local elites by an elite committed to national economic development and so it is a species of democracy turned pragmatically to the needs of the local population (better governance, better lives).

In the event, local elites resisted such national development strategies, preferring post-war links to the USA. These class-based exchanges were further shaped by inter-ethnic tensions. Latin American populations included descendants from three distinct groups: Europeans, Africans and indigenous peoples, and so class conflict intermingled with ethnic tensions. For the elite reaching out to allies in the USA was an obvious and often successful move; the balance between contending groups and state policies continues to swing back and forth.

3 Institutional theory: democracy as crisis engendered responsibility

Institutional theory was cast in terms of multiple aspects of change. Gunnar Myrdal analysed circular and cumulative causation; social change is the result of multiple small-scale interactions and, typically, a social system will continue along an established trajectory, path dependence. Society moves forward along a given development trajectory and, for the poor countries of the global south, the established path meant continuing poverty for masses of the population, but shifting the system onto some new path will require some sort of directing input. In Myrdal's case (and that of other development theorists) the input was to come from enlightened planning agents whose ethic was given by the notion of crisis, as the situation of the poor was such that action was both obvious and urgently required, action recommended in this case by a European. The ethic is one of enlightened responsibility; the approach is familiar within UNDP and sister international organizations.

4 Developmental state: democracy as elite-led national development

The ethos of the developmental state reserves a key role for the enlightened, technocratic elite and elite success is cast in terms of the provision of better lives for its local population; democracy figures as a distant goal. The goal can be cast in various terms: (1) state-socialist (China) or communitarian (Singapore) or developmental (Myanmar); here institutional reform is elite-ordered, political life is slowly broadened and reform is measured so, on the one hand, more citizens are schooled to accept the role of the elite and, on the other hand, membership of that elite is made available to wider social groups; or (2) liberal-democratic (Taiwan, South Korea) where institutional reform has been rather more forced upon the elite by popular pressure and reforms have moved in the direction of liberal democratic competitive electoral systems

Democracy: as philosophy, institution and practice

In each of the above noted cases the theory of development points to a model of democracy, that is, the models are built into the theorizing. Yet the models imply different images of humankind and the models imply different lines of policy advice for states. These models are quite different and their comparative plausibility and utility could be examined, something that has been done via criticism, as noted. But another line forward also presents itself. If most of the members of the United Nations style themselves democracies whilst evidently running a multiplicity of different systems, attention is directed to the more fundamental question of the nature of democracy itself; how to grasp the scope of the idea in order to make the notion useful in enquiries.

So in order to advance matters it is necessary to return directly to the idea of democracy: to unpack it, to display its core logic, thereby making it once again useful for analysis.

The idea of democracy can be unpacked in the following fashion.

- Democracy can be understood as a philosophical idea: it comes in varieties – debate in Europe and America often revolves around the trio of liberalism, democracy and liberal democracy – to these can be added communitarianism and developmental democracy (elite pursuit of development) – in both cases discussion starts with the collective, not individuals.
- Democracy can be understood as political theory: it deals with models of government and various institutional arrangements for recruiting required personnel – in the second case, distinctions can be drawn in terms of openness or

- closedness of recruitment – distinctions can be drawn in terms of the effective control of the rules of recruitment – open to opportunistic manipulation or not – distinctions can be drawn in terms of mechanisms of advancement within government – clear versus unclear criteria – the answers to these questions determine the first case – the model of democracy.
- Democracy can be understood as historically achieved practice: the records of nominally democratic states can be reviewed – what they have achieved and how (and what more they might be expected to seek).

1 As a philosophical idea

Understood as a philosophical idea, democracy presents itself in diverse guises and, drawing on the survey work of David Held, three main traditions can be cited: liberalism, democracy and liberal-democracy; plus two further ideas, communitarianism and developmental democracy.

With liberalism social analysis begins with discrete individuals, they are taken to have inbuilt needs and wants and these they satisfy through exchanges with the natural world and other individuals and these are secured via contracts that are made. The general social world emerges from a dense network of practical individual occasioned contracts; the business of the government is to ensure order so that these contractual relations can be sustained and democracy is thus technique, how to select the people to run the machinery of the minimum state, and a practical imperative, how to protect individuals and their contractual relationships. Liberalism is routinely presented in Western discourse as equivalent to democracy. It is a contentious claim and it is routinely couched in terms of the business of competitive elections and so their presence or absence is taken as coterminous with the presence or absence of democracy.

With republican democracy social analysis begins with relationships. It is in the dense network of their relationships that social individuals are constituted, make their lives and pursue their several projects. The business of the government is to facilitate these processes – the task is governed by the notions of liberty, equality, citizenship and law: all matters much richer than mere contractual exchanges between nominally autonomous beings. Democracy is thus a realm of obligation, how to select the citizens from within a vigorous public sphere to run the machinery of the enabling state, and an ethical imperative, how to empower all members of society so that they can reach rational consensus and flourish.

With liberal-democracy social analysis begins with individuals. It is asserted that they have inbuilt needs and wants but relations between individuals are richer than contract; democracy is part technique (filling necessary job slots) and part enabling (facilitating a rich individualism).

With communitarian democracy social analysis begins with society. It is asserted that individuals are always lodged in society and the ideal for individuals is good citizenship. Communitarian notions of democracy look to social advance as a collective endeavour – the individual and the society must be enabled to flourish.

With developmental democracy social analysis begins with society seen as lodged in wider global systems in a structurally weak position. Elite secured development will secure over time greater substantive and formal democracy; that is, better lives, more locally ordered; but in the meantime the elite must drive the project forwards.

2 As political science theory

Democracy can be understood as a political science idea: a matter of various institutional arrangements for recruiting required personnel to the core machineries of government. Questions can be raised about the openness or closedness of recruitment, the effective control of the rules of recruitment, the mechanisms of advancement within government and the responsiveness or otherwise of the machinery to the wider population. Many institutional systems are available and their associated polities are quite distinct: thus, say, Singapore versus Germany; thus, say, China versus the United Kingdom; thus, say, North Korea versus Poland – and so on.

3 As historically achieved practice

Understood as an actual historical achievement, characterizations can be offered of the quality of the democracy on offer; the extent to which elites have secured their own goals and the extent to which their stated goals match up with those of others, their neighbours or local hegemon or the general standards affirmed by international organizations such as UN. None of these judgements are, so to say, definitive; rather they are contestable reports on work in progress.

Democracy: no simple model

It is clear that there is no simple single model of a democratic polity, there is no recipe and there is no simple single standard of judgement. It is also clear that there are numerous ways in which the idea has been put to work within the core countries of global system and amongst the new states created with the collapse of global state-empires. This seems an end point to debate but that is not so, for just as theories of development carry ideals of democracy, so too do distinct intellectual traditions.

Within the classical European tradition of social theorizing, a notion of discourse democracy can be constructed; in brief, humans are rational and are able to discuss and resolve political issues. In this fashion Jürgen Habermas argues that the unfolding logic of the system and its impacts upon the life world can be characterized, that is, ideology critique can bring the deeper logic to the surface and thus facilitate progressive change as better informed citizens begin to make better choices. The approach is grounded in claims about the fundamental nature of language. In this Habermas follows a number of European social theorists in placing human language at the centre of reflection upon social life. In respect of political life there is lodged within language use a double claim: for truth, which flows from the intrinsic character of language as a formal system; and for equality, which flows from the requirements of the transmission of truth. For Habermas, language carries within it a minimum ethic – that of a rational dialogue between equals; it is the core of the ideal of democracy. In more practical terms, Habermas argues that lodged within language is the drive to full open debate along with the social conditions necessary for such debate. The scheme gives theorists a way to approach the local logics of political systems – to say something about them – tentatively, circumspectly, critically and dialogically.

However, the practical achievement of democracy is a long-term goal and there are multiple trajectories and multiple logics and multiple problems to be overcome.

Democratic ideal in context: historical trajectories in East Asia

East Asian countries entered the modern world via the episode of colonial rule. The collapse of colonial empires was violent (war, civil war and battles for power amongst potential replacement elites) and matters were made more difficult by the externally invented Cold War. Replacement elites had to begin their construction of political communities in these difficult circumstances.

East Asian replacement elites came to power in numerous ways (for example):

- in Malaysia a conservative Malay elite co-opt local elite Chinese business, suppress popular forces and inherit power from the departing colonial ruler – continuity is the key until Dr Mahathir comes to power and pursues national development;
- in Singapore an English-educated reformist socialist anti-communist clique grasps power, suppresses their popular erstwhile allies, invites in the multinational companies and pursues national development;
- in South Korea, as the Japanese withdraw the Americans suppress local popular groups in favour of the dictatorial rule of a nationalist, a long-term émigré resident of the USA; confusion results and civil war ensues, further dictatorship follows and the country is rebuilt slowly in a species of national development;
- in China a civil war between progressive groups is resolved (after the complication of foreign invasion and in the unfolding context of foreign-inspired Cold War) in favour of an elite focused on mobilizing the large peasantry against residual traditional power holders in pursuit of a socialist system – which after spectacular achievements and failures is presently reforming in pursuit of a familiar East Asian model of national development;
- and so on – throughout Southeast Asia and the wider East Asia region.

In each of these countries we can identify quite specific political communities. They have their own logics and what counts as progress is built into their systems. On this two general ideas have been presented, respectively, Asian Values and communitarian democracy; both stress the difference between East Asia and the West and both point to the importance of community (rather than any liberal marketplace).

Democracy ideal in context – divisions – ethnicity, dispersal and inequality

Whatever version of democracy is being used, it assumes a more or less coherent political community. But there are many reasons why such an assumption may not be met in practice. Any political community may include fissures, that is, differences between groups, which might lead to conflicts. There are two familiar areas of debate – ethnicity and class inequality – and a third can be added which tracks the uneven impact upon social groups of the process of deepening global linkages, enthusiastically celebrated as globalization, more accurately, perhaps, regionalization; in any case, there is significant movement of people within the global system.

1 Dispersal of social locations (and the claims of globalization theorists)

In respect of the dynamics of political communities tensions associated with ethnicity and class are familiar. They are both understood to operate within any given political community and they undermine potentially the elite pursuit of national development. However, in contrast, some theorists have pointed to the dispersal of social locations under the impact of contemporary patterns of movement and pointed to ways in which the expected coherent political community is not clearly bounded or composed of citizens with a uniform status. These theorists suggest that a political grouping can become dispersed hierarchically (with people enjoying radically different social status positions) and horizontally (with geographically dispersed and distant semi-members of the community living in other places: diasporas, émigrés, migrants and so on).

Aihwa Ong argues that neo-liberal globalization presents states with new challenges and opportunities and it presents individuals with new challenges and opportunities. State elites can react to globalization by constructing overseas networks (they can invest in production facilities overseas) or by zoning their domestic spaces to make it easier for globalized firms to take up residence (by making special economic zones or offering tax breaks to overseas firms) or by announcing new state projects (thus many small polities wish to become a 'hub economy'). In this way the familiar assumption that the state is concerned to create a unified political community is called into question as the state can accommodate or create differences within the polity.

Individual people or groups can react to contemporary patterns of movement in various ways. These different responses cut against the familiar expectation of a more or less unified political community. The highly educated middle classes can take advantage of opportunities for travel. So too can poor migrants. Others find they are tied to one place and are losing relative social power.

The population within a country, a putative political community, can become highly differentiated:

- corporate-world persons who are highly educated and mobile and thus not tied to any one political community;
- elite state-machine persons who can barter their contacts for high-level corporate influence and are thus also freed to relocate from home community;
- middle-class professionals who might be more or less tied to one place but often do have international networks that offer some chances of moving outside familiar bounds;
- other middle classes have lower skills, fewer resources or local responsibilities and are tied to one place;
- poor persons in an area often have no choice but to stay put;
- some poor can become migrant workers (legal and illegal).

Some of these phenomena could be identified – quite different social locations plus quite different life chances – in many countries in East Asia. It might be added that the ability to travel freely is a privilege of those who dwell within rich countries and it might also be added that those who stay at home can resent both the geographically mobile rich and the inflows of migrants that economic reforms can foster.

2 Ethnicity: differentiation on the basis of quasi-natural categories

Ethnic division is familiar. Populations can divide themselves from others on the basis of claims to irrevocable differences, familiarly, language or culture or race. Conflicts associated with ethnic division are also familiar.

Group self-understanding
- Reductive explanations of ethnicity point to race, that is, to something extra-social, a naturally given property – physiology is a favourite starting point, then cultural preferences are added (read as somehow natural) and often language is added (again read as natural).
- Social construction explanations argue that identity and ethnic identity are socially learned; ethnicity is a construct but people begin with particular clues (physiology, culture or language) and on the basis of these clues make available differences the basis for separate ethnic identities.
- Ethnic identities are usually ascribed within a community to minorities whilst majorities typically take their identities for granted – it is others who are ethnic.

Group self-understanding within political communities
- Ethnic groups within a political community may be not merely distinguished but characterized as privileged or underprivileged.
- Both statuses can attract criticism (that the privilege is unfair, or the underprivileged are a nuisance).
- Ethnic identity can be the basis for claims to resources or representation or with ethnonationalism to separation from the political community.

East Asian elites have had to deal with multiple ethnic minorities:

- in the process of state/nation making via co-option or mobilization or suppression;
- in the process of subsequent development via co-option or mobilization or suppression.

East Asia offers many examples of these divisions (and their destructive potential):

- *Myanmar*
  The British colonial rulers displaced the predominant position of the lowland Burmese and protected to some extent the upland minorities; with decolonization came ethnic conflict and civil war as the lowland Burmese asserted themselves against the upland minorities (and low-level warfare continues).
- *Japan*
  The Japanese home islands were home to Japanese, Ryuku islanders and Ainu from Hokkaido; in the past people from China migrated and in the modern period many people from Korea had moved to Japan; within Japanese society caste division produced an outcaste group called *burakumin*; the population is thus somewhat diverse but there is an idea of the specialness of the Japanese that inhibits the acceptance of minorities.
- *Overseas Chinese*
  This group overlaps with the dispersed diasporic communities discussed by Ong; there are many Chinese communities in Southeast Asia which are usually integrated with the local communities but, contrary to stereotypes, they are not all rich; however, they can be picked out as 'Chinese' and in times of local trouble they are liable to become scapegoats, they are blamed and have been the subject of riots and discrimination.

3 Inequality: differential life-chances

Class inequality is familiar. Conflicts around livelihood can involve:

- access: gaining access to the means of livelihood (jobs, land, tools and raw materials, credit and markets);
- control: gaining access to the means of rule setting over livelihood (bureaucracies, legislatures, landlords, company owners);
- reward: gaining access to the means of distributing rewards (business firm managements, cooperative boards, landlords).

Conflicts around these issues can be summarized as involving economic, social and political inequality, conflicts between the powerful and the less powerful.

Conflicts can find expression within the mainstream institutions of the political community (parties, pressure groups, media campaigns and legal actions) and they can find expression outside the mainstream institutional forms (strikes, go-slows, sickness, gossip or riots and rebellions).

In East Asia economic, social and political inequalities have all made their appearance:

- the decolonization period saw shifting balances in local power relationships – there were winners and losers;
- the Cold War period saw external perceptions inform outside involvements – again there were local winners and losers;
- the independence era pursuit of development has generated further problems – the pursuit of development and the process of marketization has generated winners and losers.

4 Multiple lines of tension are cross-cutting and mutually reinforcing

These various lines of tensions have sometimes overlapped, creating confused conflicts. These conflicts can be difficult to disentangle; both the manner of their starting and the manner of their stopping (or not). The following are examples:

Malayan Communist Party (MCP) struggle:

- a rebellion precipitated by circumstances of end of Pacific War and related debates about the nature of inevitable decolonization;
- MCP was a resistance army;
- MCP was supported in wartime by British;
- MCP goals were inconvenient in peacetime to Malay elite and returning British colonial economic groups;
- British authorities squeezed politically and economically the MCP and its supporters;
- MCP rebels and after twelve years is defeated.

Huk Rebellion:

- in the 1930s in Luzon the commercialization of agriculture impacted existing patron/client relationships in countryside;
- peasants formed associations to protect themselves from new commercial demands of landowners;
- in 1942 these organizations became an anti-Japanese resistance;
- returning Americans classified them as communist with enthusiastic local elite support;
- in 1946 election Huk successes were simply ignored and from 1946 to 1951 growing guerrilla warfare, but from 1952 to 1956 slow decline in fighting with subsequent intermittent problems.

Assembly of the Poor:

- a Thai peasant movement which actively promotes the interests of poor rural people;
- active and well regarded it staged a ninety-nine-day encampment in the middle of Bangkok in 1997;
- treated favourably by new Thaksin government, but later suppressed.

China and rightful resistance:

- subaltern groups in China appeal to ideas lodged in the pronouncements of the state;
- an appeal over the heads of local cadres;
- activists emerge from local situation;
- nature of claims made and activities undertaken varies according to local circumstances;
- reaction of local officials and town and provincial officials varies;
- local-level politics is fluid but as China modernizes it is a growing phenomena.

In conclusion: replacement elites have sought to build states and nations and political communities have been created which have their own logics. The dynamics of progress can be sought internally and claims to democracy investigated. There are many successes but there are many fissures, here noted as dispersal, ethnicity and inequality.

Democracy as ideal – popular dissent – masses, legitimacy and resistance

Power and authority enable elites to shape the social world; the masses accommodate to these demands; and the social world functions. The exchange is a mix of force and persuasion (and persuasion is much more effective):

- power and authority are embedded in the everyday practical social relations of groups/classes;
- power and authority are embedded in institutional arrangements;
- power and authority are asserted in the realm of ideas as Great Traditions and Little Traditions; these are ideas/ethics about how the social world is and ought to be organized – this is an important arena of exchange between elite and mass for, if the masses accept elite ideas as legitimate, then they will acquiesce but, if the masses do not accept elite ideas as legitimate, then they will use the resources of the Little Tradition in order to fashion their own responses.

Great Tradition embraces high culture: these are the most basic ideas, which are taken as constitutive of a form of life, the most fundamental commitments that are made. They are expressed in arts, literature, religion, official ideologies and so on;

they may be carried by particular institutions; they may be exemplified by particular individuals and there may be particular sites which exemplify the Great Tradition ideas.

Little Tradition embraces the resources of ordinary life, intellectual/moral; it is the sphere of the masses, celebrating and informing local ordinary life. The Little Tradition offers resources that may be used in resisting the elites.

Relations between elites and masses are not fixed, they can change, they can evolve and they can change abruptly; they can also experience long periods of relative consensus (where neither side wants to or can change the balance). The resources of Great Traditions and Little Traditions provide ideas/ethics, which can inform practical action and when problems arise in society groups turn to the resources of these traditions so as to organize their responses.

1 Chinese elites/masses and the modern world

Imperial China was organized as an agrarian bureaucratic feudal system. Great Tradition: the system was buttressed by religion/ethic of Confucianism; other religions served other functions, thus Taoism (vitalism/divination), Buddhism and Islam. Little Tradition: at local-level village life the key was family and a person fitted into the social world via family, thereafter networks of kin, clan and language group.

The 1911 Revolution ushered in a period of great change. Great Tradition ideas were drawn from the example of the modern world, thus nation, democracy and development, and elites debated the relationship between 'China' and 'modernity'. Sun Yat Sen celebrates nation, democracy and development; Chiang Kai Shek imports elements of European and Japanese fascism (celebrations of 'will' and 'moral example'); whilst Mao blends resources of classical Chinese culture with Marxism-Leninism. These elite ideas are intermixed in diverse ways in political activities involving the masses throughout the 1911–78 period of China's general crisis.

Mao, for example, remains a key element in the elite-sponsored legitimation of the People's Republic with the celebration of the Long March, the notion of Mao Zedong Thought, the Mausoleum in Tiananmen Square, the picture fixed on the wall of the Forbidden City and printed on all paper currency. There are also many examples of ideas emerging from the ordinary people: the May 4th Movement 1919; the 28/2/47 Incident; the memorials on the Death of Zhou Enlai 1976; the Tiananmen Square Incident 1989; along with many low-level protests, thus in 2005 Beijing reported 86,000 incidents of low-level violent resistance to officials or developers throughout the country

2 Southeast Asia

A realm of small shifting kingdoms and maritime empires, predominantly Malay, receives cultural inputs from China and South and West Asia and later inputs from Europe/America. A fusion of cultures with Great Traditions (Islam – Hinduism – Buddhism – Chinese folk religion – Christianity) and Little Traditions comprising a multiplicity of local-level forms of life with multiple local religions, fusing with Islam in particular.

In Southeast Asia, Michael Vatikiotis points to the role of monarchies; in Thailand, Malaysia, Brunei, Cambodia and with lower-level aristocrats, Indonesia. Here is an example of Great Tradition ideas flowing into the institutions and ideas of present-day polities. Elites mixed Great Traditions and borrowings from the modern world, making new nation-states, many developmental. Mass access restricted and there were additional Cold War problems with resistance/protest: Huk Rebellion (Philippines 1950s); Penang Consumers' Association (Malaysia 1980/90s); the Great Marxist Conspiracy (Singapore 1980s) and the Assembly of the Poor (Thailand 1990s).

Response of masses: obedience-resistance-rebellion

In recent years East Asia has undergone rapid development. The exchanges between elite and mass have taken place in the context of rapidly developing countries. The key agent has been the developmental state. Yet the East Asian developmental state has offered restricted opportunities for active subordinate access to power. But a developmental state rests on a sense of community and leaders must be able to fashion consensus and mobilize/legitimize lines of action so authoritarian control is not enough. One aspect of securing legitimacy is by generating success as material success redeems the promises elites make. But subordinates will still seek to access political power (indeed, material advance might make the subordinate classes more concerned with political power) and, if there are no effective avenues for political engagement, then politics does not go away, it goes somewhere else and reappears in novel forms.

Subaltern class responses can be summed in schematic terms:

- deferential response – accepts status hierarchy and position in it; examples: rural Malaysia (conservative traditional society) – middle-class Japan (preference for harmony);
- aspirational response – accepts status hierarchy and works to move up it; examples: urban middle-class Singapore – urban middle-class Hong Kong – both communities are strongly committed to education, hard work and material advance;
- passive – withdrawal into private realm (consumption, family or minority life style); examples could be found now in any big city in East Asia – material advance and associated social change – (more difficult in smaller communities where individuals remain more socially visible and thus liable to social pressures);
- passive – use of weapons of the weak – small scale peasant rebellions, worker riots, middle-class and/or student protests, gossip, cheating, working slowly and so on; examples from any urban/rural area in East Asia;
- active – ameliorative resistance – joining NGOs and charities; examples from any urban/rural area in East Asia;

- active – civil society – organizing party or pressure group – offering an alternative status hierarchy and offering alternative models of society (an alternative 'national past' prioritizing different groups and goals) – democratic tendency in East Asian countries – strong – often meets varieties of elite resistance; examples: student/unionists in South Korea – civil society groups in Thailand, Philippines ('people power') and Malaysia (pressure groups) – radical tendency in East Asian countries – disadvantaged groups have recourse to violence – peasant groups in Philippines – various groups in China – groups in Hong Kong – religious groups in southern Philippines and parts of Indonesia – occasional terrorist actions;
- active – rebellion – invoking ideology or ethnicity or religion; examples: Huk Rebellion in northern Philippines – Moros in southern Philippines – rebels in southern Thailand – minorities in Myanmar – East Timorese, Achinese and West Papuans in Indonesia.

East Asian modernity – retrospect

The extant polities of East Asia shifted into the modern world via the experience of colonial rule. These colonial systems disintegrated in the middle of the twentieth century and local nationalist elites took power. They have driven a number of political cultural projects and their record has been successful in general terms: societies have coalesced, economies prospered and political communities attained coherence. In brief, states have been made, nations invented and development energetically pursued. In this record much has been debated. One issue is that of the nature of the polities. One debate has revolved around the notion of democracy.

East Asian polities are not converging on the model of America (modernization and globalization), their historical trajectory does not resemble that of Latin America (dependency) and they are not converging on the rather different model of a prosperous society advocated by the United Nations or European Union (institutionalism). If their local trajectories are acknowledged then it is within the unfolding exchanges between elites and masses that an embedded idea will be found, the fundamental ethic that animates over the long run the dynamics of the polity.

A number can be identified in practice.

After Jürgen Habermas, modernity can be analysed in terms of system and life world, with debate taking place within the public sphere; such dialogue is finally underpinned by an ideal speech situation where reasoned argument is pursued; language carries a minimum ethic and critical theory is grounded, it is something more than just one more subjectively asserted ideology. In the context of comparative political analysis it serves to provide the hope for dialogue (granting evident diversity, the minimum ethic implies different peoples can talk to each other) and implies a common concern for the on-going achievement of democracy (the ethic does work, but as a deep seated imperative and not as a recipe).

Democracy: philosophy, institution, practice and dialogic critique

It is not a recipe; it is a laboriously achieved social practice.

It can be unpacked as a trio of subordinate ideas: the philosophical base of claims, the institutional mechanisms oriented towards securing such claims and the actual historical achievement of the polity in question.

East Asian trajectories are different. Local ethic, machinery and practice must be analysed in detail, for macro comparisons with America or Europe (or anywhere else for that matter) are not very helpful.

Cast in terms of the classical European tradition of social theorizing an argument can be made which lodges a disposition towards dialogic democracy in language itself; system and life-world can be distinguished, critique deployed, inhibitions to democratic functioning identified and ameliorative action proposed.

14
IMAGINED COMMUNITIES, COLLECTIVE MEMORY AND THE NATIONAL PAST

The dissolution of state-empires created a number of new states whose successor elites moved to invent nations and thereafter to pursue development; denizens of these novel political units had to be bound together in a common project, the pursuit of national development. The new nation had to be created and lodged in history and the new unit was not merely an imagined community it was also imagined in time, it had a history, it had a trajectory and it had a fundamental logic. Three ideas can uncover the logic of this process: the idea of an imagined community; plus two further ideas, which have been used to access this aspect of the business of the creation of new states and nations: collective memory and the national past. In the case of East Asia, sometime peripheral areas took the opportunity of state-empire dissolution to lodge claims to states, nations and thereafter to promise to their newly created citizens, better lives, or development. The process of creating political identities was both crucial and, so to say, out in the open; it was argued for, manoeuvred for and in more than a few cases fought for, generally, with great success.

As state-empires dissolved, the people who inhabited particular territories found themselves moving from being denizens of a large-scale multi-ethnic political-social unit to the much more restricted environment of a bounded state. Citizens in former core areas had to accommodate precipitate territorial decline and rework their ideas of themselves accordingly. And on the other hand citizens of new nation-states had to reimagine their place in the world, from being subjects located within a state-empire territory of global extent and controlled by distant masters, they became citizens of a territorially restricted state controlled – at least in principle – by their own chosen leaders. These tasks bore upon the populations of these territories but they fell most heavily upon elites, the established elites in the core areas, and newer elites in sometime peripheries, those who led their countries, or aspired to, and who had to legitimate their claims on power.

In the peripheral territories, for the people who lived within the boundaries of the newly created states, their imagined community became more restricted in its extent;

it got smaller, it inhabited a specific local space, it became more ethnically homogeneous and leadership groups assumed a clearer focus. It was a process of reimagining membership of the wider community, now a national community, and the business was advertised as one of progress, offering hope for the future. This experience – or variants of it – were repeated throughout the sometime territories of the state-empires as nations were made where they had not existed before and national pasts were invented, ancestors discovered and in some cases a pre-existing political system was legitimately reanimated, say Thailand or China; but for most peoples decolonization marked the inauguration of a novel way of belonging to the wider society.

In the sometime core territories the same general process unfolded, impacting both citizens and elites as they too came to inhabit smaller territories. They had to reimagine these units, however, where sometime peripheral peoples could read change positively, attaining independence, opening up new possibilities for the future; for the inhabitants of sometime core areas, in particular elites, the business looked like loss. Territories became smaller, familiar options were being foreclosed, and reimagining community in such circumstances required great intellectual and political imagination.

For successor elites in newly created states none of this reimagining was straightforward: elites had to invent new nations, the claims they made had to resonate with the populations they sought to lead as collective memory ran through these populations just like any other. In this context one aspect of this process of reimagining was the construction of a national past, an elite sponsored version of the history of the new country created in an exchange with collective memories. The national past points to the country's past, its present and by implication its ideal future. The national past could not simply be imposed, for ordinary people had their own recollections and there were various ways of remembering, together collective memory. The national past was constructed in an exchange with collective memory and the two intertwined in multiple fashions.

Having invented the nation it has to be sustained. The national past must be continually both reaffirmed and updated and passing events must be drawn into the overall tale as failure to update the national past opens one way for state and society to diverge, for popular dissent to grow. The role or activities of the state can dwindle (or be self-consciously reduced), so that, at best, it is merely concerned with the efficient delivery of basic services. But if the state is no longer central, that is, no longer articulates a plausible project for the future, then the legitimacy attached to the idea of the nation can move elsewhere. It can be relocated in religious community, relocated in media confections, recentred on the corporate world or relocated in local popular dissent and protest. Sustaining the nation is crucial for the legitimacy of the elite; the idea of the nation runs through common sense, it forms an element of the identities of ordinary citizens.

So, in sum, there are three ideas to consider: imagined community, collective memory and the national past; together threaded through the lives of elite and mass and working to locate citizens within the wider ordered political community and working to legitimate the power of the elite, securing their authority.

Identity: social and political

Everyone on the planet has an identity: (1) social, the person that we are (or take ourselves to be), evidenced in practical form in our routine interactions with others; and (2) political or official in the membership we have of an ordered community, evidenced in practical form in the state-issued passport or ID card that we carry.

Although an identity, social and political or formal, is something taken for granted, unremarked in ordinary life, it is nonetheless a subtle construction, not a simple given. Nor do the two elements noted here carry the same weight. The social identity is learned early in life, the latter political or formal identity is acquired much later, and it is also somewhat more self-consciously learned as figures of authority offer examples or instruction — nonetheless, it is for citizens of long-established countries something ordinary, taken for granted. Not so in the new countries that took shape during the process of state-empire dissolution. In these countries the process of constructing formal identities — memberships of nations — was played out in public in the claims of independence leaders and in the statements of departing colonial officials and perhaps also in the inchoate demands of rioters on the streets.

In terms of enquiry into the business of identity there is a long-standing debate amongst social theorists between those who would start with structures and those who would start with agents: structures could be understood as economic (say, classes) or social (say, groups) or cultural (say, traditions); and in contrast agents would be understood as individual persons or maybe groups (thus classes acting within unfolding historical processes). The debate has often been inconclusive, however another way of coming at these debates is available and it flows from essentially philosophical reflection on language. One way of putting the matter is to point out that language is a system of rules, it is trans-individual (structure) and the system of rules permits the creation of speech (agency), so every time a person speaks they invoke the available set of rules in order to make whatever point they wish to make. This idea has been picked up in a number of now familiar distinctions: thus language/speech or structure/agent or canon/text or tradition/present. Cast in these terms, individuals and communities constitute their identities through the repertoire of concepts available and these are carried in tradition, setting the limits of what can and cannot be imagined. This turns enquiry towards the resources of the disciplines of the humanities and to history and to the study of the sets of ideas/stories carried down through time, picked up, reused, reworked and then bequeathed to the successor generation.

In the present discussion of identity these distinctions will be borne in mind and the particular route into these discussions will invoke the work of Cultural Studies, in particular the work of one of the founders. Richard Hoggart's cultural studies work is an idiosyncratic empirical sociology and his writings access the social world via recollections of his own biography. The work is revealing and for present purposes it calls attention to identity as a realm of apparently mundane detail, where these mundane details serve to locate us within the wider social world.

Identity: personal and political (the role of elites)

Identity is social and each person is located in numerous social networks, such identities can be unpacked in numerous ways (given that individuals dwell in multiple networks), but here the concern is first with the ordinary personal sphere and then exchanges with the more general political networks of the social world, states, governments, elites and so on.

1 Identity – personal/formal

Identity locates us within complex social networks. It is created through social learning; most is achieved early in life and subsequent learning sits on top of the early material (otherwise, as sociologists have put it, primary and secondary socialization). The learning is very subtle. As Anthony Giddens has pointed out, all human beings are sophisticated social agents and we know how to deal with our fellow humans and we know (to a perhaps greater or lesser extent) how the world works. This sophistication in learning is thereafter replicated in sophisticated social action and thus in a sophisticated and accomplished self: identity sums this learning and related skills.

Just as it is possible to distinguish primary and secondary socialization, in a similar way it is possible to distinguish personal identity and political identity.

The former personal identity locates us within social networks with a mix of ascribed status and achieved status: age, gender, ethnicity, class and so on are clues to ascribed status, the social world puts us in our place and ideas, attitudes and dispositions are imputed to agents on the basis of these broad clues. Such imputations may be embraced or rejected but they are likely to bear down heavily on any one individual. Thereafter we can make our way in the world, accumulating achievements, thus, achieved status. The whole confection is richly elaborated enfolding a multiplicity of aspects and an extensive repertoire of social skills. It is here that we find most of the material that makes us who we are.

The later political identity locates us within the social networks that formally order the community within which we live and again it is a mix of ascribed status and achieved status. It is less elaborated. It is shaped by patterns of power and authority in the community within which we dwell. A political identity is contested comprising a mix of the claims of the powerful and our personal or group experience of how things are in routine practice. Within industrial capitalist societies the key ascribed status will be social class, perhaps supplemented by ethnicity, and these two fix most people in place: shaping life chances, shaping schedules of attitudes towards the flow of political events within the community.

2 Personal – locale, network and memory

Personal identity can be unpacked in terms of three ideas: locale, network and memory.

The notion of locale is taken from the style of work of cultural studies and it calls attention to the realm of the familiar, the taken for granted. More substantively, it points to the place where a person lives, the people whom they know in the context of day-to-day routines. In biographical terms, the place where a person was born and lived as a child, which is a rich environment with family, friends, relatives, neighbours and people in the immediate community such as teachers, officials and so on. It can be taken, in terms of social science, as the formative environment of the young but, for the adult, this would be accessible only in recollection.

The notion of network points to the wider set of people with whom a person interacts: taking a job in another town, going on holiday and meeting people or keeping touch with people via the internet, joining professional organizations and attending meetings. Middle-class professionals in industrial capitalist societies have a wide network of acquaintances and they may be located within the home country, but they might also be located in other countries. In the twenty-first century air travel is available to a mass travelling public and the internet is widely available; but it might be noted that neither are universally available and the networks of people in the global south might be geographically circumscribed, but there will still be networks.

The notion of memory points to the ways in which all the above elements are used to make a coherent sense of self. Memory is highly selective; it is a mix of active remembering and equally active forgetting. Two ideas have been used to grasp the business of memory: collective memory, the ways in which local communities remember, ideas likely to intermix with autobiographical material; and the national past, the more formal schemes constructed through an exchange of elite ideas and collective memory, a kind of contested provisional consensus in respect of the wider political community, but nonetheless, running through ordinary life.

3 Political – locale, network and memory

Political identity can be unpacked in the same way.

Thus locale comprises the political community within which individuals live, the ideas current within the immediate environment, the ideas of parents and siblings. Then the ideas current within the wider community, school, clubs and societies, then wider and more distant, newspapers, television, official announcements plus responses to figures of authority. It is within this circumscribed environment that an initial sense of a self located within a polity will be formed and perhaps also some basic stances towards the polity, thus aspiration, acquiescence or opposition, all subject to later revision and re-revision (political identities are less deep set as compared with personal identities).

Thus network comprises the ideas current in those groups, which an individual might join or with which they might interact: workplace, party, NGO and so on. These groups could be local, face-to-face, or distant, via the internet. Then travel, places and people outside the normal sphere offering new learning, new contacts and new ideas. One version of this idea was presented by Benedict Anderson: colonial pilgrimages, the ways in which those from peripheral areas of state-empires learned the ideas of the core and thereafter deployed them in contests for power.

And finally memory: those ideas current within the polity which inhabitants are invited to accept through both collective memory and the national past; ideas that locate the polity in unfolding and particular time, that is, memories are not general, they are particular and they underpin the sets of ideas of particular communities and polities.

Identity and the impacts of changing contexts

Identity locates people within complex social and political networks but these are not fixed, they change, sometimes slowly (as with the impacts of the growth of scientific knowledge and consequent novel technologies and new consumer goods), and sometimes abruptly (as with the unexpected onset of financial crises or, on a wider scale, the war-related collapse of empires). In East Asia the shift to the modern world was triggered by the arrival of foreign traders and slowly the social and political systems were remade; as social/political networks changed so did the ways in which people thought of themselves; such change continues, the unfolding shift to the modern world is open-ended.

1 Multiple reflections

There were multiple reflections amongst various groups about the shift to the modern world in East Asia as elite groups confronted the available images of the West; the same was true of elite figures in the West as they looked to the East. A mixture of correct perceptions and stereotypes could be found in both groups: thus Orientalism and Occidentalism, mutual stereotyping, mutual misunderstandings and, of course, multiple social exchanges informed by these misunderstandings.

East Asian elite ideas of the West, the images, which elites had in the late nineteenth century, were formed as they struggled to come to terms with the demands of the modern world, to grasp its essence and absorb its lessons: examples are Fukuzawa Yoichi (arguing for a modern Japan), Sun Yat Sen (arguing for a modern China) or Rabindranath Tagore (arguing for an Asia alert to its own traditions and character).

Western elite ideas of the East were shaped by the views of the incoming Westerners: examples include T.S. Raffles (an official of the East India Company, concerned to bring civilization and to record in detail nineteenth-century style the local fauna and flora), Paul Gauguin in Tahiti or, later, colonial administrator scholars, such as J.S. Furnivall, or much later, writers such as Graham Green on Vietnam or Anthony Burgess on Malaya.

Many groups produced stereotypes of the denizens of other cultures, and there are many examples. Europeans in the nineteenth century could represent the Chinese as unreliable opium smokers (thereby blaming the victims) or denizens of a recalcitrant faded civilization (Marx – battering down walls). Malays could be presented as lazy. Contrariwise, Asian critics could characterize Westerners as individualistic materialists (thereby mistaking acquisitive sojourners for the generality of Europeans or Americans).

There were also strategies for independence and progress. Examples would include nationalist movements throughout East Asia; Japan also presented the idea of pan-Asianism, which was advocated by Japanese scholars as a broad strategy of response – intellectual and practical – to the incursions of Europeans and Americans. Later, it settled into a species of Japanese nationalism as they too joined the empire builders, carving out territory in Northeast Asia.

2 The demands of the powerful

The demands of powerful elites bore down on others in society; they found expression in a number of forms.

Thus the influence of Great Traditions: these were assertions of authority and demands for obedience, the ideas of the elites inscribed in sacred texts, or found in the arts (decoration, dance, writings and so on) or located in sacred sites, perhaps of pilgrimage.

Thus the national past: the elite deployed its own ideas within the population with multiple formal and informal responses – media, official events, textbooks, films and so on. The resultant set of ideas can be tagged the national past. It is an elite-sponsored popular version of the identity of a political community: what the Japanese elite tell their population, what the Chinese elite tell their population and what the Singaporeans tell their population – a pattern repeated in every country.

Thus, relatedly, there is the business of contemporary nationalisms. Anthony Reid has offered a typology of available nationalisms. First, ethnic nationalism: culture plus language plus place plus myth issues in a claim to the naturalness of a given identity and, unlike Europeans, in East Asia the idea of race is still used. Second, state nationalism: this is a modern idea, new in the region as contemporary state nationalism is post-colonial. Third, anti-imperial nationalism: opposition to foreign rulers has been crucial in turning territories within empires into post-empire nations, thus the ideology constructs nation, and these are typically early twentieth-century ideas. Fourth, nationalism informed by reactions to foreign interventions and which invoke a pre-foreigner past in order to imagine a post-foreigner future, thus China, Korea.

All this can be pursued. The ideas and their effects (popular mobilization), how the idea of nation is presented in ordinary routine so as to foster active commitment – being a 'Chinese patriot' or being a 'loyal Singaporean' or being 'Thai respectful of the King' or being 'a true Japanese', and so on.

Thus contemporary resistance: dissident groups, for example, local-level social unrest in China, militant Islamist groups in Southeast Asia, civil society groupings in Thailand or rural peasant movements in the Philippines.

3 Absorbing the shocks

Absorbing the shocks and taking the opportunities marked the practical responses of various non-elite groups. The drivers of change were the incoming groups of traders and, whilst some locals prospered, others did not.

Groups who placed themselves in intermediate positions: those who prospered by interacting with incomers, the locals able to assist traders; locals whose form of life in time blended local and incoming cultures; groups formed by inter-marriage; and so on: examples – Chinese compradors in Hong Kong – the Straits Chinese community in Singapore.

Various dispossessed groups: those whose patterns of life were pushed aside; redundant royals, thus the Malay Royals, pushed aside and quietened with large pensions; redundant masses, pushed aside, left on the rural farms; those otherwise dispersed, as with Malay sea people.

Migrant flows and minority communities: – those who fitted into new social environments and maintained (or not) links with places of origin; examples are: Chinese migration to Southeast Asia, Indian migration into Southeast Asia, Japanese migration to Korea, Manchuria and Latin America, European and American migration to the trading cities of the region.

Identity – social movement – migration/marginal figures – losers

The modern world has been marked by flows of people, that is, migration; some occasioned by war and other civil disturbances and some occasioned by the search for better lives. Such flows were familiar in the nineteenth century and they were also familiar in the early parts of the twentieth, much of this associated with a number of catastrophic wars. Today, in the post-war world, there are flows of people: those moving for better lives (migrants); and those moving to escape troubles (refugees). Such movement is now familiar – although it has assumed newish forms, that is, organized illegal migration with routine claims for asylum; it has become an awkward issue for sending and receiving populations and elites.

1 Living in today's world

The implications of migration have impacted countries in East Asia: in social scientific terms, simple arguments about the givenness of identity are undermined, so too simple arguments about the identity-coherence of communities, but, that said, rapid change can undermine the taken-for-granted certainties of established social groups and tensions; scapegoating and violence can follow.

Mobile populations undermine the easy assumption of the natural-ness of identity; they undermine the easy argument from race (in fact, physiology) or ethnicity (the same, expressed politely) or language (claimed wrongly to be non-contingent) or culture (again, claimed wrongly to fixity) to identity. Mobile populations underscore the relational character of identity. Identity locates us within social networks (it does not somehow grow outwards from our given natural self). Identity becomes multiple and loss of simple surety can be experienced as problematical whilst claims to fixity can be used to vehicle prejudices. Thus European conservatives used to speak of rootless cosmopolitans who were viewed as a threat to traditional order; arguments revisited in Europe in recent years, following financial problems and flows of visible migrants.

Minority communities can be long established or relatively new. There are many examples of both types: Chinese in Indonesia, Malays in Singapore, Koreans in Japan, Indians in Fiji, Karen, Hmong, Wa and others in the border areas of Mynamar and Thailand, Montagnards in Vietnam, Javanese migrants in Kalimantan, or, rather differently, affluent foreign professionals in Singapore and Hong Kong. East Asia is home to many minority groups and their relationships with host majority communities can be difficult. Thus prejudices, a mix of status ascription plus discrimination, offer particular readings of a person or groups identity; such identities can be imputed on the basis of a perceived ethnicity; if that ethnicity or identity is low status within the majority community then discrimination may follow and once initiated the process can easily become self-reinforcing.

Diasporic communities are constituted by family relocation. Trans-state linkages are created along with the maintenance of discrete ethnic identities within host communities. Once again there are many examples: Hong Kong people migrating to Canada or Taiwanese people migrating to America or Vietnamese migrating to Australia.

There are also flows of popular culture and within East Asia there are networks of imports and exports; from Japan, Korea, Hong Kong and Taiwan throughout the region. These regional producers also export to North America and Europe and the region also imports from North America and Europe: commercial media, high-status fashion goods.

2 Marginal groups

The contemporary global system is also home to weaker groups: those who are today's marginal groups, those who have been left behind or pushed aside.

Many people in East Asia are not rich urban dwellers; rather they are relatively poor rural people. The implications of urban bias for the rural poor are negative; they get left behind. These rural areas can be home to a multiplicity of language groups and a multiplicity of cultural groups – in the past, tagged plural societies. Many examples: Thailand's rural poor, Myanmar's minority groups, Fiji's indigenous groups, New Zealand's Maori people, Australia's aboriginals and the rural poor in China and throughout Southeast Asia.

The urban poor are another group: they comprise slum dwellers or informal settlements or urban villages. There are many examples: slums, Bangkok, Manila and Jakarta; or squatter settlements, for example in Malaysia; or migrant urban villages in big cities in China; and so on.

In urban and rural communities there are those judged to have failed or have been judged to be not worthy: for example, Japan's *burakumin* or Southeast Asia's sex trade workers.

Liquid modernity

Zygmunt Bauman has argued that today's world offers many opportunities for movement. It has created new opportunities but has done so at a cost: linkages with place and community are weakened and the individual is thrown back on their own resources. Such structural changes impact social groups differentially. In rich areas, there are winners and losers – roughly, the corporate world, in particular finance, has benefited from these changes – highly educated middle-class professionals have also found these changes acceptable. But less well educated people and the poorly educated masses have not found these changes to their liking and employment has become precarious, so too other aspects of ordinary life. The gap between elite and mass has been noted, thus the distinction between the one per cent and the rest. In America and Europe this condition has provoked a backlash against ruling elites; multiple anxieties have coalesced around the issue of inward migration, in particular irregular movement from relatively poor areas to relatively rich. In the second decade of this century the poorer members of society in these latter areas have signalled their non-acceptance. President Trump, Brexit and what are labelled by commentators as 'right-wing populists' in many mainland European countries are read as symptomatic.

Identity – rich, layered and suffused with memory

Personal identity is constituted in terms of the exchange of locale, network and memory: it is rich in detail; it is suffused with memory; and it is always local, fixing individuals in place, geographical, social, cultural, and at a macro scale, historical (hence talk of generations in social commentary). The same argument works (albeit revised) for social groups: communities have identities (village, town or city); formal organizations have identities (the tax man, the police or health service); and industries have identities (coal or steel or aerospace or finance).

The same argument works (again, albeit revised) for political communities. A series of layers can be posited. Their make-up will vary from place to place, but they will run from local and particular to the non-local and general. In the contemporary global system the last noted would be – in principle if not in fact – a state and at this point denizens of the state will be invited to accept a national identity, membership of an imagined community.

Elites must secure the support or acquiescence of the populations that they rule; mechanisms of hard social control (laws, rules etc.) can be supplemented by mechanisms of soft social control (ideas, images etc.) and in this last noted area memory plays a role.

Three key ideas to discuss: imagined community, collective memory and the national past.

Imagined community: Benedict Anderson argues that membership of a community involves an exercise in sympathetic imagination, he writes of a deep horizontal comradeship, adding that membership in the nation is inclusive. Anderson traces its roots to the early settlers in North America when local print sources plus the experience of being tagged as provincials fed an idea of America, a national imagined community. Thereafter, the idea was available for others to use: in Latin America, in Europe and recently with decolonization throughout the Global South.

Collective memory: Maurice Halbwachs has dealt with the multiple ways in which communities remember (active remembering plus active forgetting) at individual, group and community levels. Memories are passed on down the generations in this fashion. The process is piecemeal, untidy, low-key and so on.

The national past: Agnes Heller has dealt with elite-sponsored version of the events dealt with by collective memory. The national past runs through common sense, it is experienced in ordinary life as something taken for granted but it is a stylized history turned to the legitimation of the extant political system. The national past offers a statement about where the polity came from, where it now is and what in principle is the outline of its ideal future. The national past lodged a polity in unfolding time, in history.

East Asia: imagined community, collective memories and national pasts

The notion of collective memory points to the ways in which human societies remember, it is a social process and these memories are transmitted down the generations in a number of ways: individual memory (recollection or testimony); family memory (documents, memorabilia); corporate or civic memory (records, archives, memorials); and national state (archives (open/closed), public records, memorial sites, official remembrance and official statements – national pasts). All these social mechanisms transmit the past into the present; it is a highly contingent process but it can be simplified (thus, popular/elite memory) and it can be returned to its substantive context, that is, the unfolding process of the shift to the modern world and, more particularly, the recent history of the dissolution of state-empires and the creation of new nations and states.

Anthony Reid writes of three elements: pre-colonial, colonial and then post-colonial; as the cultures of the earlier forms of life have blended into the latter, so today's contemporary forms are layered.

East Asia: before contact

Elite and popular memories of the period prior to colonial rule are available only as matters of recollection, or story telling of one sort or another. In Northeast Asia, mainland Southeast Asia and Southeast Asia the resources available would be indirect: sacred texts, bureaucratic records, the arts, architecture and folk memory. The past can be read into the present day in unexpected ways; for example, Hong Kong citizens celebrate traditional Chinese festivals but they do so in a rich, cosmopolitan world city; or Thai and Cambodian nationalist groups squabble about border areas around ancient temple sites – so the deep past does run on into the present.

The past can also be carefully packaged and presented to a contemporary audience. Thus major tourist sites – Angkor Wat, Xi'an's terracotta warriors, Confucius's home town, memorial sites for Mao – not deep past, but heritage. And the process of reconstruction can be picked up in popular media/arts: in Thailand, popular films dealing with Siamese wars against Burmese; in Japan, Kurasawa's movies, thus *Seven Samurai*; or in China, movies about the Wars of the Three Kingdoms; and so on.

TABLE 14.1 East Asia: major conflicts, 1911–91[1]

1911–14	Chinese Revolution
1914–16	Yuan Shikai Interval
1916–26	Warlord Era
1918–41	First-phase anti-Colonial Movements
1926–28	Northern Expedition
1927–37	First Chinese Civil War
1931–34	Jiangxi Soviet
1931–32	Japanese invasion of Manchuria
1932–37	Japanese expansion in Northern China
1937–45	Sino-Japanese War
1941–45	Pacific War
1945–50	Indonesian Revolution
1946–51	Huk Rebellion
1946–49	Second Chinese Civil War
1946–54	First Indo-China War
1948–60	Malayan Emergency
1950–53	Korean War
1963–66	Konfrontasi
1965–68	Indonesian Coup
1966–69	Cultural Revolution
1954–93	Cambodian wars
1954–75	Laos conflicts
1954–75	Second Indo-China War
1978–91	Third Indo-China War

Note
1 List first assembled at CUHK, published in P.W. Preston, 2010, *National Pasts in Europe and East Asia*, London, Routledge.

The colonial period

Thus elite and popular memories of the period of colonial rule, and whilst these are also mostly matters of recollection and stories, there are great stocks of materials: records, photographs, memoirs, paintings and so on, all dealing with the Dutch colonial sphere, the British colonial sphere, the French colonial sphere and the American colonial sphere.

The colonial period is best seen as the means whereby peoples in East Asia shifted into the modern world and the episode has marked them profoundly. It has been read into their respective national pasts, as noted earlier, but a note can be added on the self-conscious recollection of the process: folk memories, arts and humanities.

Thus the period is available in reconstruction: in film – for India, Merchant and Ivory; in China, films and television soaps dealing with the Sino-Japanese War; or in novels – for Africa, Joseph Conrad; in China the long period from the Opium War to the foundation of New China is recalled as a Hundred Years of Humiliation (the Kuomintang celebrated National Humiliation Day, the CCP discarded the idea, resurrected it as National Defence Day), and the end time of colonial rule is available in film – thus Bernardo Bertolucci's *The Last Emperor* or Chang Yuen Ting's *The Soong Sisters*.

TABLE 14.2 East Asia: casualties, 1911–91[1]

Warlords and civil war, 1916–37	4,000,000
Chinese civil war, 1945–49	2,500,000
Sino-Japanese and Pacific War	12,600,000
Southeast Asia Occupations	5,000,000
Korean War, 1950–53	2,800,000
First Indo-China War, 1945–54	600,000
Second Indo-China War, 1960–75	2,700,000
Indonesian Regime Change, 1965	500,000
Third Indo-China War, 1978–91	1,500,000
Total	31,200,000

Notes
1 The list of wars is assembled from the work of historians. The data is also from multiple sources, but see in particular these websites:
World History at KMLA, http//www.zum./de/whkmla/military;
Source List and Detailed Death Tolls for the Twentieth Century Hemocylism, http//users.erols.com/mwhite28/warstat1.htm;
Secondary Wars and Atrocities of the Twentieth Century, http//users.erols.com/mwhite28/warstat1.htm;
en.wikipedia.org/wiki/List_of_wars_and_anthropogenic_disasters_by_death_toll;
necrometrics.com/wars19c.htm.
List first assembled at CUHK, published in P.W. Preston, 2010, *National Pasts in Europe and East Asia*, London, Routledge.

Decolonization and development

Thus elite and popular memories of the process of decolonization: the Dutch colonial sphere, the British colonial sphere, the French colonial sphere and the American colonial sphere. Again, a wealth of material is available in the form of documents, official, corporate and private, photographs, private and commercial, film, mostly commercial. The episode is historically recent, so that oral history is available and as the episode is recent, it is not settled in recollection, that is, it can be contentious.

Thus elite and also popular memory memories of the drive for state, nation and development led by new successor elites, inheriting assorted legacies, establishing novel projects and then ensuring new trajectories are established.

The collapse of the state-empire system was violent and local-level opposition was given its chance with the 1941 opening of the Pacific War; state-empires were swept aside and local populations had to adapt, that is, collaborate; local elites could seek advantage, that is, collaborate in expectation of independence.

The end of the Pacific War brought further violence as returning colonial powers sought either to recover their former territories or to shape successor regimes. There were numerous violent conflicts and again there are popular memories of anti-colonial independence struggles; local elites sought independence, now in conflict with sometime colonial masters yet buttressed in their determination by wartime experiences.

The slow process of withdrawal on the part of former colonial masters was – as noted – accompanied by violence, but as territories became independent this sort of violence subsided. Local elites were established in power and the broader context offered further problems and opportunities in the guise of the Cold War. Here memories diverge along bloc lines; popular memories of further struggles as elites continued to seek sovereign independence and popular memories of economic growth as elites contrived the developmental state strategy of advance.

Individual experiences – mass and elite – differed. In time official recollections were put in place, national pasts were created, noting the business of securing independence, laying claim to a deeper history than colonial life and plotting a route to the future.

Having written a national past, a set of substantive claims, the construction has to be maintained and updated. Unfolding events have to be drawn into the national story, the story will need to be reworked from time to time and any inflection points in the unfolding historical trajectory will need to be interpreted (thus, for example, China and the episode of the Cultural Revolution followed by the reforms of Deng Xiaoping see the country redirected and its past re-evaluated – or Malaysia with the riots of 1969 followed thereafter the idea of NEP – or recently Thailand, the experiment with liberal-democratic party elections is vetoed by the elite's coup).

Thus, once again, in highly schematic terms – extant national pasts:

- China – foreign incursions, local collapse, multiple wars until finally China 'stands up' – further successes – China Dream;

Collective memory and the national past **249**

- South Korea – colonial rule, Cold War division and national recovery;
- Japan – late development, failed empire and deep continuity in recovery as Japanese uniqueness is sustained;
- Taiwan – resistance to communism, maintenance of traditional cultures, a novel independence created;
- Indo-China – a quartet or polities – colonial rule or pressures, civil wars, external involvement plus national liberation and recovery;

FIGURE 14.1 Lim Bo Seng Memorial, Singapore, December 2009.

- Thailand – local elite-sponsored reforms, no formal colonial rule and deep national continuity – King, religion and place;
- Philippines – elite rule, an America-inflected nationalism;
- Malaysia – colonial rule, conflicts and deep Malay national continuity;
- Singapore – vulnerable, few resources, local efforts and upshot is a self-created trading nation;
- Indonesia – colonial rule and the creation of a new nation;
- Myanmar – colonial rule, loss and recovery of Burmese priority.

FIGURE 14.2 Kranji, Singapore, December 2009.

FIGURE 14.3 School, Sichuan, November 2016.

Citizens of new nation-states had to learn new identities; schematically, the shift from subjects within a multi-ethnic trans-global state-empire, to citizens of a bounded state. The notion of identity can be unpacked – locale, network and memory are the basic elements, thereafter, collective or national identities can be added to the mix.

Contemporary debates – politics, economics and the invocation of identity

Trying to grasp the form of life of another culture is anything but straightforward – the shift to the modern world has over several centuries radically remade human forms of life – social scientists have been one group trying to make sense of these macro-level changes and the reactions of discrete populations – one style of popular work has run with bi-polar characterizations – thus characterizations have moved from civilization versus barbarians through the Asian Values debate to the business of forms of life. East Asia has produced its own counterparts and Orientalism has been matched by Occidentalism. A number of recent reiterations of these debates can be identified: Japan versus the USA (around the issue of trade), the crony capitalism debate or, more recently, the China versus America debate (around the issue of status in the global system).

This style of debate rumbles on: orientalist work versus occidentalist work; one set of stereotypes deployed against another. It is unhelpful. It has gone through quite distinct phases: the early days of state-empire expansion (European traders reached East Asia and brought back travellers' tales – exotics of one sort or another – Chinese mandarins saw violent foreigners); the later phases of colonial expansion (White race and Yellow Race); the high tide of colonial rule (rational administrators versus less competent local rulers); period of decolonization (rulers and rebels); and latterly the period following the dissolution of state-empires and the creation of new states and nations (East versus West etc.).

In place of these oppositions what is really at stake is an adequate interpretive grasp of the multiplicity of forms of life within the contingent global (non)system.

Retrospect

By way of a summary note: the dissolution of state-empires was accompanied by the emergence of successor elites that went on to create states, build nations and pursue national development; events fed into collective memory and an elite-sponsored exchange between elite goals and collective memories created national pasts; these constructions bind elite and mass in pursuit of elite-sponsored goals.

Elite-sponsored goals have typically revolved around some sort of ideal of national development; populations have been mobilized and one aspect of such mobilizations is an appeal to the past, the national past.

The record for the region is good.

15
PERFORMANCE, PROBLEMS AND MOOTED REFORMS

The region has advanced rapidly. In the years since 1945/49 the countries that make up the region have at various times recorded sustained high rates of economic growth; first Japan, then the Four Tigers, later Southeast Asia and, over recent decades, China. The growth has been accompanied by wrenching social change: rural–urban migration on a massive scale with all the consequent social changes attached; large-scale pollution problems; along with a spread of domestic political problems, the inevitable accompaniment of such broad programmes of social reconstruction. Foreign powers have also left their mark on the region through wars of colonial withdrawal and related ill-considered exercises in Cold War politics. All that said, the record is one of great and sustained success and there is little reason to suppose that it cannot continue; however, there is also reason to acknowledge that such success was not achieved by accident and nor will its continuity.

In 1945/49, at the end of the Pacific War and the Chinese Civil War, the territories of the region faced great difficulties. At first there was the immediate business of recovery from wartime killing and destruction plus the experience of trauma for those who survived. This involved the repatriation of foreign soldiers and their civilian associates to their home countries; securing food and medical and welfare supplies; and receiving returning authorities of former colonial powers, in the initial form of military administrations. Then the difficult business of bringing colonial rule to an end: thus the matter of the crystallization of successor elites, thus the business of carving out a discrete space from the disintegrating territories of empire, creating a state, mobilizing the resident population as a nation and then organizing a drive for development, implementing thereby the basic post-empire deal where the elite ask for support in return for making better lives for the newly minted citizens.

These difficulties can be further unpacked and their scale spelled out by noting the interaction of local politics, that is, the domestic concerns of successor elites and their newly claimed populations, with the demands of foreign powers. And setting aside the demands of neighbouring newly minted states, there were two groups in particular who laid claim to an interest in the affairs of new states. First, elements of the populations of the departing state-empires including politicians and spooks concerned with geo-security, corporate world actors concerned with economic links and sometime sojourners, concerned with social and maybe emotional links with their sometime postings. All these groups could be accommodated by successor elites; they were, if not welcome, then well known and the end of empire was an agreed process, not an abrupt exchange of rulers followed by new projects. In some contrast, the second, a grouping of foreigners, comprised the great powers, the USSR and the USA. It is clear that their economic and political power was not the same: the latter was much more economically powerful, but at that particular time their military and diplomatic power was much more equal. After 1945/49 their relationship soured and with the 1950s invasion of South Korea by the forces of the DPRK, the nascent Cold War, which had been announced in Fulton Missouri in 1947, was now underway in East Asia. It took the form of open warfare. It also took the form of covert struggles, where allies received support, whilst non-allies were undermined. This great-power competition ranged across East Asia, impacting the domestic concerns of successor elites and making their task that bit more complicated; Japan and the Tigers were given significant military and more importantly economic aid of one sort or another whilst the allies of the USSR fared rather less well.

Local successor elites had to read and react to these shifting and sometimes treacherous circumstances for, notwithstanding the demands of foreign powers, the basic domestic deal of elite support in exchange for better lives had to be honoured. And, in general, with some spectacular exceptions, that deal has been honoured for the countries of the region have experienced dazzling success.

The region has been successful – but it is not all of a piece. Disaggregating the region there are a number of discrete historical trajectories. Successor elites played the hands they were dealt in different ways and consequently the new countries in the region have different records. The differences show up in the standard data produced by the UNDP and the World Bank. The intellectual roots of these judgements, published in tables of technical data, combine institutional and liberal market ideas. The UNDP and World Bank data represent what might be tagged a macro consensus, forged amongst international civil servants (the country representatives and employees of these organizations). Thereafter, a richer set of judgments can be made by using the records of the new countries and then judging them against domestic claims, judging them comparatively within the region and finally judging them internationally against the most general tenets of modernity (perhaps, in part, exemplified by those countries that shifted into the modern world earlier in history). And these are obviously not simple judgements, nor anything other than contestable; thus, by way of illustrations of the differences in historical track records: Japan (global economic power); China (global power); Cambodia (poor/LDC); Singapore (trading city); Hong Kong (transferred colony) and so on.

The success of the countries of the region was greeted in the 1970s and 1980s with a discussion of the notion of the developmental state. And today, overall, the region is highly successful but that success disguises significant country and local-level differences.

Successor elites: on-going issues

As state-empires dissolved away, successor elites sought to build states, create nations and pursue development. The key to the claim to power of new elites was the promise to their populations that they would create better lives for everyone so development issues come to the fore. In short, economic growth (plus the administrative machineries necessary to deliver such growth), thereafter there are issues of schedules of social reform and social costs and finally, questions about the resultant form of life, as an independent nation-state implies the existence of a distinct people, raising issues of culture.

So, a rough agenda: *first*, economic growth and political reform issues; *second*, social issues such cities, migration, burgeoning growth and environmental degradation; *third*, culture and the exchanges between indigenous and imported strands that together constitute the contemporary polities; and *fourth*, as states are always elements within a system of states, the position of the newly created states within the wider global system.

Economic and political issues

The region has seen very rapid economic growth and very many people now lead better material lives. Unfortunately this economic growth has fostered inequality and it has also seen catastrophic pollution.

1 Rapid economic growth – triumphs, explanations and sustainability

Two standard routes into this debate, plus one novel and influential idea plus one recently added issue. So, the first route into the question is cast in market-economics terms, paradigmatically, the work of the World Bank. A report published each year records market-economic data and success is cast in these terms. The second route into the question is cast in holistic pattern of life terms, paradigmatically the work of the UNDP. A report published each year reports on pattern of life data and success is cast in these terms. The novel and influential idea, albeit one with an intellectual pedigree reaching back to Friedrich List, was the notion of the developmental state; and the recently added issue concerns the sustainability of particular development models. These matters have been pursued over the last forty or fifty years (*Silent Spring – The Limits to Growth –* and so on) and the arguments presented are now mainstream; it is noted that past development has had environmental and social costs and it is argued that development should be environmentally cost-neutral and thus sustainable.

256 East Asia: success and its costs

FIGURE 15.1 Hong Kong Central, August 2009.

The World Bank, along with the IMF and the GATT (General Agreement on Tariffs and Trade, forerunner of WTO), was called into being by the Bretton Woods 1944 agreement. It was an institutional element of the American-sponsored vision for a liberal-democratic and liberal market future global system, a replacement for the failed liberal system of the 1930s. The designers of the project and the Bank had their thinking shaped by the experience of the Great Depression and the American government's response, the New Deal. This initiative legitimated state intervention and deficit financing; in brief, economies could be managed. The Bank and the IMF were based in Washington, which was the seat of the American federal government and associated financial institutions; in other words the Bank was shaped to encourage liberal markets. The remit of the Bank was to finance long-term economic growth and its earliest work was done in war-torn areas following 1945/49 and then, with the dissolution of sometime state-empires, its attention turned to the new states of what would come to be tagged the Global South; that is, it was concerned with development. It has accumulated a somewhat mixed reputation: for preferring infrastructure; for preferring market solutions; for endeavouring to apply recipe knowledge whereby ideas made in Washington were exported to their development customers in the Third World.

The record of East Asia was noted by the World Bank in a 1983 publication entitled *The East Asian Miracle*, which reviewed the performance of the region in detail. The record was noted (it was in their own data) and explanations sought and these, somewhat predictably, were cast in terms of local planning agencies (for their existence could hardly be denied and in any case, in those areas occupied after the Pacific War by the USA, planning had been a condition of the receipt of aid) and policy makers having got the prices right. The governments were praised for facilitating rapid growth. Interestingly, when the regional economies went into crisis in 1997 as a credit bubble collapsed, these same commentators gleefully pointed to the same governments, now tagged centres of crony capitalism. Events have moved in two directions since then: local states have built up reserves of currency and made swop agreements (so as to defend better against speculators) and the prevailing influential theory has become globalization; local states, however, continue their national development trajectories.

The UNDP has paid attention to the details of the lives of those living in the Third World and this is reflected in the data that it publishes on health, education, social welfare and the like. The picture painted is rather different to the main lines of argument presented by commentators (and the Bank). Thus it is the case that the big picture of great success should be modified to acknowledge the lives of those who have not prospered quite so obviously, including rural dwellers, the urban poor, migrant workers, those working within the informal sector, those living in slum areas and so on. The work of UNDP also calls attention to the differential impact of decades of economic growth upon populations in patterns of inequality – age-related, gender-related, majority/minority related and so on. When examined in detail, social patterns are very varied. And the pace of change has thrown up unexpected problems. In China, rural–urban migration has left rural villages with skewed age patterns – many old people plus some very young but with few if any adults of working age – so has created left-behind children, raised by elderly grandparents. In Thailand, differences in life-chances between the rural north and Bangkok coupled to the presence of American and other armed forces bases during the Indo-China wars encouraged a large sex industry. Again, in the Philippines skewed life chances encourage local people to overseas travel as migrant workers. Cast in these terms, for development experts, the region's success is both marvellous and distinctly unfinished.

Chalmers Johnson theorized the particular experience of Japan in terms of the notion of the developmental state. Johnson unpacked the post-1945 record and took note of the key players. The SCAP authorities had removed the old pre-war and wartime elite of soldiers, politicians and industrialists and they had inaugurated an ambitious reform programme; however, the SCAP numbers were slight and they issued their instructions via the remaining cadres of the Japanese state, that is, civil servants or bureaucrats. The demands of the SCAP authorities had to be interpreted by the central bureaucrats as they issued instructions down the hierarchy and the central bureaucrats also had the task of allocating scarce resources, both material and financial (cash or credit) so, unwittingly, they came to occupy a very powerful position within the post-1945 Japanese system of governance.

One key ministry, identified by Johnson, was the ministry responsible for economic planning, that is, MITI. It was, on this argument, Japan's great good fortune that the inhabitants of MITI were dispassionate, efficient and far-sighted technocrats and their control of access to resources and the removal or downgrading of other centres of power courtesy of SCAP's purge of war-time elites, meant that they could marshal a collective project on the part of Japanese politicians, industrialists and people. They picked up on a long-term Japanese elite goal, one affirmed since the days of Meiji, that is a strong economy and a strong country, and cashed in practice in the post-1945 days as the pursuit of national development.

MITI is not the whole of the story of Japanese post-1945 recovery; unsurprisingly, other factors came into play. Domestically, the SCAP authorities curbed the post-1945 trades unions (suppressing strikes); and externally, so to say, the decision of the USA to go to war in Korea to sustain their client regime in Seoul meant that local Japanese industry received a flood of orders for war-related materials and at the same time, and for the same reason, the progressive reformers in SCAP gave way to the realists. Japan was not to be reformed; rather it was to be made into an American-oriented bastion of anti-communism in Northeast Asia.

That said, the model of state-directed industrialization was exported around the sometime Japanese colonial sphere – now officered by the USA – where a series of nationalist and heavy-handed regimes were able to put the model into effective practice: thus Chiang Kai Shek, thus Park Chung Hee, thus the business elites of Hong Kong and further south, the PAP regime in Singapore and the government of Mahathir Mohammed in Malaysia and, for a period, the Thaksin government in Thailand.

The model has proved effective. It has a long pedigree. It reaches back to the late nineteenth-century German Historical School, one key figure being Friedrich List, the theorist of late industrialization.

But there have been costs, in particular around the idea of sustainable development. In the post-war sphere of the USA, the West, the general atmosphere was one of great confidence. The USA was by pre-war standards extraordinarily well off with full employment, welfare provisions and the arrival of a consumer society. The confidence was replicated in rather different ways in the countries that had been allies of the USA, Western Europe, in particular. In both territories populations enjoyed hitherto unfamiliar prosperity; it was theorized in a 1958 publication by J.K. Galbraith entitled *The Affluent Society*.

One aspect of that success was provided by industry. The war years had forced the development of natural science-based industry for the production of war materials. These natural scientific innovations were now turned to consumer goods; they included labour saving procedures for local city governments, one of which was a way of dealing with grass verges along roads. In the past these had been dealt with by labour, that is, the grass was cut, but now it was determined that the grass could be controlled by spraying with herbicide as it was quicker and cheaper to just kill the grass.

In 1962 Rachel Carson published *Silent Spring*, an early classic of what was to become the environmental movement. The book tracked the implications of the widespread use of agri-chemicals and showed that introducing poisons into the

Performance, problems and mooted reforms **259**

FIGURE 15.2 Changi Airport, December 2008.

natural environment had consequences; in this case as the herbicides moved up the food chain they killed wild birds. In the 1960s there were further influential texts including Paul and Ann Ehrlich's work and then the Club of Rome published *The Limits of the Earth*, at which point the modern environmental movement had arrived.

In the context of development where arguments had been cast in terms of the overriding importance of economic growth or where the environment was

260 East Asia: success and its costs

FIGURE 15.3 Beijing Airport, July 2009.

mentioned as having little priority, now it was argued that growth had to be sustainable because there was little point in growing the economy if the result was environmental degradation (air, water and land pollution) and consequent human ill-health.

In the rapidly developing countries of East Asia this message was not at first well received but acute problems have driven the issue up the elite's political agenda;

thus Japan and Minimata disease; thus China and city smog; thus Southeast Asia and the problem of haze – and so on.

The basic deal for successor elites was support in exchange for better lives for their populations and it would be difficult to say that they have not delivered; however, local populations now bear the social costs of environmental damage and the most extensive problems – inevitably – are in China, but here there are signs that the elite has taken note and is initiating ameliorative action.

2 Political systems – pressures – reform possibilities

The wars that accompanied the dissolution of state-empires produced a number of new states and most of these were successor states to European and American empires, inheriting territory in part or whole. There were a number of strands of debate in respect of the appropriate institutional machinery of the successor states and these debates were clouded by the rivalries of the Cold War: thus, proponents could argue for variant forms of liberal democracy (Singapore or Malaysia) or proponents could also argue for variant forms of elite-led party-state systems (thus China) or eccentric variants (thus North Korea). Proponents could also argue for hybrid systems, thus guided democracy (Indonesia) or emergency rule (Taiwan, South Korea) or even species of continued colonialism (Macau, Hong Kong) where liberal democracy was nodded to but more or less ignored.

One issue that clouded these debates was the manner of achievement of new nation-states. This has often involved more or less violent episodes; thus the states were new and had emerged via violence. It produced one highly particular context-shaped status, that of 'father of the nation' and great authority could accrue to such a status, plus great power. Thus, for example, Lee Kuan Yew, or Mao Zedong or Ho Chi Min or Kim Il Sung or Sukharno and so on, Plus, on the part of populations or critics, there could be great reluctance to remove them from power where that was for whatever reason judged correct.

In America and Europe the default setting of debates about politics were liberal democratic; parties, elections, separation of powers and so on and most of the sometime empire holdings of the Europeans and Americans opted for some variants of this model. However, in the USSR matters were cast in terms of the machinery of party-state systems with internal democracy and thus political debate restricted to the double-bureaucracy. This was true also of China; after the end of the civil war a party-state system was constructed. And in the sometime territories of Japan in Northeast Asia hybrid patterns emerged, deference was paid to ideas of liberal democracy whilst variant forms of state-centred systems were created. In this way the Cold War division of East Asia found expression in different forms of governance.

In East Asia, given the differences in forms of life (or, levels of living) between and within countries, debates about governance revolve around a narrow set of issues: (1) the effectiveness of the state machinery (can it do its basic job of providing security and advances in material welfare for the people it controls?);

(2) the responsiveness of the state machinery (can it deal with changing requirements of the people it controls?); and (3) the openness or not of the system to critical inspection (recalling Alasdair MacIntyre on the machineries of ideological universe maintenance: if the elite can block debate, then within the ambit of the elite's world view, everything makes sense). All this opens up a number of further questions: recruitment to key positions (party or family or corporate network and so on), open-ness to popular influence (liberal-democracy) or effectiveness of internal scrutiny (party-state).

All these debates take place within the unfolding shift to the modern world in East Asia. States do not have the choice of standing still and elites must read and react to enfolding circumstances, demands that come from internal and external sources. The former are likely to be the more demanding.

Over the long period of the still unfolding shift to the modern world reform programmes have typically taken the form of securing for the population in general greater access to the decision making machineries of the state. It might be added that such democratizing progress is not easy, nor is it swift and nor is it guaranteed (the shift to the modern world is contingent; after Jürgen Habermas, a disposition can be argued for, but historical practice is something else altogether).

In East Asia questions about reform include multiple issues.

In Japan there are debates about the peace constitution. The nationalist right wing argue that it should be revised so as to allow Japan the right to use force and the nationalists also defend the use of the Yasukuni Shrine to memorialize the war dead of the modern era. Contrary positions are held by the political left who argue that the peace constitution plus episodes of Hiroshima and Nagasaki place Japan in a unique position to argue for peaceful politics. A secondary suggestion is using the Meiji Shrine as the national memorial. These somewhat charged debates intersect with debates about political life where criticism of the iron triangle is familiar, as is criticism of the LDP. But critics seem to make little headway as political players circle around these issues (recently long-serving Prime Minister Abe was an effective right-winger from an established political family).

In South Korea there are debates about the state and the role of the *chaebol*. The record of South Korea is one of many years of military rule plus popular opposition (demonstrations/repression) and dramatic economic growth. The state is a variant form of developmental state with links to large private conglomerates but critics suggest that their day is done, that they are corrupt and now indefensible (thus 2017 saw public scandals involving sunken ferry boats, corporate malfeasance and, more bizarrely, a scandal about nuts served on an aircraft).

In Taiwan there are debates about identity and independence. The trajectory of modern Taiwan begins with Japanese colonialism in the late nineteenth century; the island was developed as a colony for around fifty years. It passed to the control of the mainland's Kuomintang in the late 1940s and thereafter it developed within the American sphere as a military dictatorship until reforms came late in the twentieth century. A number of issues are intertwined: the notion of a distinct Taiwanese identity; the international status of Taiwan; and the relationship with Beijing which lays claim to the island, thus recently there have been manoeuvrings around the status of the 'one China principle'.

In China the reform of the party-state machinery has been discussed by David Shambaugh. The party-state reforms as newer social groups acknowledged and more members drawn in: all in the context of the creation of wide swathes of private enterprise so local commentators can speak of a mixed economy. The related issues revolve around upgrading the local economy, cast in terms of avoiding the middle-income country trap. In 2013 the development programme known as OBOR was announced, this will guide overseas investment plans throughout the region, linking China with Eurasia and Europe (Silk Road) and China with Southeast Asia, East Africa and again Europe (Maritime Silk Road). Thereafter, wider strategic issues come into play; that is, the role of China within the changing global economic and security architecture.

Social issues: the new cities of East Asia

Human settlements have been shaped by distinct patterns of life; the key is livelihood, and the key to human livelihood until very recently has been agriculture. Settlements have been small villages or small market towns; occasionally there would be settlements devoted to symbolic or administrative purposes, religion or government, and these are one starting point for the development of cities. But cities are difficult to organize and expensive to service, they require a great deal of collective effort, so for most of human history most people lived in rural areas. One activity that favoured urban growth was trade; in the modern era trade has increased, so too trading cities. Mike Davis points out that cities have grown quickly in the modern era, until around the start of twenty-first century the majority of human population had become city dwellers.

1 Cities prior to the emergence of the modern world

In Europe pre-modern cities were organized around the institutions of the Christian church (a supranational organization) and the landed estates of powerful families (kings, princes, family retainers, servants, labourers and so on). In this environment cities were symbolic sites, places of government, places of religious power/pilgrimage, and, as they required servicing, they were also places of trade. A similar pattern is found in other civilizations in Latin America, in the Middle East, in South Asia and in China. It is a mixture of overarching symbolic and material power resting on the economic base of agriculture and supplemented by trade.

However, as it happens, a matter of accident, the modern world takes shape within the cities of Europe as they become:

- centres of commerce (as economic networks expand, so traders become more important within society and so class relations shift);
- centres of natural science (early commercial traders encouraged practical research to assist trade);

- centres of politics (as commercial trade and natural science grow, so does political role of city and power drifts from settlements on landed estates to the now growing cities).

As natural science develops and technology advances cities change:

- they become centres of industry (industrial factory production is a novelty – economically, socially and politically);
- cities begin to grow quickly, and overall populations increase rapidly, and there is rural–urban migration, but in the nineteenth century urban growth was often unplanned;
- problems multiplied: working patterns were new (industrial factory development was unregulated with no zoning law, no environmental law, no workplace regulation, no welfare benefits); health and welfare were low priorities (as working and living conditions changed standards were often poor with high morbidity and mortality rates); public health faced disease and epidemics (concentrated populations in poor conditions provided ideal environments for diseases); and social order was problematical (as old social structures changed a novel individualism was noted alongside the rise of novel class groups and both strained inherited political structures).

Patterns of life found expression in the urban form (the layout of the settlement and the types of buildings):

- in pre-modern cities the urban form would be organized around ideas of political authority (castles, government districts, gardens and parks for the rich) or sacred authority (temples and related sacred objects/sites) and the accommodations of ordinary people would be of secondary importance;
- in early modern cities there was slow development of urban infrastructure and slow development of urban spatial segregation; the familiar pattern of first-world cities emerged with elegant squares, middle-class housing areas, slums and the slow replacement of narrow medieval streets;
- in the nineteenth century industrial cities emerged with more ordered forms: government and public buildings, industrial areas, new middle-class housing, workers housing, parks and gardens for masses and commercial areas to serve citizens;
- now in the twenty-first century the patterns are changing again with urban cores, extensive suburbs and now even wider semi-urban peripheries.

Urban forms are created by their populations; the keys are livelihood, social mores and politics. Urban building types depend not only upon livelihood (that is, the functions which are served by the buildings) but also on location (where the buildings are in the local landscape) and available materials (thus, wood, stone, brick or, lately, glass and concrete).

2 Cities in East Asia

There were significant East Asian cities prior to rise of modern world; some were large with populations measured in hundreds of thousands, Edo had a population of over one million. They were pre-industrial with economic bases in agriculture plus extensive craft skill-based activity plus trading. The cities were orderly and prosperous. In Northeast Asia the core of the cities would be bureaucratic governmental buildings (Beijing); in Southeast Asia the core of the cities would be sacred sites (Bangkok, Angkor), or trading centres (the core settlements of Malay maritime empires such as Mataram or Srivijaya or Johor-Riau and so on).

East Asian cities were changed during the shift to modern world. During the colonial era significant new cities were developed and as the colonial powers were interested in trade, trading ports became the new key cities. Each city formed a link in a chain joining metropolitan core to distant colonial periphery; each city drew its hinterland into the wider state-empire system. So colonial port cities had a crucial double function. For example, in respect of the British empire in the Far East, trading cities were established, either new or on the basis of extant pre-modern local settlements, in a chain joining London with the Mediterranean, West Asia, South Asia, Southeast Asia and, eventually, Hong Kong (and thus Qing China).

The layout of these cities reflected their novel economic role as they drew colonial territories into the global trading system. The number of foreigners was always small relative to the local population either as it existed or as it became once the settlement was established. The foreign minority (traders, administrators, missionaries, soldiers and so on) were the key to the function of the new settlement; absent the foreigners there was no trading city. Contrariwise, absent the flows of inward migration the city would be starved of personnel and linkages and unable to access its hinterland or service the trading port. Colonial port cities depended upon both groups and over time accommodations were made: colonial cities were hybrid formations.

The new settlements had new layouts to reflect economic activity (port facilities, military defence constructions and infrastructure – road, water and so on). They had new spatial segregation to reflect social divisions including traditional local settlement areas along with foreign enclaves. There were novel commercial/industrial areas and dockyards/railways. There were novel colonial government areas (plus new laws to fix spatial arrangements in place – property, lease and so on). Plus long-distance inward migration produced distinctive receiving areas (China-towns or Indian-quarters or Native areas and so on). Looking at these settlements, colonial bureaucrat-scholars spoke of plural societies.

East Asian cities in market-oriented East Asia changed after decolonization; economics and migration played key roles. Economic policy focused on export-oriented industrialization; there was extensive new building and urban infrastructure (dockyards, airports, roads, services and so on). New development zones were identified; major facilities like airports were built; social welfare provisions included schools, hospitals, shopping centres and housing. All were mostly manufactured out of concrete in the international style or recently post-modernist style, hence the urban patterns of Hong Kong, Singapore, South Korea and Taiwan. In Japan much concrete was poured but there were also many low-rise suburbs.

There was significant rural–urban migration as the drive for industrial development drew in migrants: migration from outside the countries was now controlled but migration from domestic rural areas was not. As new industries drew in new

FIGURE 15.4 Consumption, Singapore, December 2009.

populations, the inward migration put pressures on urban facilities. Informal sector activity grew, so too areas of informal settlement. New forms of spatial segregation developed. Informal settlements (sometimes, slums) grew and have remained in Thailand, Malaysia, Indonesia and the Philippines: middle-class areas and rich enclaves have developed in the form of gated communities; and in recent years special economic zones have been planned and built (often to process for export but also to encourage local high-tech industrial development).

East Asian cities in socialist-oriented East Asia also changed after decolonization. In China until the end of the Mao period rural–urban migration was blocked as the household registration system prevented easy movement. The larger urban areas did not grow significantly but the population grew in rural areas and small towns; there was equality of provision of facilities as basic needs were met in work, housing and welfare; the state socialist version of the international style. In China after the reform period began in 1978 restrictions on place of residence were relaxed and there is now rural–urban migration to the economically growing cities; export processing zones kick-started the reform process and state socialist planning adapted to new demands as export zones were joined by high-tech zones, new airports, new housing areas, condominiums and shopping malls.

Cities in East Asia now display the benefits of industrial capitalist economic development with higher material living standards for many (but not all), modern urban facilities such as transport, housing, welfare and leisure facilities; capital cities have also become sites for the dazzling work of internationally renowned architects, but these cities also display problems typical of very rapid development, including pollution, congestion, inequality and social distress and class/spatial segregation.

3 Environmental costs of rapid growth

The costs associated with some fifty years of headlong industrialization and urbanization have been very high, with air pollution in cities (and covering whole areas in China and Southeast Asia), water pollution (poisoned rivers and ground waters) and land poisoned by industrial waste.

The costs of industrialization and urbanization can be directly observed in pollution in all its forms, but they can also be subtle, with a cumulative loss of biodiversity. Environmental strength is weakened as forests are cleared to be replaced by monocultures (desertification, dust bowls and so on), fisheries are weakened or in the extreme destroyed (thus, North Sea, or Southeast Asian shrimp fisheries or coral stocks, or at the extreme Canadian Grand Banks fishery simply collapsed) and as environmental strength is weakened it has short-term impacts on humans, as noted above. It also has more subtle longer-term impacts as the environment that supports humans is weakened, hence anxieties about aerosols' impact on ozone layer and today concerns for fossil fuel usage and consequent global warming. These issues are debated in international meetings but it is difficult to acknowledge and apportion blame (for past episodes of pollution), or to agree the scale of

FIGURE 15.5 Recycling, Zhenjiang, Spring 2017.

contemporary problems (hence the reported lobbying activities of fossil fuel corporations and 'climate change denial'), or to agree future action to tackle upcoming pollution problems (hence disquiet amongst climate scientists).

Culture: culture as ideas, culture as praxis

The shift to the modern world up-ends established forms of life but it does not wholly obliterate them, it remakes them. Cultural practices run on into the new modern dispensation: Chinese people do not stop being 'Chinese', Malay people do not stop being 'Malay' and so on.

1 Cultural practices – shifting, changing and adapting

Many cultural practices and associated ideas have been sustained through into the present configuration of the modern world, forms of life: (1) there are continuities in fishing or farming or commerce (hence the continued use of artisanal fishing, small-scale farming, informal banking networks, relational contracting and so on); (2) politics (personal relations, networks or 'big man' traditions and so on); or (3) society (Chinese folk religion celebrations, Chinese traditional medicine or distinctive regional food cultures and so on).

Some cultural practices/ideas have been noted and memorialized: (1) national treasures and historical sites/relics (links to ideas of national pasts and also links to theme park culture); (2) in Australia, the affirmation of rights of indigenous Australians and reconstruction of Aboriginal culture (thus, dot painting, a recent invention); or (3) in China, explicit recognition of minority nations.

Some cultural practices and ideas bend with the impacts of shift to modern world: (1) the modern world is secular; it impacts local religious ideas everywhere

FIGURE 15.6 Beijing smog, December 2015.

and their sphere of routine application shrinks (births, marriages and deaths and minimum requirements of religious observation), as they are not relevant to the routines of everyday life, and disputes about them are provoked; (2) the modern world is highly ordered and this impacts forms of living everywhere, hence local accommodations to familiar state requirement of ID cards (opposed in UK, familiar in mainland Europe), CCTV surveillance of population (accepted in UK, opposed in many places in mainland Europe), use of face-recognition software for surveillance (spreading around planet); (3) the modern world had produced a vibrant consumer culture; there are assorted reactions to spread, whether to resist, embrace or modify, here there are multiple examples (Japan: floating world, electric geisha, J-pop, manga, family restaurants; South Korea: K-pop; Singapore: casinos, F1 race, tourist resorts).

2 Contemporary polities in East Asia – summary and comparison

Historically, the peoples of the broad territory of East Asia inhabited long-established successful and sophisticated cultures. In the north, centred on China, a civilization with a recorded history reaching back some two and a half thousand years, a group of polities; today, Japan, North and South Korea, Taiwan. Then, in Indo-China along the valleys of the Chao Phraya and Mekong Rivers, civilizations of similar vintage also embracing the influence of China; today, Vietnam, Thailand, Cambodia and Laos. And to the south, the Malay world, a series of shifting kingdoms embracing a broad archipelago of some thousands of islands and melding local cultures with imports from the north and importantly from the west, including Indian and Arabian lands; today, Malaysia, Singapore, Indonesia, Brunei and the Philippines.

All these territories were impacted by the arrival of the modern world. At first it took the form of aggressive trading companies, then later equally determined and sometimes violent European and American states: the upshot being the formal absorption of the region in the nascent and rapidly deepening industrial-capitalist system. The state-empire system comprised cores and peripheries. In the East Asian peripheries colonial rule reached down into extant forms of life – the nature and extent of reconstruction varied – determining in colonial port cities (Singapore or Hong Kong) – largely invisible in rural areas (the eastern parts of Malaya – the highlands of Burma or Indo-China – more or less disruptive in the established centres of extant civilizations (the sea-coast and riverine settlements of Qing Empire). In time these exchanges generated a double reaction comprising learning and resistance: the state-empire system was beset with tensions and over the period 1911–45 it was engulfed in crisis so that from 1945 it quickly dissolved away; new states emerged and successor elites took their inherited legacies, colonial era learning and embarked on novel projects of state making, nation inventing and the pursuit of development.

The newly created polities were cultural hybrids with the precise mix depending on the reach of colonial reconstructions, the resilience (or luck) of pre-contact indigenous cultural forms and the particular enthusiasms for modernity embraced by successor elites. All these strands of ideas and praxis fed into the construction of new polities. So, today, East Asia is made up a number of variant forms of modernity, each showing the marks of its particular route to the still unfolding modern world.

3 Schematic sketches: presently unfolding routes to the modern world[1]

a) Northeast Asia

- As regard the Japanese polity: the institutional structure is dominated by the iron triangle of bureaucrats, parties and business; the emperor serves as head of state, religious organizations of Shinto and Buddhism are active and the population is ethnically (more or less) homogeneous. There is a public sphere and there is a vigorous commercial and popular culture. The social ethic is one of harmony derived from a Confucian legacy. The ideal lodged in the system can be summarized as an elite-led search for a consensus, via extensive consultations, and with popular agreement or acquiescence, which is focused finally on the family of the Japanese.
- As regards the South Korean polity: the institutional structure includes the state bureaucracy, the military and the corporate world; there is a public sphere and a vigorous commercial and popular culture. Social order is sustained in terms taken from Confucian legacy of hierarchy, harmony, education and stress on family. The ideal lodged in the system is one of the collective pursuit of national development.
- As regards the North Korean polity: the institutional structure is that of a party-state, the army is a key organization. The embedded ideal is self-reliant socialist development; commercial and popular cultures are weak.
- As regards the Taiwanese polity: the institutional structure of the polity includes the state bureaucracy, the army and the corporate world; there is a public sphere and a vigorous commercial and popular culture. The embedded ideal derives from Confucianism and includes hierarchy, education, consensus and the pursuit of national secure development.
- As regards the Chinese polity: the institutional structure is that of a party-state, governance is hierarchical and bureaucratic; economic activity includes SOEs and a corporate sector; there is a vigorous commercial and popular culture. The embedded ethic centres on state-sponsored pursuit of peaceful development for the Han Chinese nation.

b) Southeast Asia

- As regards the Philippines polity: the institutional structure includes a weak state, landed families, associated business groups, the army and the Catholic Church; there is a sharp divide between the elite and a diverse mass; there is a contested public sphere; and there is a vigorous commercial and popular culture. The embedded ideal combines an American inheritance that produces a superficial liberal democracy with a deeper local client patron system.
- As regards the Malaysian polity: the institutional structure is corporatist with elite-level ethnic-based cooperation; the polity is fissured by ethnicity, religion and material wealth. There is a constrained public sphere but there is a vigorous

commercial and popular culture. The embedded ideal of elite cooperation is oriented towards national development but presently embraces divergent strands, liberal market and Islamic.
- As regards the Singaporean polity: the institutional structure is corporatist with elite-level direction oriented towards national development; mass acceptance amongst a mobilized population; the public sphere is constrained but there is a vigorous commercial and popular culture. The embedded ideal is elite-directed national development.
- As regards Brunei: the institutional structure is absolute monarchy; the dominant religion is Islam; the population small, rich and acquiescent.
- As regards the Indonesian polity: the institutional structure includes the army, bureaucracy and Islamic faith; the social world is plural with Java culturally central; the recently opened up public sphere is energetic and there is a vigorous commercial and popular culture. The embedded ideal is national development, cast for a long period in terms of Pancasila, but lately more influenced by Islam.

c) Mainland Southeast Asia

- As regards the Thai polity: the institutional structure centres on the army, the bureaucracy and the palace, plus there is an influential Buddhist religion; the polity is deeply fissured (metropolitan-centred elite-supporting yellow shirt parties and provincial popular-oriented mass red shirt parties; civil society is heavily constrained, commercial and popular culture are subdued. The embedded ideal is conservative and includes reverence for established authority (thus monarchy, army and Buddhist religion) and the social status quo.
- As regards the Vietnamese polity: the institutional structure is that of a party-state system and governance is hierarchical; there is a diverse popular culture. The embedded ideal is a Confucian-inflected state socialism.
- As regards the Cambodian polity: the institutional structure is quasi party-state system with a monarchy as head of state; the country is poor. Buddhism and animism are present. The embedded ideal looks to hierarchy, elite networks and pursuit of development.
- As regards the Laos polity: the institutional structure is that of a party-state system; the country is poor with many ethnic groups. Buddhism and animism are prevalent. The embedded ideal favours hierarchy and looks to state socialist pursuit of development.
- As regards the Myanmar polity: the institutional structure includes army and Buddhist religion. There are multiple ethnic minorities. The country is poor. The embedded ideal has been cast in terms of a Burmese road to socialism, lately reworked as political and economic reforms are pursued; thus, idea of development becomes more prominent.

4 In more detail: Singapore shopping and Japanese harmony

The PAP project was cast in terms of national development (elite coherence, a disciplined population and a clearly delineated place in the world) but the paradox is that as they pursue material advance they lodge themselves ever more deeply within global structures. During the colonial period the flow of people through Singapore was largely unregulated and Singapore at the moment of independence inherited a diverse population both settled and sojourners. In recent years flows of inward and outward migration have attracted renewed attention – loss of educated people – long established flows of labourers from the region – novel inward flow has involved maids – such flows of people are not likely to diminish; nor will the flows of ideas/goods.

The country is rich and consumerism has grown, and material and non-material goods are available in abundance. Yet consumerism cuts against the task of inscribing the PAP project in the routine lives of the population; it presents population with new spheres of expression; and it presents state with problems of discipline. Grasping consumption is awkward and as Singapore becomes richer the elite worry about excess and Westernization. Japanese imports are unproblematic. American imports are problematic. But examination of consumption practices reveals that imports do not work on locals mechanically; the experiences they offer are read into local culture and examination of practices suggests imports are both inevitable and unproblematic. It is not the imports per se; it is how they call into prominence some features of life in Singapore, in particular inequalities and changing social mores.

In Singapore, individualism and privatism are evident. The Singaporean middle classes are wealthy and they can disengage and turn to family. Contemporary capitalism invites the creation of consumer societies and consumerism becomes a novel social practice/culture. The consumer marketplace offers consumers choices and consumers are invited to select. The portfolio of consumption practices generates a species of individualism through differentiation from others within the confines provided by available consumption goods. The local provision of shopping malls has grown rapidly in recent years and these are spaces for consumption and display. Class division is evident. The pursuit of material advance within a global capitalist system brings consumption into the heart of routine social practice (people become 'consumers'), feeds into the structural patterns of the society (some consume more than others and inequality grows) and becomes more visible (consumption is always in part conspicuous consumption and choosing life-style entails differentiation). Such class division can feed through into politics and routine class oppositions – for the PAP the emergence of class division and class-consciousness is unwelcome as it cuts against elite-desired social harmony

Singapore is embedded within global flows of goods/ideas. The traffic is not simply from the West to Singapore. There are East Asian regional flows of great significance, and popular culture is imported from Japan, Taiwan, Korea and Hong Kong. It becomes part of the blend of contemporary Singaporean cultural practice.

Singapore is rich; like all rich cities it borrows ideas and practices from elsewhere and makes them its own. Capitalist modernity might homogenize; capitalist modernity might be variously indigenized; Singapore is its own place but the business of indigenization is subtle and the self-conscious efforts of the state can look like pastiche: once upon a time Singapore marketed itself as 'instant Asia', more recently the city is presented as a major business hub, a 'five-star Hotel Singapore', a centre for cosmopolitan talent serving regional and global networks.

In a similar interpretive vein, John Clammer has written on the subtle adaptations made by Japanese people as they accommodate the demands of the modern world. Japan is the only non-Western country to effectively establish an autonomous industrial economy and society. The Japanese political-cultural and social projects are deeply humanist: (1) persons are taken to be lodged within social contexts and natural contexts (a humanistic decentring of self which recalls the core ideas of classical European sociology); (2) persons are taken to have reason, emotion and aesthetic sensibilities, and routinely and inevitably to be limited in skills and fallible in practice; (3) the social world is taken to revolve around overlapping networks of personal relationships, including family, group and organization; and (4) that a reasonable aspiration is for individual achievement within these multiple social contexts.

Clammer has suggested that the key to grasping the culture of Japan is to understand the mix of historically constituted formality and a deep humanism – an attempt to extend personal concern and reciprocity to the society as a whole. Clammer notes that the mix of modern industrial capitalism and tradition has caused comment. A recent attempt to grasp these matters has been cast in terms of modernity and postmodernity. But postmodernism is a Western notion; it comes in many varieties; and applied to Japan it looks odd. This is not a society of expressive individualism. The Japanese decentred self is located in community, everyday life is humanistic and the personal is widely reproduced (in school, office or club). There has been no epochal shift rather, as socially constructed cultural practices are continually reworked, so enfolding tradition is reaffirmed. Japan has its own cultural logic. Japanese society remains humanist, this logic binds individual and community.

Or, in brief, culture, as praxis and idea, shifts and changes as structural pressures impinge upon existing forms of life. Nothing is static and forms of life adapt, traditions adapt, embracing novelty whilst sustaining, perhaps in novel forms, the inheritance of the past.

East Asia's place in the world

East Asia entered the modern world via the experience of absorption within the geographically extensive territories of European state-empires and this episode can be unpacked as a series of phases. Thus there was a sequence comprising early contact, absorption, formal colonial rule, rebellion, dissolution and the formation of independent states. A further set of phases can be identified which in broad terms detail the trajectories of these now independent states: the early phase of overlapping Cold War demands and developmental state advance; the post-Cold War phase, which saw the overlapping of neo-liberalism and the developmental state; and now in the early twenty-first century a new phase may be in the offing. In East Asia the drive for economic advance continues but the European and American elite enthusiasm for neo-liberalism has been defied by popular electoral rebellions; these rebellions are widespread and they will have some impact upon elites. Three policy areas present themselves: trade, migration and the rise of China; there could be European and American restrictions placed on trade and migration, suggesting a turn inwards. The rise of China as a significant global power will also generate a response; at present it is easier to think of restrictions rather than further opening. And the rise of China could exercise the minds of those elites ruling around the northern edges of the Pacific Ocean.

All these changes/trends would impact East Asia but this does not signal any regional turning inwards, rather the reverse, as all three areas of debate point to an increasing salience for the region. However, whilst it does make sense to speak of an East Asian region it does not make sense to ignore the many tensions, which cut against cooperative progress.

East Asia – shifting locations within the global system

East Asia entered the modern world via the experience of absorption to a greater or lesser extent into European and American systems of state-empires. These state-empires encompassed large territories, they were organized in hierarchies of cores and peripheries and embraced multiple ethnic groups held together by violence and the over-arching idea of empire, trade and modernity.

The dissolution of these over-arching systems gave rise to the current pattern of sovereign states; each the home of a nominal nation, each with an elite committed one way or another to some species of development, that is, to elite-sponsored projects that point to a better life for their citizens. In the years following the Pacific War such goals were cast in two broad terms: state socialism or alternatively liberal market capitalism. America provided the model and resources for the members of the latter group which prospered; in time the former group, which had looked to an uneasy double-centre in Moscow and Beijing, embraced market-oriented reforms and they too have prospered.

These trends were accentuated during the years following the end of the Cold War, which was abrupt in Europe, thus 1989, but slower in East Asia (with significant hangovers and unresolved issues), and claims were made that neo-liberalism was now the evident vehicle for globalization and the end of history itself.

However, in the second decade of the twenty-first century there were signs that the era of neo-liberal globalization was in question with political troubles in Europe, surprising electoral results in the USA and signs of distress in East Asia with pollution, corruption and popular protests of one sort or another. It may be that established success will now go forwards in the post-neo-liberal era but at present it is not clear how this will be shaped in any of the regions.

In Europe and America there could be greater elite and popular scepticism about the benefits of trade, so too scepticism about migration. There could be greater elite and popular anxieties about security, and this could impact East Asia directly. And in East Asia there could be elite-level domestic and regional concerns to further integrate the region or at least deepen its protection from unwanted impacts from Europe and America. There might also be elite-level concerns to assert their status in the global system.

A tentative agenda of structural pressures can be readily identified as changing circumstances bear directly on local elites:

- trade – issues of geo-economics;
- security – issues of geo-strategy;
- soft power – issues of culture and cross-cultural perceptions.

The shift to the modern world is on-going. The region continues to be subject to these system demands; however, where, in its earliest exchanges with the pressures for change, and where, in the main exchanges, the region was submerged within colonial empires, now, following the dissolution of state-empires, the elites of the region are free to read and react to enfolding circumstances in pursuit of gaols set by themselves, not outsiders of one sort or another. Cast in these terms, reading the situation in the second decade of the twenty-first century, two crucial processes would seem to be in train: first, the rise of China to the status of global power; and, second, the comparative decline of the USA. Commentators have drawn parallels with shifting state-empire relations in the late nineteenth century and in these cases they led to conflicts that ran on for decades and in the end destroyed the pre-eminent positions that had been enjoyed by the protagonists.

However, against such pessimistic speculations, it should be recalled that the region in general is rich, it is orderly and there is little reason to expect dramatic domestic change. The future for the moment looks like the consolidation of a period of remarkable advance, however, the wider global system is less secure as a period of reaction against neo-liberalism is in train in America and Europe. It may be that the relatively benign international environment within which countries in East Asia have prospered could change and that being so, the future would look more problematic.

East Asian modernity: retrospect and prospect

In East Asia the unfolding shift to the modern world can be characterized in terms of a number of phases, albeit very simply, ignoring the detail of local histories. Thus, the phase of the irruption of European state-empires into the region; then the phase of ordered colonialism with its hierarchies of cores and peripheries and its distinctive peripheral forms of life; and then the rolling crisis of the early twentieth century leading to the dissolution of state-empires. Thereafter, there was the local elite seizure of territory and thereafter the construction of states, the creation of nations and the pursuit of development. The record is mixed. The current situation shows a spread of diverse problems but against all this East Asia is now one of three powerful regions within the global economy: thus North America, Europe and now East Asia.

The extant polities of East Asia shifted into the modern world via the experience of colonial rule. The colonial systems disintegrated in the middle of the twentieth century and local nationalist elites took power. They have driven a number of political cultural projects and their record has been successful in general terms; societies have coalesced, economies prospered and polities attained coherence. In brief, states have been made, nations imagined and development pursued. This record has been much debated. One issue is that of the nature of the polities: one debate has revolved around the notion of democracy, but East Asian polities are not converging on the model of the United States of America (modernization/globalization) and they are not converging on the rather different model of the European Union. If their local trajectories are acknowledged, then it is within the unfolding exchanges between elites and masses that an embedded idea will be found; the fundamental ethic that animates over the long run the dynamics of the polity. A number can be identified in practice – for example, in Japan or China or Singapore. Looking to the future, after Jürgen Habermas, language carries a minimum ethic and in the context of comparative political analysis it serves to provide the hope for dialogue (granting evident diversity, the minimum ethic implies different peoples can talk to each other) and implies a common concern for the on-going achievement of a discourse democracy (the ethic does work, but as a deep seated imperative and not as a recipe).

Note

1 These brief sketches cannot be taken too seriously, the point here is that different historical trajectories produce different polities – the comparison is what counts here. For a more detailed discussion (from which these notes are taken) see P.W. Preston, 2014, *After the Empires: The Creation of Novel Political-Cultural Projects in East Asia*, London, Palgrave, chapter 7.

AFTERWORD

I have carried this book project around on my travels. It has been constructed on the basis of lecture notes produced for classes which I have given in various universities, in particular the Chinese University of Hong Kong (CUHK), where I had a mix of local students, Hong Kongers in the main, and international students, mostly from America and Europe. The lecture courses were designed to introduce people to the dynamics of change in the region and to provide a base for their own further work. This book was begun in the delightful surroundings of CUHK, which is located on a hilltop in the New Territories, overlooking Tolo Harbour and at a distance the open sea. Further work was accomplished in the sometimes smoky environs of Beijing Normal University, located in a determinedly urban environment, some twenty minutes by foot from the Behai Lakes. Some further work was done in a trio of cafes in the neighbourhood of Ramkhamhaeng University in Bangkok; one of these was a familiar chain, albeit unusually spacious and civilized, the others independents, set amongst trees and flowers. And finally the basic text was completed whilst sitting in the spectacular new library of Jiangsu University, which is set amongst beautiful parkland surroundings in Zhenjiang on the Yangtze River. The book was finally finished back in England over the course of a rainy summer. The book grows out of teaching and research: the former noted, the latter available in a series of books, all addressing, one way or another, core preoccupations with the ways in which diverse groups of people make sense of their changing social circumstances.

FIGURE A.1 Café, Bangkok, March 2014.

ANNEX 1

Population, GDP and Gini coefficient

Countries	Population	GDP	Gini
China	1376.0	13,400	422
Taiwan	23.5	47,000	336
North Korea	25.2	•	–
South Korea	50.3	34,387	–
Japan	126.6	35,804	321
Vietnam	93.4	5,668	376
Laos	6.8	5,341	379
Cambodia	15.6	3,278	308
Thailand	68.0	15,345	379
Malaysia	30.3	25,308	463
Singapore	5.6	80,192	–
Myanmar	53.9	•	–
Indonesia	257.6	10,385	395
Brunei	0.4	66,647	367
East Timor	1.2	2,126	316
Philippines	100.7	6,926	430

Sources: Data is derived from UNDP, 2016, *Human Development Report*, New York, UNDP. Taiwan data from www.indexmundi.com/taiwan_gdp_per_capita_(ppp).html and CIA Fact Book, accessed August 2017.

ANNEX 2

Health and education

Countries	Health		Education	
	Life[1]	Budget[2]	Secondary[3]	Budget[4]
China	19.4	3.1	75	–
Taiwan	–	–	–	–
North Korea	16.8	•	•	–
South Korea	24.3	4.0	91.4	4.6
Japan	25.8	8.6	91.8	3.8
Vietnam	22.4	3.8	71.7	6.3
Laos	16.6	0.9	36.4	4.2
Cambodia	17.1	1.3	19.6	2.0
Thailand	21.4	5.6	43.3	4.1
Malaysia	19.3	2.3	77.1	6.1
Singapore	25.1	2.1	78.6	2.9
Myanmar	16.7	1.0	23.8	–
Indonesia	16.5	1.1	47.3	3.3
Brunei	21.4	2.5	68.6	3.8
East Timor	16.9	1.3	•	–
Philippines	16.8	1.6	71.6	3.4

Sources: Data is derived from: UNDP, 2016, *Human Development Report*, New York, UNDP. Taiwan data: Life expectancy 80; Literacy 98%; data from *CIA Fact Book*, accessed August 2017.

Notes
1 Life is life expectancy at age 60 years.
2 Budget is public health expenditure as % of GDP.
3 Secondary is % of population with some secondary education.
4 Budget is government expenditure as % of GDP.

ANNEX 3

Rural and urban employment

Countries	Working[1]	Agriculture[2]	Services[3]
China	67.6	2.5	47.0
Taiwan	–	–	–
North Korea	74.2	•	–
South Korea	58.6	6.1	69.5
Japan	57.3	3.7	69.1
Vietnam	76.7	46.8	32.0
Laos	76.1	71.3	20.2
Cambodia	80.5	54.1	29.6
Thailand	70.6	41.9	37.5
Malaysia	61.5	12.2	60.3
Singapore	65.0	0	70.6
Myanmar	74.3	•	–
Indonesia	63.4	34.3	44.8
Brunei	62.3	0.6	80.8
East Timor	39.3	50.6	39.8
Philippines	60.4	30.4	53.6

Sources: Data is derived from UNDP, 2016, *Human Development Report*, New York, UNDP. Taiwan data: Labour force by sector; Agriculture 4.9%; Industry 35.9%; Services 59.2%. Data is from *CIA Fact Book* accessed August 2017.

Notes
1 Working is % population over 15 who are working/employed.
2 Agriculture is % in employment in agriculture.
3 Services is % in employment in services.

ANNEX 4

Military expenditures

Countries	Expenditure GDP[1]	Expenditure total[2]	Active personnel[3]
China	1.9	215,176	2,183
Taiwan	1.9	9,924	215
North Korea	•	•	1,190
South Korea	2.7	36,777	630
Japan	1.0	46,126	247
Vietnam	2.4	5,017	482
Laos	•	•	29
Cambodia	1.8	370	124
Thailand	1.5	5,880	361
Malaysia	1.4	4,169	109
Singapore	3.4	9,959	73
Myanmar	•	•	406
Indonesia	0.9	8,183	396
Brunei	3.8	403	7
East Timor	1.3	26.2	1
Philippines	1.3	3,899	125

Data sources: (1) SIPRI Military Expenditures Database, www.sipri.org/sites/default/Milex-share-ofGDP.pdf (accessed August 2017); (2) SIPRI Military Expenditures Database, www.sipri.org/databases/milex (accessed August 2017); (3) IISS Chapter Ten: Country Comparisons and Defence Data. The Military Balance, 2017, London, Routledge, www.dx.doi.org/10.1080/04597222.20171271217 (accessed August 2017).

Notes
1 Expenditure GDP is % on defence.
2 Expenditure total is total figure in US$ millions (2015).
3 Active personnel is total active armed forces (000s).

ANNEX 5

China's twentieth century in twelve films

Zhang Yimou, 1992, *Raise the Red Lantern*
Bernardo Bertolucci, 1987, *The Last Emperor*
Cheung Yuen Ting, 1997, *The Soong Sisters*
Lu Chuan, 2010, *City of Life and Death*
Ang Lee, 2008, *Lust, Caution*
Steven Spielberg, 1988, *Empire of the Sun*
Chen Kaige, 1993, *Farewell my Concubine*
Zhang Yimou, 1994, *To Live*
Jia Zhangke, 2001, *Platform*
Jia Zhangke, 2008, *Still Life*
Wong Kar Wai, 2000, *In the Mood for Love*
Wong Kar Wai, *2046*

ANNEX 6

East Asia's twentieth century in twenty films

Zhang Yimou, 1992, *Raise the Red Lantern*
Bernardo Bertolucci, 1987, *The Last Emperor*
Zhang Yimou, 1987, *Red Sorghum*
Cheung Yuen Ting, 1997, *The Soong Sisters*
Lu Chuan, 2010, *City of Life and Death*
Ang Lee, 2008, *Lust, Caution*
Steven Spielberg, 1988, *Empire of the Sun*
Alexander Sokurov, 2005, *The Sun*
Chen Kaige, 1993, *Farewell my Concubine*
Tran Ahn Hung, 1994, *The Scent of Green Papaya*
Phillip Noyce, 2002, *The Quiet American*
Joshua Oppenheimer, 2013, *The Act of Killing*
Zhang Yimou, 1994, *To Live*
Jia Zhangke, 2002, *Platform*
Jia Zhangke, 2008, *Still Life*
Wong Kar Wai, 2000, *In the Mood for Love*
Wong Kar Wai, *2046*
Sofia Coppola, 2003, *Lost in Translation*
Ang Lee, 1995, *Eat Drink Man Woman*
Peter Greenaway, 1996, *The Pillow Book*

BIBLIOGRAPHY AND FURTHER READING

Acharaya, A. 2000. *The Quest for Identity: International Relations of Southeast Asia*, Oxford University Press.
Alatas, S.H. 1997. *The Myth of the Lazy Native*, London, Frank Cass.
Anderson, B. 1983. *Imagined Communities*, London, Verso.
Anderson, W. 2014. *The Grand Hotel Budapest* (film).
Backhouse, R. 2002. *The Penguin History of Economics*, Harmondsworth, Penguin.
Baker, C. and Phongpaichit, P. 2005. *A History of Thailand*, Cambridge University Press.
Bayly, C.A. 2004. *The Birth of the Modern World 1780–1914*, Oxford, Blackwell.
Beeson, M. and Stubbs, R., eds. 2012. *Routledge Handbook of Asian Regionalism*, London, Routledge.
Benjamin, G. 2015. 'The Unseen Presence: A Theory of the Nation-state and its Mystifications', *Inter-Asia Cultural Studies* 16.4.
Bickers, R. 2011. *The Scramble for China: Foreign Devils in the Qing Empire 1832–1914*, London, Allen Lane.
Billig, M. 1995. *Banal Nationalism*, London, Sage.
Block, F. 1990. *Post-industrial Possibilities: A Critique of Economic Discourse*, University of California Press.
Bourdieu, P. 2008. *Sketch for a Self Analysis*, Cambridge, Polity.
Briant, A. 2017. 'Diary (Oil Industry Corruption), *London Review of Books* 39.2, 19 January 2017.
Bryant, C. 1985. *Positivism in Social Theory and Research*, London, Macmillan.
Burgess, A. 1964. *The Long Day Wanes: A Malayan Trilogy*, New York, Norton.
Canadine, D. 2001. *Ornamentalism: How the British Saw Their Empire*, London, Allen Lane.
Case, W. 2002. *Politics in Southeast Asia: Democracy or Less*, London, Curzon.
Chen, N. 2002. 'Regionalism in China', in Preston, P.W. and Haacke, J. eds. *Contemporary China: The Dynamics of Change at the Start of the New Millennium*, London, Routledge Curzon.
Chen, P. 1983. *Singapore: Development Policies and Trends*, Oxford University Press.
Christiansen, F. and Rai, S. 1996. *Chinese Politics and Society*, London, Prentice Hall.
Chua, B.H. 1995. *Communitarian Ideology and Democracy in Singapore*, London, Routledge.

Chua, B.H., ed. 2000. *Consumption in Asia: Lifestyle and Identities*, London, Routledge.
Chua, B.H. 2003. *Life is not Complete without Shopping*, National University of Singapore Press.
Cipolla, C. 1985. *Guns, Sails and Empires: Technological Innovation and the Early Phases of European Expansion*, Sunflower University Press.
Clammer, J. 1995. *Difference and Modernity*, London, Kegan Paul International.
Clammer, J. 1997. *Contemporary Urban Japan*, Oxford, Blackwell.
Clark, C. 2013. *The Sleepwalkers*, Harmondsworth, Penguin.
Colley, L. 1992. *Britons: Forging the Nation*, Yale University Press.
Conrad, J. 1899. *Heart of Darkness*, London.
Coppola, F.F. 1979. *Apocalypse Now* (film).
Cummings, B. 1997. *Korea's Place in the Sun*, New York, Norton.
Cummings, B. 1999. *Parallax Visions: American-East Asian Relations at the End of the Century*, Durham, Duke University Press.
Cummings, B. 2017. 'A Murderous History of Korea', *London Review of Books* 39.10.
Darwin, J. 2009. *The Empire Project*, Cambridge University Press.
Davies, T. 1988. *Distant Voices, Still Lives* (film).
Durkheim, E. 1893. *The Division of Labour in Society*, Paris.
Fanon, F. 1967. *The Wretched of the Earth*, Harmondsworth, Penguin.
Finkelstein, N. 2000. *The Holocaust Industry*, London, Verso.
Frank, A.G. 1998. *Re-Orient: Global Economy in the Asian Age*, University of California Press.
Galbraith, J.K. 1958. *The Affluent Society*, Harmondsworth, Penguin.
Gay, P. 2008. *Modernism: the Lure of Heresy*, New York, Norton.
Gellner, E. 1964. *Thought and Change*, London, Weidenfeld.
George, S. 1984. *Ill Fares the Land*, Harmondsworth, Penguin.
Giddens, A. 1979. *Central Problems in Social Theory*, London, Macmillan.
Gipoloux, F., ed. 1994. *Regional Economic Strategies in Southeast Asia*, Tokyo, Maison Franco-Japonais.
Godement, F. 1997. *The New Asian Renaissance: From Colonialism to the post Cold War*, London, Routledge.
Goldmann, L. 1969. *The Human Sciences and Philosophy*, London, Cape.
Goschca, C. 2016. *The Penguin History of Modern Vietnam*, London, Allen Lane.
Green, G. 1955. *The Quiet American*, London, Heineman.
Gudeman, S. 1986. *Economics as Culture*, London, Routledge.
Habermas, J. 1989. *The Structural Transformation of the Public Sphere*, Cambridge, Polity.
Hacohen, M.H. 2000. *Karl Popper: The Formative Years 1902–1945*, Cambridge University Press.
Halbwachs, M. 1992. *On Collective Memory*, University of Chicago Press.
Halliday, F. 1990. *Cold War, Third World*, London, Hutchison.
Hasegawa, T. 2005. *Racing the Enemy: Stalin, Truman and the Surrender of Japan*, Harvard University Press.
Haslam, J. 1999. *The Vices of Integrity: E.H. Carr 1892–1982*, London, Verso.
Hastings, M. 2008. *Retribution: The Battle for Japan 1944–45*, New York, Alfred Knopf.
Hay, C. 2002. *Political Analysis*, London, Palgrave.
Held, D. 1987. *Models of Democracy*, Cambridge, Polity.
Heller, A. 1984. *Everyday Life*, London, Routledge
Herr, M. 1997. *Dispatches*, New York, Alfred Knopf.
Hirst, G. and Thompson, G. 1992. *Globalization in Question*, Cambridge, Polity.
Hodgson, G. 1988. *Economics and Institutions*, Cambridge University Press.

Hodgson, G. 2000. 'What is the Essence of Institutional Economics?', *Journal of Economic Issues* 34.2.
Hoggart, R. 1958. *The Uses of Literacy*, Harmondsworth, Penguin.
Huang, X. 2009. *Politics in Pacific Asia*, London, Palgrave.
Inglis, F. 1993. *Cultural Studies*, Oxford, Blackwell.
Janick, A. and Toulmin, S. 1973. *Wittgenstein's Vienna*, New York, Simon and Shuster.
Jessop, B. 1988. *Thatcherism*, Cambridge, Polity.
Johnson, C. 1995. *Japan: Who Governs? The Rise of the Developmental State*, New York, Norton.
King, A.D. 1990. *Urbanism, Colonialism and the World Economy: Cultural and Spatial Foundations of the World System*, London, Routledge.
Lam, W.M. 2004. *Understanding the Political Culture of Hong Kong*, New York, M.E. Sharpe.
Lieberthal, K. 1995. *Governing China: From Revolution through Reform*, New York, Norton.
Lieven, A. 2004. *America Right or Wrong: An Anatomy of American Nationalism*, London, HarperCollins.
Low, L. 2001. 'The Singaporean Developmental State in the New Economy and Polity', *The Pacific Review* 14.3.
Ma, N. 2007. *Political Development in Hong Kong*, Hong Kong University Press.
MacIntyre, A. 2007. *After Virtue: A Study in Moral Theory*, 3rd edn, University of Notre Dame Press.
Mackerras, C., ed. 1995. *Eastern Asia*, London, Longman.
Mackerras, C., ed. 2003. *Ethnicity in Asia*, London, Routledge Curzon.
Macpherson, C.B. 1973. *Democratic Theory: Essays in Retrieval*, Oxford University Press.
Maddison, A. 2007. *Contours of the World Economy*, Oxford University Press.
Mayer, A. 1981. *The Persistence of the Old Regime*, New York, Croom Helm.
Meek, J. 2017. 'Somerdale to Skarbimerz', *London Review of Books* 39.8, 20 April 2017.
Mirowski, J. 1988. *Against Mechanism: Protecting Economics from Science*, New Jersey, Rowman and Littlefield.
Moore, B. 1966. *The Social Origins of Dictatorship and Democracy*, New York, Boston Beacon.
Muller, J.W., ed. 2002. *Memory and Power in Post-war Europe*, Cambridge University Press.
Mumford, L. 1961. *The City in History*, New York, Harcourt.
Noyce, P. 2002. *The Quiet American* (film).
O'Brien, K. and Li, L. 2006. *Rightful Resistance*, Cambridge University Press.
Ong, A. 1999. *Flexible Citizenship: The Cultural Logics of Transnationality*, Duke University Press.
Oppenheimer, J. 2012. *The Act of Killing* (film).
Oppenheimer, J. 2014. *The Look of Silence* (film).
Ormerod, P. 1994. *The Death of Economics*, London, Faber and Faber.
Parkin, F. 1972. *Class Inequality and Political Order*, London, Paladin.
Pomeranz, K. 2000. *The Great Divergence: China, Europe and the Making of the Modern World Economy*, Princeton University Press.
Porter, R. 2000. *Enlightenment: Britain and the Creation of the Modern World*, London, Allen Lane.
Preston, P.W. 1994. *Discourses of Development*, Aldershot, Avebury.
Preston, P.W. 1997. *Political-Cultural Identity*, London, Sage.
Preston, P.W. 2000. *Understanding Modern Japan*, London, Sage.
Preston, P.W. 2007. *Singapore in the Global System*, London, Routledge.
Preston, P.W. 2009. *Arguments and Actions in Social Theory*, London, Palgrave.
Preston, P.W. 2010. *National Pasts in Europe and East Asia*, London, Routledge.

Preston, P.W. 2014. *After the Empires*, London, Palgrave.
Preston, P.W. 2016. *The Politics of China–Hong Kong Relations*, Cheltenham, Edward Elgar.
Preston, P.W. 2017. *Political-Cultural Developments in East Asia: Interpreting Logics of Change*, London, Palgrave.
Preston, P.W. and Haacke, J. eds. 2003. *Contemporary China: The Dynamics of Change at the Start of the New Millennium*, London, Routledge Curzon.
Raferty, G. n.d. 'In the Garden of England' (song).
Rigg, J. 1997. *Southeast Asia: The Human Landscape of Modernization and Development*, London, Routledge.
Rorty, R. 1989. *Contingency, Irony and Solidarity*, Cambridge University Press.
Rostow, W.W. 1960. *Stages of Economic Growth*, Cambridge University Press.
Rungrawee, C. 2004. 'Politics of Representation: A Case Study of Thailand's Assembly of the Poor', *Critical Asian Studies* 36.4.
Scott, J.C. 1985. *Weapons of the Weak*, Yale University Press.
Shambaugh, D. 2008. *China's Communist Party: Atrophy and Adaptation*, University of California Press.
Sheehan, N. 1988. *A Bright and Shining Lie*, New York, Vintage.
Streeck, W. 2016. *How will Capitalism End?* London, Verso.
Streeten, P. 1972. *The Frontiers of Development Studies*, London, Macmillan.
Stubbs, R. 2005. *Rethinking Asia's Economic Miracle: The Political Economy of War, Prosperity and Crisis*, London, Palgrave.
Sum, N.L. and Jessop, B. 2013. *Towards a Cultural Political Economy*, Cheltenham, Edward Elgar.
Swedberg, R. 1987. 'Economic Sociology: Past and Present', *Current Sociology*, Vols. 31 and 35.
Tarling, N. 1993. *The Fall of Imperial Britain in Southeast Asia*, Oxford University Press.
Tett, G. 2009. *Fool's Gold*, London, Little Brown.
Trocki, C. 1999 *Opium, Empire and the Global Political Economy: A Study of the Asian Opium Trade 1750–1950*, London, Routledge.
Varoufakis, Y. 2017. *And the Weak Suffer What they Must: Europe, Austerity and the Threat to Global Stability*, London, Vintage.
Vatikiotis, M. 2017. *Blood and Silk: Power and Conflict in Modern Southeast Asia*, London, Weidenfeld.
Wade, R. and Veneroso, F. 1998. 'The Asian Crisis: High Debt Model versus Wall Street, Treasury, IMF Complex', *New Left Review*, March/April.
Wallerstein, I. 1974. *The Modern World System*, New York, Academic.
Wee, C.J.W.L. 2000. 'Capitalism and Ethnicity: Creating Local Cultures in Singapore', *Inter Asia Cultural Studies* 1.1.
Williams, R. 1976. *Keywords*, London, Fontana.
Winch, P. 1990. *The Idea of a Social Science and Its Relation to Philosophy*, 2nd edn, London, Routledge.
World Bank. 1983. *The East Asian Miracle*, Oxford University Press.
World History at KMLA: History of Warfare, at www.zum.de/whkmla/military.
Worsley, P. 1984. *The Three Worlds: Culture and World Development*, London, Weidenfeld.
Yahuda, M. 2011. *The International Politics of the Asia Pacific*, 3rd edn, London, Routledge.
Zheng, Y. 2010. *The Chinese Communist Party as Organizational Emperor: Culture, Reproduction and Transformation*, Cheltenham, Edward Elgar.

Some useful journals/periodicals/websites

Asian Survey
British Library (web-images)
Bulletin of Concerned Asian Scholars
China Quarterly
Contemporary South East Asia
Critical Asian Studies
Harvard-Yenching Library (web-images)
Imperial War Museum (web-images)
Inter-Asia Cultural Studies
Journal of Asian Studies
London Review of Books
Modern Asian Studies
New Mandala (web-commentary)
Pacific Affairs
Pacific Review
RSIS Commentary (web-commentary)
Sojourn
South China Morning Post
The Economist
The Financial Times
University of Texas at Austin Perry Castaneda Library (web-images)

Some further possible reading

On development in the region

Maddison, A. 2007. *Contours of the World Economy*, Oxford University Press.
Rigg, J. 2002. *Southeast Asia: The Human Landscape of Modernization and Development*, London, Routledge.
World Bank. 1993. *The East Asian Miracle: Economic Growth and Public Policy*, Oxford University Press.

On regions

Beeson, M. and Stubbs, R., eds. 2012. *Routledge Handbook of Asian Regionalism*, London, Routledge.
Katzenstein, P. 2005. *A World of Regions: Asia and Europe in the American Imperium*, Cornell University Press.

On political culture

Anderson, B. 1983/2016. *Imagined Communities*, London, Verso.

On war

Max Hastings, M. 2008. *Retribution: The Battle for Japan 1944–45*, New York, Alfred Knopf.

Hasegawa, T. 2005. *Racing the Enemy: Stalin, Truman and the Surrender of Japan*, Harvard University Press.

Dower, J. 1999. *Embracing Defeat: Japan in the Aftermath of World War II*, London, Allen Lane.

On security

Yahuda, M. 2011. *The International Politics of the Asia Pacific*, London, Routledge.

On history

Bayly, C. 2004. *The Birth of the Modern World 1780–1914*, Oxford, Blackwell.

Bickers, R. 2011. *The Scramble for China: Foreign Devils in the Qing Empire 1832–1914*, London, Allen Lane.

Cummings, B. 1997. *Korea's Place in the Sun*, New York, Norton.

Darwin, J. 2009. *The Empire Project: The Rise and Fall of the British World System*, Cambridge University Press.

Spence, J. and Chin, A. 1996. *The Chinese Century: A Photographic History*, London, Harper Collins.

Tarling, N., ed. 1992. *The Cambridge History of Southeast Asia: Vol. 4. From World War Two to the Present*, Cambridge University Press.

INDEX

Africa 80, 83, 84, 87, 123, 154, 161, 167, 221, 247, 263
agency 9, 30, 40, 41, 42, 63, 237
agriculture 55, 57, 61, 149, 150, 152, 154, 163, 229, 263, 265, 282
Algeria 88
anthropology 11, 34, 41, 77, 86, 137, 212
ASEAN 75, 119, 123, 128, 141, 174, 176, 178, 182–5, 196, 197, 199, 211, 220
Asian Financial Crisis 21, 123, 124, 127, 149, 166, 178, 199
Australia 177, 179, 220, 243, 268

Bangkok 157, 215, 230, 243, 257, 265, 278, 279
Beijing 72, 106, 115, 124, 140, 165, 177, 181, 182, 184, 186, 217, 231, 262, 265, 269, 275, 278
Beijing Olympics 124, 125, 181, 184, 186
Britain 23, 28, 37, 38, 61, 88, 191, 288, 289
Burma 70, 91, 99, 102, 105, 106, 112, 113, 119, 270

Cambodia 48, 70, 75, 100, 107, 108, 112, 121, 128, 136, 175, 176, 179, 183, 218, 232, 246, 254, 272, 280, 281, 282, 283
Chiang Kai Shek 99, 118, 140, 231, 258
Chinese Communist Party 64, 70, 106, 117, 121–3, 213, 289
collective memory 69, 73, 74, 78, 83, 87–9, 135, 139, 203, 218, 235, 236, 239, 240, 241, 245, 247, 249, 251, 287
colonialism 45, 51, 55, 67, 70, 71, 76, 109, 142, 143, 167, 205, 212, 221, 261, 262, 276, 287, 288
colony 62, 72, 86, 98, 109, 118, 208, 254, 262
comfort women 75
Commonwealth 89
Cultural Revolution 115, 122, 186, 246, 248
cultural studies 12, 15, 29, 237, 239, 286, 288, 289, 290

Darwin, C. 23, 24, 64, 85
decolonization 137, 139, 140, 165, 178, 186, 219, 228, 229, 236, 229, 248, 252, 265, 267
democracy 17, 22, 48, 72, 91, 120, 130, 132, 133, 139–44, 191, 193, 200, 208, 210, 213–34, 261, 262, 271, 277, 286–8
Deng Xiaoping 115, 122, 126, 208, 209, 248
Dilthey, W. 12, 13
Durkheim, E. 25

economics 11, 15, 21, 28, 29–41, 43, 124, 126, 146, 148, 161, 164, 176, 198, 251, 255, 276, 286–8
education 102, 116, 145, 154, 159–63, 232, 257, 271, 281
Engels, F. 16
Enlightenment 4, 6, 21, 22, 23, 26, 27, 46, 133, 288
environment 5, 16, 18, 27–30, 39, 46–8, 77, 78, 115, 121, 122, 132, 137, 138, 152, 163, 166, 167, 171, 183, 184, 219,

235, 239, 242, 255, 258, 259, 260, 263, 264, 267, 276, 278
ethnicity 57, 64, 69, 141, 180, 226, 227, 230, 233, 238, 242, 243, 271, 288, 289
European Union 4, 16, 21, 28, 75, 98, 123, 127, 134, 165, 170, 177, 178, 185, 191, 192, 195, 199, 200, 233, 277

France 25, 28, 51, 88, 107, 137, 192
Frankfurt School 15, 17, 132
Furnivall, J.S. 240

Gadamer, H-G. 13
Germany 17, 25, 28, 34, 51, 80, 87, 90, 192, 224
globalization 4, 42, 146, 164, 166, 168, 169, 178, 186, 187, 188, 189, 191, 192, 194–201, 219, 220, 226, 233, 257, 275, 275, 271, 287
Great Leap Forward 115

Hapsburg Empire 6, 83
health 42, 102, 149, 154, 158–66, 244, 257, 260, 264, 281
historical institutionalism 20, 31, 33, 35, 40, 45
historical trajectories 19, 29, 31–6, 44, 45, 47, 48, 75, 101, 125, 142, 147, 169, 185, 216, 225, 233, 248, 254, 274
Hobbes, T. 3, 4, 22, 61
Ho Chi Minh 28
Hong Kong 70, 71, 85, 88, 105, 106, 115, 120, 126, 127, 137, 162, 187, 217, 232, 242, 243, 236, 254, 256, 258, 261, 266, 370, 273, 278, 289
Huk Rebellion 73, 141, 179, 229, 232, 233, 246
human livelihood 3, 12, 17, 22, 24, 32–9, 40, 41–7, 52, 56, 101, 139, 148, 193, 196, 198, 208, 212, 218, 228, 263, 264

identity 69, 71, 102, 143, 182, 205, 212, 213, 227, 237–44, 251, 162, 286, 288
imagined community 69, 102, 212, 235–7, 244, 245
inequality 122, 133, 146, 159, 160, 171, 187, 193, 194, 201, 203, 206, 228, 255, 257, 267, 273, 288
India 57, 58, 70, 84, 88, 89, 105, 106, 109, 120, 206, 208, 240, 242, 243, 247, 265, 270
Indonesia 68, 70–4, 78, 81, 88, 98, 100, 102–20, 136, 141, 175–9, 214–20, 232, 233, 243, 246, 247, 250, 261, 267, 270, 272, 280, 282, 283

industrial capitalism 3, 15, 17, 24, 25, 34, 41, 47, 49, 51, 52, 56, 57, 69, 75, 77, 78, 91, 136, 140, 149, 198, 257, 274
International Monetary Fund (IMF) 134
Italy 51, 141

Japan 24, 25, 44, 48, 51, 55, 62–7, 71–8, 80–2, 90–8, 100, 102, 105–20, 122–8, 136, 140, 149, 165, 174–85, 190, 207–18, 231, 240, 251, 258, 261, 266, 270, 280–8, 291

Konfrontasi 73, 74, 246
Korea (DPRK) 71–3, 98, 110, 117, 118, 123, 175, 176, 179, 180–4, 215, 218, 224, 261, 270, 271, 280–3
Korea (ROK) 71–3, 102, 110, 115, 117, 126, 128, 141, 175, 176, 179, 180–6, 210, 215–18, 222, 225, 233, 254, 261, 262, 270, 271, 280–3
Kuhn, T. 6, 9, 10
Kuomintang 71, 73, 111, 122, 208, 247, 262

Laos 48, 70, 100–8, 121, 128, 179, 183, 218, 270, 272, 280, 281–3
Lee, Kuan Yew 28, 91, 115, 120, 171, 261
Locke, J. 22, 61, 147, 166, 194, 220, 267
London 9, 35, 54, 63, 83, 96, 112, 165, 165, 175, 192, 194, 246, 247, 265, 283, 286, 287, 288, 289, 290, 291
Long March 67, 140, 231

Malacca 63
Malaya 58, 73, 74, 85, 100, 105, 106, 119, 120, 179, 213, 214, 229, 240, 246, 270, 286
Malaysia 63, 68, 70, 98, 100, 102, 113, 126, 136, 141, 175–9, 214–18, 220, 225, 232, 243, 248, 250, 258, 261, 267–71, 280–2
Malthus, T. 23, 37, 80
Manchuria 63, 65, 67, 75, 80, 110, 112, 210, 213, 242, 246
Manila 99, 243
Mao Zedong 28, 71, 115, 119, 121, 122, 186, 208, 209, 216, 231, 243, 246, 261, 267
Marx, K. 8, 15, 17, 23, 24, 28, 37, 52, 56, 71, 79, 131, 135, 136, 140, 141, 212, 231, 232, 241
migration 26, 34, 35, 82, 127, 144, 154, 157, 163, 168, 178, 187, 242, 244, 253, 255, 257, 264, 265, 266, 267, 273, 275, 276
Mill, J.S. 23, 37

modernity 28, 43, 46, 47, 51, 52, 56, 75, 76, 78, 86, 89, 90, 121, 134, 183, 194, 203, 217, 233, 244, 254, 270, 274, 275, 276, 287
modernization 46, 104, 110, 131, 141, 145, 146, 168, 169, 178, 189, 190, 193, 195, 200, 205, 219, 220, 233, 277, 289, 290
Moscow 72, 275
Myanmar 88, 97, 106, 113, 119, 141, 175, 176, 183, 215, 218, 222, 228, 233, 243, 270, 272, 280, 281, 281, 283

National Past 16, 33, 63, 69, 73, 74, 78, 83–90, 103, 122, 135, 139, 140, 203, 214, 218, 233, 235–52, 268, 288
Netherlands 88
Nixon, R. 181

Okinawa 180
Open Door 80, 81, 82, 85, 178
Opium War 59, 82, 84, 112, 140, 208, 240, 247, 289
Ottoman Empire 92

Pangkor Engagement 63, 105
Pearl Harbour 75
Pearl River Delta 199
Philippines 56, 63, 71, 73, 81, 82, 99, 100, 102, 113, 121, 141, 152, 176, 178, 179, 187, 213, 215, 216, 218, 220, 233, 241, 250, 251, 267, 270, 271, 280–3
Popper, K. 68, 287
poverty 144, 159, 160–3, 193, 221

Qing Empire 82, 84, 91, 110, 111, 118, 121, 182, 208, 210, 265, 270, 286, 291

regionalism 127, 128, 175, 195, 198, 199, 286, 290
Rhee, S. 117, 118
Ricardo, D. 23, 24, 37, 164
Rorty, R. 14, 289
rural 26, 35, 58, 119, 125, 137, 139, 141, 145, 149, 150, 154, 158, 178, 203, 211, 219, 230, 232, 241, 242, 244, 253, 251, 264, 266, 267, 270, 282
Russia 16, 61, 80, 90, 110, 117, 124, 176, 186, 184, 209, 210

Sakhalin 63, 71, 80, 110, 210
SCAP (Supreme Commander for the Allied Powers) 72, 113, 257, 258
Shandong 80
Shanghai 96
Siam 63, 71, 91, 105, 107, 110, 246

Singapore 44, 55, 61, 70, 85, 91, 100, 105, 113–20, 141, 155, 175, 214–18, 220, 224, 232, 249, 261, 266, 270–7, 280–3, 286–9
Smith, A. 23, 37, 75
sociology 11, 14, 15, 28, 29, 34, 35, 41, 145, 212, 237, 278, 289
Soviet Union 16, 21, 28, 67, 68, 98, 104, 112, 117, 119, 121, 146, 181, 199, 246
state-empires 48, 64–8, 75, 76, 81–6, 90–6, 100–4, 130, 134, 173, 184–6, 205, 210–17, 224, 235, 240, 248, 252–5, 261, 274–6
structure 6, 16, 17, 20–3, 29, 35, 42–7, 52, 57, 62, 64–9, 77–9, 90, 96, 102, 116, 133, 134, 136, 147, 156, 158, 203, 207, 219, 256, 264, 271–3
Sukarno 120
Sun Yat Sen 71, 91, 121, 140, 208, 209, 231, 240

Taiwan 63, 71, 73, 93, 98, 102, 110–18, 123–8, 175, 176, 179–85, 190, 209, 213–15, 222, 243, 249, 261, 262, 266, 270–3, 280, 281–3
Thailand 48, 62, 100–5, 110, 111, 141, 175–9, 214–18, 220, 233, 241–6, 250, 267, 278, 289–3, 289
Tiananmen Square 140, 181, 217, 231
Tokugawa 209, 210
Tokyo 65, 88, 90, 182, 210, 287

urbanization 149, 154, 156, 267

Vienna Circle 6, 7
Vietnam 48, 55, 70, 74, 75, 108, 112–19, 121, 146, 174–9, 218, 243, 272, 280, 281–3, 287
violence 42, 44, 48, 64–8, 70, 77, 81–6, 92, 100–6, 121, 122, 132–8, 141, 158, 175, 181–7, 208, 212, 214, 233, 242, 248, 261, 275

Washington 72, 73, 96, 165, 171, 181, 192, 256
Weber, M. 25, 34, 126, 132, 135
Winch, P. 10, 14, 196, 289
Wittgenstein, L. 7, 13–15, 196, 288
WTO (World Trade Organization) 22, 164, 256

Xi, Jinping 122, 177, 208
Xinjiang 112, 176

Yasakuni Shrine 112, 176